Darling!

Five days before the wedding!

Woo-Woo!

me

THREE PLAYS

MY HEART'S IN THE HIGHLANDS
THE TIME OF YOUR LIFE
LOVE'S OLD SWEET SONG

By William Saroyan

THE TIME OF YOUR LIFE

MY HEART'S IN THE HIGHLANDS

PEACE, IT'S WONDERFUL

THE TROUBLE WITH TIGERS

LOVE, HERE IS MY HAT

LITTLE CHILDREN

THREE TIMES THREE

INHALE AND EXHALE

THE DARING YOUNG MAN ON THE
FLYING TRAPEZE

WILLIAM SAROYAN

Three Plays:

MY HEART'S IN THE HIGHLANDS

THE TIME OF YOUR LIFE

LOVE'S OLD SWEET SONG

HARCOURT, BRACE AND COMPANY
New York

first edition

PRINTED IN THE UNITED STATES OF AMERICA
BY QUINN & BODEN COMPANY, INC., RAHWAY, N. J.

To the American Theater, with love

We are indebted to the editors of *The Stage* and *Town and Country* for permission to reprint HOW AND WHY TO BE A PLAYWRIGHT and THE ONE EASY LESSON

INTRODUCTION

In the sequence of plays written by me "Love's Old Sweet Song" is the fourth. The first and second are "My Heart's in the Highlands" and "The Time of Your Life." These three plays have been produced in New York and are published in this book. The third and fifth plays, as yet unproduced or unpublished, are "The Hero of the World" and "Something About a Soldier." All of these plays, excepting "My Heart's in the Highlands," were written sometime after March, 1939. A sixth play, "Sweeney in the Trees," was completed on the last day of 1939.

My work has always been the product of my time. Although the world was at peace when I wrote "My Heart's in the Highlands," there was every indication that it would be at war again before long. The poet of this play, Ben Alexander, speaks to the world on the subject of war as follows: "Go ahead. Fire your feeble guns. You won't kill anything. There will always be poets in the world."

The shadow of impending war is over the whole of my second play "The Time of Your Life," and its central character, Joe, spends most of his time examining maps, guns, and the effect of contemporary reality (which includes the constant likelihood of war) on the little and unknown human beings of the world, and on their natural instinct to live gracefully and decently. The Arab of this play says over and over again: "No foundation. All the way down the line."

The theme of my third play, "The Hero of the World," is the effect of this world-disorderliness on both ordinary and superior human beings, canceling the integrity and dignity of the first, and destroying the faith and personal force of the second, leaving man in art speechless, unwilling to act, incapable of accepting responsibility to himself and to society.

"Love's Old Sweet Song" is my fourth play.

I began to write my fifth play, "Something About a Soldier," on September 3, 1939, when it was evident that the war which the world for twenty years had been making inevitable was now to come about. Art and religion would not be able to stop the war any more than they would be able to stop tomorrow. In this play a man of seventy who has lived a truly civilized life, along with his adopted son of eleven, who has not so much as begun to live consciously at all, declare war against the political leaders of the world. These two, the old and the young, build a trench in their front yard, put on military uniforms, and appear to be making fools of themselves, but only because their foolishness is on a much smaller scale than the historical foolishness of the world. At first the man is regarded as crazy. We, too, at first regard large-scale trouble-makers as crazy. Crazy or sane, however, their persistence, their energy, and the support of millions of simple human beings reduces any aberration in them to something that is irrelevant. And soon after my soldier's declaration of war, his seeming craziness also becomes irrelevant. Since World War II had unquestionably arrived and would unquestionably do its damage, and there was nothing

2

I or you could do about it, I found it necessary to foresee its end and to return to the essential labor of art.

As far as it is possible to do so, in writing my sixth play, "Sweeney in the Trees," I dismissed the war. It had started; consequently it would end. All of us were disgraced once more, and the most (as well as the least) we could do was seek to bring the spirit of man together again.

Wars, for us, are either inevitable, or created. Whatever they are, they should not wholly vitiate art. What art needs is greater men, and what politics needs is better men. If the creation and execution of vast active human projects are necessary for the health of the people, and for the security of the state, they must be the work of men more imaginative than militarists and politicians, and men less fond of their own privacy than artists. Art and politics must move closer together. Reflection and action must be equally valid in good men if history is not to take one course and art another. The weakness of art is that great poems do not ennoble politics, as they certainly should, and the trouble with politics is that they inspire poets only to mockery and scorn.

Art can no longer afford to be contemptuous of politics, and it appears to be time politics took a little instruction from art. Not only is the individual an inhabitant of the world, so also is the nation, and as the world goes, so goes the individual and the nation. What is necessary is greater art in the determining of how the world shall go. During this war we have come to accept all manner of artless and base behavior simply because of the tremendous quantity of it in operation. This is historically inevitable. Whatever beauty there may be in a vast military success, it is no beauty that can delight anything in us excepting that which is most uncultivated or inhuman. There is no longer occasion, how-

3

ever, for us to grieve foolishly over the destruction of half a million lives in so short a space of time as twenty days.

We have always believed that art should be one thing, religion one thing, politics one thing, morality one thing, and so on. This kind of isolation of entities, while convenient, is, I believe, foolish. All things must come together as one, which is man. The functioning of all things should be to the glory of living. Art is answerable to politics, and politics is answerable to religion, and all are answerable to man, so that when there is disgrace in life, as there is now, we are all guilty, the poet with the statesman, the general with the Pope, and so on. If we can pretend that evil is unnatural or that it is undesirable, all men who are conscious, all functioning men, all men with superior natural endowment, all men of thought, all men of action, all men of faith, must be responsible for the occurrence of evil. Force is the simplest and easiest method in the world by which to settle any kind of dispute. Intelligence and grace, however, are the means of canceling disputes, which are unimaginative creations, not realities. Political systems, however deeply and emotionally integrated in the legend and behavior of a people, are worthless when they can survive only at the cost of the actual lives of the people whom they claim to protect. And yet we know one political system or another is still necessary for the management of the world. For this reason, art must enter the arena. It must be part of one large thing: the world and its management, life and its instruction. Art must not be a separate and special thing. The intention of art has always been to deepen, extend, elevate, ennoble, strengthen, and refresh the experience of living. It cannot begin to do these things until it accepts part of the management of the

4

physical life of man, which is now in the hands of inferior men.

There are many sound arguments in favor of all of the things of life and the world, seemingly good or seemingly bad. There is no argument against grace, however, and the way of art, and the companion of art, is grace. This is a word, I think, which must now begin to take the place in our vocabulary of a word long since outworn and for the time being dangerous, if not useless: *truth*. Truth, in our time, has so many variations it has become an actual nonentity. Except statistically, we know no truth, because we have little grace and less honor. There are arguments in favor of war, and I am sure there could be arguments in favor of disease and death. There are times, even in the healthiest of lives, when destruction appears to be more compelling than construction, when death seems more in order than life. Part of the infinite wonder of man is the simultaneous reality of varying and contradictory states. In the flux of inner reality, however, the good and positive appear to be much more abundant and natural than the evil and negative. To have been born is surely our end. To die is beside the point. And to live is our pleasure and law. There may be exhilaration in death, but most of us prefer to survive exhilaration. Most of us cannot help enduring our emotions.

As the conscious individual has intelligence and conscience, in addition to instinct, so also has the mass. What it lacks in quality, it makes up in quantity. Simple and relatively uncultivated men of energy who find themselves in the leadership of great masses very often contain within themselves both the intelligence and instinct of the whole mass, plus a compulsion to be somehow superior and immortal. These men are seldom actually evil, although they

5

may seem to be. They are naive. They are not to be scorned or dismissed by men individually superior. While no member of the mass is deprived of his *special* individuality until he dies or is killed, that individuality is so nearly the same as the individuality of millions of others, he and the millions are essentially one, and this one, numbering hundreds of millions, has its model in the *uncultivated* man who is their leader. This man knows which way the mass wishes to go, or can be led, and therein is his superiority—and his essential inferiority. If he leads, he *cannot* lead to anything like a worthy destination, and if he fulfills the wish of the mass, that fulfillment will carry him and the mass to death or disgrace. The instinct of the mass in our time is toward regimentation. Toward the security of narrower limits. The mass appears to be either fearful or unappreciative of the kind of individual freedom the poet, for instance, must insist upon. For the mass this instinct may or may not be proper. Improper or proper, the mass appears to be fearful of exposure to leisure and individual choice. It appears to want the time of its life carefully mapped out and organized, and it appears to want its behavior dictated. (There are good arguments in favor of all this. There are better arguments in favor of truly superior men exerting a truly superior influence.) Without completely abandoning old techniques (which would swiftly bring about even greater chaos), the imperative requirement of our time is to restore faith to the mass and integrity to the individual. The integration of man is still far from realized. In a single age this integration can be immeasurably improved, but it is impossible and useless to seek to imagine its full achievement. Integration will begin to occur when the individual is uninhibited, impersonal, simultaneously natural and cultured, without hate,

6

without fear, and rich in spiritual grace. Strong men of poor, coarse, or undeveloped sensibilities usually find themselves in control of the mass. Strong men of rich sensibilities usually find themselves in control of themselves. This situation would be equitable and satisfactory only if we found it possible to accept as perfectly natural all the kinds of mass behavior which now shock and disgust us. If it were possible or desirable for a man to inhabit only his own personal world, without regard for the lesser (and greater) world of the mass, the present distribution of balance would offend no one. It becomes increasingly true, however, that the most superior man in the world finds a valid variation of himself in the most inferior man in the world, and is hurt by that which hurts this man.

We may feel grateful that the war is on, since we know its beginning is its end, and once again our chance has come to *attempt* the establishment of a not *too* ambitious style of human order, and yet one at least a little finer than the one which created the war. Man wages his wars against himself. It is the same war each of us must wage within himself: good in conflict with evil. In the world the strong are better than the weak only if the strong have love for the weak, and in ourselves virtue is true only if we recognize vice and know it to be an inseparable part of virtue. We cannot begin to be truly good until we know we cannot be *constantly* good. It is hard to imagine anything more likely to be offensive to nature than permanent goodness. What we need is a better proportion of grace and a more generous distribution of understanding.

The majesty of art lies in its simultaneous aloofness and democracy, its *aloneness* and fraternity, and its quietude and tumult. Art begins by being a personal exercise in grace for

7

its creator. Before all others, it refines its maker. The inner calisthenics of art tempers and gives form first to the spirit of the artist. It is the similar affection for and need of form in the many which has carried art into the world, and it is according to the needs of the living that art is given its texture and shape. The first creator of art is one's world and time. The material of art is provided by the world abundantly but chaotically. The labor of art is to take this material and instruct it in grace and form. In ratio to the rawness of the material, art exercises its discipline, its precision, and its faith. Insofar as the world lacks these things, art must provide them. And it must do so blandly, with delight, with ease, and with casualness. It must entertain as it instructs. Its instruction cannot be direct. Since its boundaries are form, and since its cargo is pleasure, in order to accomplish more than the trivial and tentative, art must know deeply and intimately the grief, the despair, and the frustration of its time. It must know the sources of these things and the destinations of them. The source of the grief of man is the monotony of peaceful living. The source of his despair is his lack of resourcefulness and imagination. The source of his frustration is the pain he suffers in the attempt and failure to escape boredom. True escape for man can be provided only by art. To taste life in its full flavor he has not the experience or equipment or style. To accept only as much as he has the equipment to enjoy he has not the discipline or courage. And therefore to evade his defeat, he is eager to enter into any project which provides a substitute somehow or anyhow for the fullness his dream needed. Such a substitute is participation in war, directly or indirectly, as soldier, instructed, in order, and close to ultimates, murder or death, obvious and immediate triumph or failure; or as

8

bystander, excited by war, pleased, frightened, or fretted. Naturally, when there is war in the world the artist's material in addition to being raw is complex, and very hard to work with. The ecstatic pitch, which art itself seeks to reach, now exists in the world, but is such a base ecstasy that it cannot be given back to the world as great art. What usually happens, therefore, is that artists, at such times, either give up and join the others in bluffing or fretting, or sink deeper and deeper into remoteness and inutility, doing work which is repetitious and beside the point. It is a mistake to imagine that we are *forced* into unpleasant activities, such as war. Our absence of vigilance and industry when there was time to instruct ourselves and the world in alternatives to war is at least partly responsible for the repetition of war. Behavior repeats itself, and great behavior cannot begin to repeat itself until it has *once* occurred, and it cannot begin to occur until art has made it as natural, as easy, and as inevitable as war has been for a long time. *During* a war there is absolutely no chance for correction, just as *after* a gun has been fired there is no chance to deprive its shell of its destination. After the explosion of a gun the most any of us can do is protect our eardrums. We are not forced into unpleasant activities. We either allow them to come about or we encourage them to come about.

There are many who believe art cannot do anything about history. I am not one of these. I believe art can do a good deal about history. Art cannot charge with the infantry or roll along with the armored car units of an army, but there has always been less charging and rolling in history than quietude and conversation; fewer parachute jumps and power dives, less strafing and bombing than poems and the reading of them.

9

In a time of war if art abandons its labor, war wins its victory, and cheap history tells the fable of the world. If it is impossible for art to reach the soldier who is on the verge of killing or being killed, it can get ready for the soldier's son. If art cannot improve the tone and meaning of the statesman's radio speech, it can anticipate his burial and be ready for his successor. If the world is amuck and there is no one for art to talk to, it can prepare itself for the next generation. War is tentative. Aberration is tentative. Art is not tentative.

It is true that as long as there are poets in the world war can kill nothing.

The world now provides art new and more difficult material. Art has no alternative but to accept this material and to remove from it all foolishness, all feebleness, and all foolish and feeble fantasy.

WILLIAM SAROYAN

San Francisco
June 1, 1940.

My Heart's in the Highlands

To the pure in heart.

To the poet in the world.

To the lowly and great, whose lives are poetry.

To the child grown old, and the child of childhood.

To the heart in the highlands.

PREFACE

The theatre is and always has been a place visited by more or less normal people who, by the grace of God, are out of pain and in a mood to compare their experience in living with the experience of others—with the experience of the people who appear in a play or with the experience of the man who wrote the play. Or both. Or with the experience of the people in the theatre, from their response to the play.

There are many reasons for a man to go to a theatre and see a play. One man goes to escape dying of boredom. Another goes in order to escape being eager, personally, about all things. To relax and rest and watch others being eager. One man goes to dream. Another goes to be awakened. Another goes because there isn't anything else to do at the time, and many years ahead. Still another goes because it's a social affair—a good chance to put on the fancy clothes and feel fine.

I go to the theatre to see still another variation of the world. To see another dimension of human reality. If what I see is false, it's no matter to me, because I *know* it's false. If it's true, fine: I'm delighted. Art comes from the world, belongs to it, can never escape from it. The world is interesting to me. Therefore the theatre is interesting to me. I may not like a play, but it can't bore me. This is so because I am a writer.

I know there are others who can take the theatre this way.

They are not all writers. On the contrary, very often the dullest people in the world are writers—of one sort or another. There are great numbers of people in the world who can't be bored. They are usually the ones who are themselves not bores. Most often, however, what they usually are, are children.

The child race is fresh, eager, interested, innocent, imaginative, healthy and full of faith, where the adult race, more often than not, is stale, spiritually debauched, unimaginative, unhealthy, and without faith.

A number of drama critics sincerely regretted they couldn't understand this simple play, and a number were bored by it. It is perfectly all right with me for any man who must be bored with this play to be bored with it. I believe I understand people well enough to know that a perfectly fine human being could be bored with this play, or be confused by it, or could regard it as preposterous. Or even as preposterous nonsense. He could, by a generous exercise of the imagination, be regarded himself as not insane or dull-witted, either. I would recommend rest, recreation, and reading, however.

If this play can bore a man, I would like to know if any play could escape boring him, or if anything at all could. Here is a play as real as a street corner. As natural as the earth or sidewalk underfoot, the sky overhead. As true as any fable in the literature of the world. Any man who could be bored with this play could be bored with the sudden vision of the Good Lord negotiating a substantial body of water on foot.

The meaning of the play is the meaning of reality itself. It is not a meaning which I or anyone else can express in phrases beginning, "Well, it means—" You simply don't say

14

of any real thing, whether it is the whole world, a city like New York, an ocean, a bird flying, a man dying, or a child entering the world, that it has a meaning. That kind of explaining I leave to those intellectual giants who can explain everything—and understand nothing.

As for the message and moral of the play it is the simplest and oldest in the world:

It is better to be a good human being than to be a bad one. It is just naturally better.

As I see it, the basic trouble with the American theatre is that the element of "play" has been completely forgotten by American playwrights and completely left out of their plays. American plays, in fact, are not plays. They are, as a rule, essays at one or another of the many variations of reality, usually sorrowful. As a rule they are dull and depressing. They make a visit to the theatre a pleasure only because after the two or two-and-a-half hours of headache, it is delightful to get out into the open air and breathe a moment of plain, unmechanical, worldly reality.

I have a reputation as one who enthusiastically praises and recommends his own work. The reputation is justified. I believe in my work and am eager for others to know about it. I think it will do them good to know about it. If talk of this kind makes a braggart of me, that, I suppose, is something I shall have to continue to be. Nevertheless, all I have ever argued for has been impersonal. My right to be myself is relatively a feeble right for me to quarrel for. In the realm of world events it is not exactly the most important struggle of the day. In the realm of my own life, however, I do not hesitate to say that it is by all odds the most important matter of all. Stop one good man from functioning and you stop all men, which may or may not be Fascism, but is certainly something vicious as far as I am concerned, and something I will not personally tolerate.

The only way I can argue impersonally for integrity and reality, truth and imagination, in art, in living, and in the theatre, is to argue specifically—with my own work as a basis for comparison.

The value that comes from my being myself—that is to say, honest, unspoiled and continuously concerned about valid potentialities in living and in art—is a value of some importance to everybody. In the theatre, for instance, if I can get by with it (and it is truly something you have to put over, unfortunately), it is likely that others, perhaps more talented, will be encouraged to make the attempt. The result, possibly, will be that the greatest country in the world will become, in art as well as in its day-to-day life, truly the greatest country in the world. As it should be.

I am convinced there is no place in the world like America. It is the first place in the world of its kind, and I for one don't want it to begin to be the last. There never has been such a place. There never has been such a people. Any of us who does not try to do something about it, or make something of it, is a failure—as an artist and as an American. It doesn't make any difference what we do, or how well it is received.

I am now five years an American writer. Several weeks an American playwright. Yet all I know is that I have not so much as made a real beginning. The important truth—the *true* truth—is still in the stage of an expected and hoped-for arrival. I don't want this truth to be forced to arrive somewhere where it won't be able to make itself known. In a factory worker, for instance, who won't be able to tell anybody about it—in a sensibility and mind, that is, which will be innocent but uncommunicative. Just because we're writers doesn't mean that we shall be less than the people of the world. We may be their superiors in technical skill—in being able to articulate what little we know—but we can never afford to be their inferiors in spirit, as we seem to be now.

I would like to see the boys who really know how to write plays really write them, instead of throwing them together out of the shabby devices which they have come to believe are sure-fire. I would like them to remember, for instance, that nothing has ever been more sure-fire than truth and integrity. You can fool all of the people all of the time, but you can fool only the fool in them, which is no great feat of heroism, and nothing to get any blue ribbon for.

To say there is no American theatre at all is false, and to some degree silly. To say there is not yet an American theatre *equal* to the dramatic materials provided by the American environment and people, however, is very true, and to a small degree profound.

The day-to-day drama of American life following its beautiful destiny is far away from the American drama, wallowing, as it were, in its present unconsciousness, or more correctly going insignificantly mad, or ga-ga, in its busy mechanicalism.

American life is still a total stranger to American dramatic art.

It is about time for ten or eleven (or maybe one or two) experts in the theatre—playwrights, directors, actors, scene designers, composers, and others—to introduce American reality to American dramatic art.

I feel confident that the two will get along famously.

A great but simple and more or less dimensionless reality

is constant, of course, where there are people and cities, villages, and dwellings. The greater reality, the truer, deeper and more pertinent reality of a people and place, however, can be established—by isolation, emphasis, and magnification—only by men of good will, good vision, and great humanity.

Although these men must be naturals (that is, first writers), I believe they must learn everything good and valuable to be learned from the men in the theatre who are technical experts, but, unfortunately, little else.

The present theatre is tricky as a consequence of great technical skill being wasted on second-hand material synchronized out of third-rate sensibilities. It doesn't have to remain tricky. Producers with as much sensibility as money are on the scene, and appear to be as willing to gamble on a work of freshness as on a work of artificiality.

This is all anybody who writes plays needs to know.

There is no such thing as experiment. There is only good and bad art. When a good thing appears to be very new, it is more likely that it is only something that has been forgotten, and is now suddenly remembered. A classic is simply a first work, the beginning of a tradition, and an entry into a fresh realm of human experience, understanding, and expression.

I believe "My Heart's in the Highlands" is a classic.

It is surely impertinent for me to believe that the greater and truer American theatre shall begin its life after the appearance and influence of this play, but God forgive me, that is what I believe.

I know the play itself is relatively a trifle, but I also know of no one else who hopes for more for the American theatre than myself, and plans to do something about fulfilling these hopes personally.

I regret very much that to speak the truth in our day appears to be bad taste. I find, however, that even at the risk of seeming to be a boor I must still say what I truly believe.

I believe that time, with its infinite understanding, will one day forgive me.

WILLIAM SAROYAN

New York City

MY HEART'S IN THE HIGHLANDS

BY ROBERT BURNS

My heart's in the Highlands, my heart is not here,
My heart's in the Highlands a-chasing the deer,
A-chasing the wild deer and following the roe—
My heart's in the Highlands, wherever I go!

Farewell to the Highlands, farewell to the North,
The birthplace of valor, the country of worth!
Wherever I wander, wherever I rove,
The hills of the Highlands forever I love.

Farewell to the mountains, high cover'd with snow;
Farewell to the straths and green valleys below;
Farewell to the forests and wild-hanging woods;
Farewell to the torrents and loud-pouring floods!

MY HEART'S IN THE HIGHLANDS

NOTE

My Heart's in the Highlands was offered as a Group Theatre production at the Guild Theatre in New York City on April 13, 1939.

This play has grown out of one of my short stories. The story was called "The Man with the Heart in the Highlands," and was published in December, 1936, in a book called "Three Times Three." A one-act play bearing the title of the story was published in *The One-Act Play Magazine*, edited by William Kozlenko, who suggested to me that the story contained a play, and again in "Contemporary One-Act Plays," a book published by Scribner's and also edited by Mr. Kozlenko. After the appearance of the shorter play, I could not resist the impulse to carry out the theme to its present completion.

In the production of a play there are many people a writer admires and wants to thank. A play may or may not be literature before it is played, but it is certainly not a play until it is played, and it is most truly a play only while it is being played. The effective playing of a play puts to work many people. It is a group activity. I wish to express my gratitude to Harold Clurman, founder and director of the Group Theatre; Robert Lewis, director of the play; Herbert Andrews, who did the sets and costumes; Paul Bowles, who composed the music; Michael Gordon, who lighted the play; the cast: Jackie Ayers (*The Boy with*

23

the *Double-Decker Ice Cream Cone*), Philip Loeb (*Ben Alexander*), Sidney Lumet (*Johnny*), Art Smith (*Jasper MacGregor*), William Hansen (*Mr. Kosak*), Hester Sondergaard (*Johnny's Grandmother*), James O'Rear (*Rufe Apley*), Loren Gage (*Philip Carmichael*), Phil Brown (*Henry*), Harry Bratsburg (*Mr. Wiley*), Nicholas Conte (*The Real Estate Agent*), John O'Malley (*The Husband*), Catheryn Laughlin (*The Wife*), Mae Grimes (*Esther Kosak*), Peter Leeds (*A Guard*), Charles De Shein (*Another Guard*), and Eda Reis, Eileen Detchon, Undine Forrest, Charles Henderson, Mary Liles (*Good Friends and Neighbors*); the Group Theatre Staff: Kermit Bloomgarden, General Manager; Emanuel Eisenberg, Press Representative; Morton Nathanson, Associate Press Representative; Leo Rose, Company Manager; Michael Gordon, Production Manager; Philip Mathias, Stage Manager; Ruth Young, Executive Secretary; Moe Jacobs, Master of Properties; William Kellam, Master Carpenter; Henry Linck, Master Electrician; the musicians: Sol Dzuzga, cornet; Max Marlin, director and Hammond electric organ; Ben Storch, oboe and English horn; Sam Gershek, drums and sound effects; the Guild Theatre, for sponsoring the play; and the people who saw the play, for seeing it.

To all these, my sincere regards and thanks. I had fun. I hope you did, too.

W. S.

24

THE PEOPLE

JOHNNY
His father, BEN ALEXANDER, the poet
Johnny's grandmother
JASPER MAC GREGOR, the man with the heart in the high-
lands
MR. KOSAK, the grocer
ESTHER, his beautiful daughter
RUFE APLEY, the carpenter
PHILIP CARMICHAEL, the young man from the Old People's
Home
HENRY, the morning paper route carrier
MR. WILEY, the mailman
MR. CUNNINGHAM, the real estate agent
The Young Husband and Wife, and Their Baby
Good Friends and Neighbors
A dog

THE PLACE

A house on San Benito Avenue in Fresno, California.
Mr. Kosak's grocery store.

THE TIME

August and November, 1914.

AN old white, broken-down, frame house with a front porch, on San Benito Avenue in Fresno, California. There are no other houses near by, only a desolation of bleak land and red sky. It is late afternoon of a day in August, 1914. The evening sun is going down.

JOHNNY, aged nine, but essentially ageless, is sitting, dynamic and acrobatic, on the steps of the porch, dead to the world and deep in thought of a high and holy order. Far away a train whistle cries mournfully. He listens eagerly, cocking his head on one side like a chicken, trying to understand the meaning of the cry and at the same time to figure out everything. He doesn't quite make it and when the cry ends he stops being eager. A fourteen-year-old boy on a bicycle, eating an ice-cream cone and carrying newspaper bags, goes by on the sidewalk in silence, oblivious of the weight on his shoulders and of the contraption on which he is seated, because of the delight and glory of ice cream in the world. JOHNNY leaps to his feet and waves to the boy, smiling in a big humanitarian way, but is ignored. He sits down again and listens to a small overjoyed but angry bird. After making a brief forceful speech of no meaning, the bird flies away.

From inside the house is heard the somber voice of JOHNNY's FATHER reciting poetry of his own composition.

27

JOHNNY'S FATHER

The long silent day journeys through the sore solemn heart, and—

(Bitter pause)

And—

(Quickly)

The long silent day journeys through the sore solemn heart, and—

(Pause)

No.

(He roars and begins again)

Crippled and weeping, time stumbles through the lone lorn heart.

(A table or chair is pushed over in anger. A groan. Silence)

(The boy listens. He gets up and tries to stand on his head, fails, tries again, fails, tries again, and succeeds. While he is standing on his head he hears the loveliest and most amazing music in the world: a solo on a bugle. The music is "My Heart's in the Highlands."

The bugler, a very old man, finishes the solo in front of the house. The boy leaps to his feet and runs up to the old man, amazed, delighted and bewildered)

JOHNNY

I sure would like to hear you play another song.

MAC GREGOR

Young man, could you get a glass of water for an old man whose heart is not here, but in the highlands?

28

JOHNNY

What highlands?

MAC GREGOR

The Scotch Highlands. Could you?

JOHNNY

What's your heart doing in the Scotch Highlands?

MAC GREGOR

My heart's grieving there. Could you get me a glass of cool water?

JOHNNY

Where's your mother?

MAC GREGOR

(Inventing for the boy)
My mother's in Tulsa, Oklahoma, but her heart isn't.

JOHNNY

Where is her heart?

MAC GREGOR

(Loud)
In the Scotch Highlands.
(Soft)
I'm very thirsty, young man.

JOHNNY

How come the members of your family are always leaving their hearts in the highlands?

MAC GREGOR

(In the Shakespearean manner)
That's the way we are. Here today and gone tomorrow.

29

JOHNNY

    (Aside)
Here today and gone tomorrow?
    (To MacGregor)
How do you figure?

MAC GREGOR

    (The philosopher)
Alive one minute and dead the next.

JOHNNY

Where's your mother's mother?

MAC GREGOR

    (Inventing, but angry)
She's up in Vermont, in a little town called White River, but her heart isn't.

JOHNNY

Is her poor old withered heart in the highlands, too?

MAC GREGOR

Right smack in the highlands. Son, I'm dying of thirst.

    (JOHNNY'S FATHER comes out of the house in a fury, as if he has just broken out of a cage, and roars at the boy like a tiger that has just awakened from evil dreams)

JOHNNY'S FATHER

Johnny, get the hell away from that poor old man. Get him a pitcher of water before he falls down and dies. Where the hell are your manners?

JOHNNY

Can't a fellow try to find out something from a traveler once in a while?

30

JOHNNY'S FATHER

Get the old man some water, God damn it. Don't stand there like a dummy. Get him a drink, I tell you, before he falls down and dies.

JOHNNY

You get him a drink. You're not doing anything.

JOHNNY'S FATHER

Not doing anything? Why, Johnny, you *know* I'm getting a new poem arranged in my mind.

JOHNNY

How do you figure I know? You're just standing there on the porch with your sleeves rolled up.

JOHNNY'S FATHER

(Angry)

Well, you ought to know.

(Roaring)

You're my son.

(Amazed)

If you shouldn't know, who should?

MAC GREGOR

(Blithely)

Good afternoon. Your son has been telling me how clear and cool the climate is in these parts.

JOHNNY

(Bewildered, but eager to learn)

(Aside)

Holy Moses, I didn't say anything about the climate. Where's he getting that stuff from?

31

JOHNNY'S FATHER

    (The aristocrat, grandly)

How do you do? Won't you come in for a little rest? We should be honored to have you at our table for a bite of supper.

MAC GREGOR

    (The realist)

Sir, I'm starving. I shall come right in.

        (He moves to enter the house. JOHNNY gets in his way, looking up at him)

JOHNNY

    (The romantic)

Can you play "Drink to Me Only with Thine Eyes"? I sure would like to hear you play that song on the bugle. That song is my favorite. I guess I like that song better than any song in the world.

MAC GREGOR

    (The disillusioned)

Son, when you get to be my age you'll know songs aren't important, bread's the thing.

JOHNNY

    (The faithful)

Anyway, I sure would like to hear you play that song.

        (MAC GREGOR goes up on the porch and shakes hands with JOHNNY'S FATHER)

MAC GREGOR

    (History in the making)

My name is Jasper MacGregor. I am an actor.

32

JOHNNY'S FATHER

(*Delighted*)

I'm mighty glad to make your acquaintance.

(*The imperial giver of orders*)

Johnny, get Mr. MacGregor a pitcher of water.

(JOHNNY *runs around the house*)

MAC GREGOR

(*Dying of thirst, sighing, but telling the truth nevertheless*)

Charming boy.

JOHNNY'S FATHER

(*Ordinary statement*)

Like myself, he's a genius.

MAC GREGOR

(*Roaring, from fatigue*)

I suppose you're very fond of him?

JOHNNY'S FATHER

(*Delighted to be alive*)

We are the same person— He is the heart of my youth—
Have you noticed his eagerness?

MAC GREGOR

(*Delighted to be still alive*)

I should say I have.

JOHNNY'S FATHER

(*Proudly and with anger*)

I'm the same way myself, although older and less brilliant.

(JOHNNY, *running, returns with a pitcher of water which he hands to the old man. The old man*

33

*throws back his shoulders, lifts his head, his nostrils
expand, he snorts, his eyes widen, he lifts the pitcher
of water to his lips and drinks all the water in one
long swig, while* JOHNNY *and his* FATHER *watch with
amazement and admiration. The old man breathes
deeply, looks around at the landscape and up at the
sky and to the end of San Benito Avenue where the
evening sun is going down*)

MAC GREGOR

(*Reflection, sadly; weariness, softly*)

I reckon I'm five thousand miles from home. Do you think
we could eat a little bread and cheese to keep my body and
spirit together?

JOHNNY'S FATHER

(*Napoleon*)

Johnny, run down to the grocer's and get a loaf of French
bread and a pound of cheese.

JOHNNY

(*The voice of doom*)

Give me the money.

JOHNNY'S FATHER

(*Statistics, poetic, with pride*)

You know I haven't got a penny, Johnny. Tell Mr. Kosak
to give us credit.

JOHNNY

(*The unwilling dutiful son*)

He won't do it. He's tired of giving us credit. He says we
don't work and never pay our bills. We owe him forty
cents.

34

JOHNNY'S FATHER

(*Impatient, irritated*)

Go on down there and argue it out with him. You know that's your job.

JOHNNY

(*Defending his rights*)

He won't listen to reason. He says he doesn't know anything about anything. All he wants is the forty cents.

JOHNNY'S FATHER

(*Napoleon*)

Go on down there and make him give you a loaf of bread and a pound of cheese.

(*Gently, pleading, flattering*)

You can do it, Johnny.

MAC GREGOR

(*Impatient and hungry*)

Go on down there and tell Mr. Kosak to give you a loaf of bread and a pound of cheese, son.

JOHNNY'S FATHER

Go ahead, Johnny. You've never failed to leave that store with something or other. You'll be back here in ten minutes with food fit for a King.

(*For his own amusement*)

Or at least a Duke of some kind.

JOHNNY

I don't know. Mr. Kosak says we are trying to give him the merry run-around. He wants to know what kind of work you do.

35

JOHNNY'S FATHER
> (*Furiously*)
Well, go ahead and tell him.
> (*The hero*)
I have nothing to conceal. I write poetry, night and day.

JOHNNY
> (*Giving in at last*)
All right, but I don't think he'll be impressed. He says you never go out and look for work. He says you're lazy and no good.

JOHNNY'S FATHER
> (*Roaring*)
You go on down there and tell that great-hearted Slovak he's crazy, Johnny. You go on down there and tell that splendid scholar and gentleman your father is one of the greatest unknown poets living.

JOHNNY
He won't care, Pa, but I'll go. I'll do my best. Haven't we got anything in the house?

JOHNNY'S FATHER
> (*Mock-tragically, roaring*)
Only popcorn.
> (*To* MAC GREGOR)
We've been eating popcorn four days in a row now. Johnny, you've got to get bread and cheese if you expect me to finish that long poem.

JOHNNY
I'll do my best.

36

MAC GREGOR

Don't take too long, Johnny. I'm five thousand miles from home.

JOHNNY

I'll run all the way, Mr. MacGregor.

JOHNNY'S FATHER

(*For the amusement of the good Lord*)

If you find any money on the way, remember we go fifty-fifty.

JOHNNY

(*Delighted with the comedy*)

All right, Pa.

(JOHNNY *runs down the street*)

The inside of Mr. Kosak's Grocery Store. MR. KOSAK *is sleeping on his folded arms when* JOHNNY *runs into the store.* MR. KOSAK *lifts his head. He is a fine, gentle, serious man with a big, blond, old-fashioned mustache. He shakes his head trying to waken.*

JOHNNY

(*The diplomat, as it were*)

Mr. Kosak, if you were in China and didn't have a friend in the world and no money, you'd expect somebody over there to give you a pound of rice, wouldn't you?

MR. KOSAK

What do you want?

37

JOHNNY

I just want to talk a little. You'd expect some member of
the Aryan race to help you out a little, wouldn't you, Mr.
Kosak?

MR. KOSAK

How much money you got?

JOHNNY

It's not a question of money, Mr. Kosak. I'm talking about
being in China.

MR. KOSAK

I don't know nothing about nothing.

JOHNNY

How would you feel in China that way, Mr. Kosak?

MR. KOSAK

I don't know, Johnny. What would I be doing in *China?*

JOHNNY

Well, you'd be visiting there. You'd be hungry and five
thousand miles from home and not a friend in the world.
You wouldn't expect *everybody* to turn you away without
even a pound of rice, would you, Mr. Kosak?

MR. KOSAK

I guess not, but you ain't in China, Johnny, and neither is
your Pa. You or your Pa's got to go out and work sometime in your lives, so you might as well start now. I ain't
going to give you no more groceries on credit because I
know you won't pay me.

JOHNNY

Mr. Kosak, you misunderstand me. This is 1914, not 1913.

38

I'm not talking about a few groceries. I'm talking about all them heathen people around you in China, and you hungry and dying.

MR. KOSAK

This ain't China. You got to go out and make your living in this country. Everybody's got to work in America.

JOHNNY

Mr. Kosak, suppose it was a loaf of bread and a pound of cheese you needed to keep you alive in the world, would you hesitate to ask a Christian *missionary* for these things?

MR. KOSAK

Yes, I would. I would be ashamed to ask.

JOHNNY

Even if you knew you would give him back *two* loaves of bread and *two* pounds of cheese instead of one loaf and one pound? Even then, Mr. Kosak?

MR. KOSAK

Even then.

JOHNNY

Don't be that way, Mr. Kosak. That's defeatist talk, and you know it. Why, the only thing that would happen to you would be death. You'd *die* out there in China, Mr. Kosak.

MR. KOSAK

I wouldn't care if I would. You and your Pa have got to pay for bread and cheese. Why don't your Pa go out and get a job?

39

JOHNNY

> (*Swift abandonment of the intellectual attack for the human one*)

Mr. Kosak, how are you?

MR. KOSAK

I'm fine, Johnny. How are you?

JOHNNY

Couldn't be better, Mr. Kosak. How are the children?

MR. KOSAK

They're all fine, Johnny. Stepan is beginning to walk now.

JOHNNY

That's great. How's Angela?

MR. KOSAK

Angela's beginning to sing. How's your Grandmother?

JOHNNY

She's fine. She's beginning to sing too. She says she'd rather be an opera singer than Queen of England. How's your wife Martha, Mr. Kosak?

MR. KOSAK

Oh, swell.

JOHNNY

I can't tell you how glad I am to hear that everything is fine at your house. I know Stepan is going to be a great man some day.

MR. KOSAK

I hope so. I'm going to send him to high school and see that he gets every chance I didn't get. I don't want *him* to have trouble all *his* life, too.

40

JOHNNY

I have great faith in Stepan, Mr. Kosak.

MR. KOSAK

What do you want, Johnny, and how much money you
got?

JOHNNY

Mr. Kosak, you know I didn't come here to buy anything.
You know I enjoy a quiet philosophical chat with you
every now and then.
(Quickly, pleading)
Let me have a loaf of French bread and a pound of cheese.

MR. KOSAK

You got to pay cash, Johnny.

JOHNNY

And Esther? How is your beautiful daughter Esther?

MR. KOSAK

She's all right, Johnny, but you got to pay cash. You and
your Pa are the worst citizens in this county.

JOHNNY

I'm glad Esther's all right, Mr. Kosak. Jasper MacGregor
is visiting our house. He's a great actor.

MR. KOSAK

Never heard of him.

JOHNNY

And a bottle of beer for Mr. MacGregor.

MR. KOSAK

I can't give you a bottle of beer.

41

JOHNNY

Sure, you can.

MR. KOSAK

I can't. I'll let you have one loaf of French bread and a pound of cheese, but that's all. What kind of work does your Pa do when he works, Johnny?

JOHNNY

My father writes poetry, Mr. Kosak. That's the only work my father does. He's one of the greatest writers of poetry in the world.

MR. KOSAK

When does he get any money?

JOHNNY .

He never gets any money. You can't have your cake and eat it too.

MR. KOSAK

I don't like that kind of work. Why doesn't your Pa work like everybody else, Johnny?

JOHNNY

He works harder than everybody else. My father works twice as hard as the average man.

(MR. KOSAK hands JOHNNY a loaf of French bread and a pound of cheese)

MR. KOSAK

Well, that's fifty-five cents you owe me, Johnny. I'll let you have some stuff this time, but never again.

JOHNNY
    (At the door)
Tell Esther I love her.
    *(JOHNNY runs out of the store. MR. KOSAK swings at
    a fly, misses, swings again, misses, and, objecting to
    the world in this manner, he chases the fly all
    around the store, swinging with all his might)*

    *The house. JOHNNY'S FATHER and the old man are
    looking down the street to see if JOHNNY is coming
    back with food. His GRANDMOTHER is standing on
    the porch also eager to know if there is to be food.*

MAC GREGOR
I think he's got some food with him.

JOHNNY'S FATHER
    (With pride)
Of course he has.
    *(He waves at the old lady on the porch who runs
    into the house to set the table. JOHNNY runs to his
    FATHER and MAC GREGOR)*

I knew you'd do it.

MAC GREGOR
So did I.

JOHNNY
He says we got to pay him fifty-five cents. He says he's not
going to give us any more stuff on credit.

43

JOHNNY'S FATHER

That's *his* opinion. What did you talk about?

JOHNNY

First I talked about being hungry and at death's door in China. Then I inquired about the family.

JOHNNY'S FATHER

How is everyone?

JOHNNY

Fine. I didn't find any money, though. Not even a *penny*.

JOHNNY'S FATHER

Oh, that's all right. Money isn't everything.

(*They go into the house*)

The living room. They are all at the table after supper. MAC GREGOR *finds crumbs here and there which he places delicately in his mouth. He looks around the room to see if there isn't something more to eat.*

MAC GREGOR

That green can up there, Johnny. What's in there?

JOHNNY

Marbles.

MAC GREGOR

That cupboard, Johnny. Anything *edible* in there?

JOHNNY

Crickets.

44

MAC GREGOR

That big jar in the corner there, Johnny. What's delectable in there?

JOHNNY

I got a gopher snake in that jar.

MAC GREGOR

Well, I could go for a bit of boiled gopher snake in a big way, Johnny.

JOHNNY

(Defiantly, protector of animals)
Nothing doing, Mr. MacGregor.

MAC GREGOR

Why not, Johnny? Why the hell not, son? I hear of fine Borneo natives eating snakes and grasshoppers. You haven't got a half dozen fat grasshoppers around, have you, Johnny?

JOHNNY

Only four.

MAC GREGOR

Well, trot them out, son, and after we've had our fill, I'll play "Drink to Me Only with Thine Eyes" for you. I'm mighty hungry, Johnny.

JOHNNY

So am I, but I don't want anybody killing them innocent animals. They got rights the same as anybody else.

JOHNNY'S FATHER

(To MAC GREGOR)
How about a little music? I think the boy would be delighted.

45

JOHNNY
(*Leaping to his feet*)
I sure would, Mr. MacGregor.

MAC GREGOR

All right, Johnny. Bread. Bread. My God, how savagely it quarrels with the heart.
(MAC GREGOR *gets up and begins to blow into the bugle. He blows louder and more beautifully and mournfully than anybody ever blew into a bugle. Eighteen* NEIGHBORS *gather in front of the house and cheer when he finishes the solo: "Drink to Me Only with Thine Eyes"*)

JOHNNY'S FATHER
(*Delighted, for amusement*)
I want you to meet your public.

(*They go out on the porch*)

The house. The crowd is looking up at JOHNNY'S FATHER, MAC GREGOR and JOHNNY.

JOHNNY'S FATHER

Good neighbors, and friends, I want you to meet Jasper MacGregor, the greatest Shakespearean actor of our day.
(*Pause*)
I believe.

MAC GREGOR
(*The actor*)
I remember my first appearance in London in 1851 as if

46

it was yesterday. I was a boy of fourteen from the slums of Glasgow. My first part was a courier in a play, the title of which I have unfortunately forgotten. I had no lines to speak, but moved about a good deal, running from officer to officer, and from lover to his beloved, and back again, over and over again.

RUFE APLEY, THE CARPENTER

(*Regretfully interrupting the great speech*)
How about another song, Mr. MacGregor?

MAC GREGOR

Have you got an egg at your house?

RUFE APLEY

I sure have. I've got a *dozen* eggs at my house.

MAC GREGOR

Would it be convenient for you to go and get one of them dozen eggs? When you return I'll play a song that will make your heart leap with joy and grief.

RUFE APLEY

I'm on my way already.
(*He goes*)

MAC GREGOR

(*To the crowd*)
My friends, I should be delighted to play another song for you on this golden-throated bugle, but time and distance from home find me weary. If you will be so good as to go, each of you to his home, and return in a moment with some morsel of food, I shall be proud to gather my spirit together and play a song I know will change the course of each of your lives, and change it, mind you, for the better.

47

(*The people go. The last to go is* ESTHER KOSAK, *who hears the speech out, then runs.* MAC GREGOR, JOHNNY'S FATHER, *and* JOHNNY *sit on the steps and remain in silence, and one by one the people return, bringing food to* MAC GREGOR: *an egg, a sausage, a dozen green onions, two kinds of cheese, butter, two kinds of bread, boiled potatoes, fresh tomatoes, a melon, tea, and many other good things to eat*)

Thank you, my friends, thank you.

(*He stands solemnly, waiting for absolute silence, straightens himself, looks about him furiously, lifts the bugle to his lips and is irritated by the swift and noisy return of* ESTHER KOSAK, *bringing an eggplant. When there is silence, he plays "My Heart's in the Highlands, My Heart is not Here." The* PEOPLE *weep, kneel, sing the chorus, and go away.* MAC- GREGOR *turns to the father and son*)

(Grandly)

Sir, if it is all the same to you I should like to dwell in your house for a long time to come.

JOHNNY'S FATHER

(Delighted and amazed)

Sir, my house is your house.

(*They go into the house*)

The living room. Eighteen days later, MAC GREGOR *is lying on the floor, face up, asleep.* JOHNNY *is walking about quietly in the room, looking at every-*

48

body. His FATHER is at the table, writing poetry. His GRANDMOTHER is sitting in the rocking chair, rocking. There is a knock on the door. Everybody but MAC GREGOR jumps up and runs to it.

JOHNNY'S FATHER
(At the door)
Yes?

YOUNG MAN
I am looking for Jasper MacGregor, the actor.

JOHNNY'S FATHER
What do you want?

JOHNNY
Well, ask him in anyway, Pa.

JOHNNY'S FATHER
Yes, of course. Excuse me. Won't you please come in?

(The YOUNG MAN enters)

YOUNG MAN
My name is Philip Carmichael. I am from the Old People's Home. I have been sent to bring Mr. MacGregor home.

MAC GREGOR
(Wakening and sitting up)
Home? Did someone mention home?
(Roaring)
I'm five thousand miles from home, always have been, and always will be. Who is this young man?

YOUNG MAN
Mr. MacGregor, I'm Philip Carmichael, from the Old People's Home. They've sent me to bring you back. We

49

are putting on our annual show in two weeks and need you for the leading role.

MAC GREGOR

(*Getting up with the help of* JOHNNY'S FATHER *and* JOHNNY)

What kind of a part is it? I can't be playing young adventurers any longer.

YOUNG MAN

The part is King Lear, Mr. MacGregor. It is perfect for you.

MAC GREGOR

(*The actor, with a job again*)

Good-by, my beloved friends.

(*He returns from the porch*)

In all the hours of my life, in all the places I have visited, never and nowhere have I had the honor and pleasure to commune with souls loftier, purer, or more delightful than yours. Good-by.

(*The* OLD MAN *and the* YOUNG MAN *leave the house.*

There is a moment of silence, full of regret and loneliness)

JOHNNY'S FATHER

(*Hungry, loudly*)

Johnny, go on down to Mr. Kosak's store and get a little something to eat. I know you can do it, Johnny. Get ANYTHING.

JOHNNY

(*Hungry, loudly, and angry*)

Mr. Kosak wants eighty-five cents. He won't give us anything more without money.

50

JOHNNY'S FATHER

Go on down there, Johnny. You know you can get that
fine Slovak gentleman to give us a little something to eat.

JOHNNY

(With despair)

Aw, Pa.

JOHNNY'S FATHER

(Amazed, roaring)

What? You, my son, in a mood like that. Come on. I
fought the world this way before you were born. After you
were born we fought it together, and we're going to go on
fighting it. The people love poetry but don't know it, that's
all. Nothing is going to stop us, Johnny. Go on down there
now and get us something to eat.

JOHNNY

All right, Pa. I'll do my best.

(He runs to the door)

The house. It now has a large sign: "For Rent."

It is a moment before daybreak of a day early in
November, 1914. There is a suggestion of Winter
coming. High in the sky a flock of geese flying south
make their call. JOHNNY is sitting on the steps of
the front porch with his chin in his hand. He hears
the geese, listening carefully, leaps to his feet and
looks into the sky for them. The sound decreases,
then ends. JOHNNY goes back to the steps of the
porch and sits down. As the sun rises, a big solemn

51

smile comes over his face. He looks out of the corner of his eye at the morning's light as if it were a quiet friend with whom he was on terms of perfect understanding. As the light increases, this play between JOHNNY and the sun grows, like a theme of music, bringing him to his feet, turning his face to the light. He lifts his arms, and very solemnly begins turning somersaults. He then runs around the house lickety-split and returns on the other side, almost dancing.

A freight train goes by not far enough away not to make the earth tremble.

The light of morning increases.

A newspaper route carrier arrives on foot, whistling.

He is the typical small-town morning route carrier: about thirteen years old. He is in that somber and dignified state which comes over men who have done their work. His paper bags are empty. Night is over. His daily wage has been earned. The papers have been left at the doors of the readers. Another day has come to the world. He has walked two hours through dark streets to morning. The song he is whistling is soft and full of understanding. It is a song of his own composition, a morning song.

JOHNNY
    (Running down the steps)
Hello.

THE BOY
    (Stopping)
Hello.

52

JOHNNY
    What was that song?

THE BOY
    What song?

JOHNNY
    That you were whistling?

THE BOY
    Was I whistling?

JOHNNY
    Sure. Didn't you know?

THE BOY
    I guess I'm always whistling.

JOHNNY
    What was it?

THE BOY
    I don't know.

JOHNNY
    I wish I could whistle.

THE BOY
    Anybody can whistle.

JOHNNY
    I can't. How do you do it?

THE BOY
    There's no *how* to it. You just whistle.

JOHNNY
    How?

53

THE BOY

Like this.

> (*He whistles a moment, obviously improvising, a tour de force of technique*)

JOHNNY

> (*With admiration*)

I wish I could do that.

THE BOY

> (*Pleased and eager to make an even better impression*)

That was nothing. Listen to this.

> (*He gives the melody a sort of counterpoint, two tones, and a bit of syncopation*)

JOHNNY

Can't you teach me to do that?

THE BOY

You can't teach whistling. You just do it. This is another way.

> (*He whistles a little melody, the loud newsboy's style, but keeps it soft*)

JOHNNY

> (*Trying to whistle*)

Like that?

THE BOY

That's the way to start. Keep it up and after a while your mouth'll take the right shape and you'll be whistling before you know it.

JOHNNY

Honest?

54

THE BOY
    Sure.

JOHNNY
    Is your mother dead?

THE BOY
    How did you know?

JOHNNY
    My mother's dead too.

THE BOY
    Yeah?

JOHNNY
        (With a sigh)
    Yeah. She died.

THE BOY
    I don't remember my mother. Do you remember your
    mother?

JOHNNY
    I don't exactly remember her. Sometimes I dream about
    her, though.

THE BOY
    I used to, too.

JOHNNY
    Don't you any more?

THE BOY
        (Disillusioned)
    Naaaah. What good does that do you?

JOHNNY
    My mother sure is beautiful.

55

THE BOY

Yeah, I know. I remember. You got a father?

JOHNNY

(Proudly)
Oh, sure. He's in the house now, sleeping.

THE BOY

My father's dead, too.

JOHNNY

Your father, too?

THE BOY

(Matter-of-fact)
Yeah.

(They begin bouncing an old tennis ball back and forth to each other)

JOHNNY

Haven't you got anybody?

THE BOY

I got an aunt, but she ain't really my aunt. I was brought up in an orphanage. I'm adopted.

JOHNNY

What's an orphanage?

THE BOY

That's a kind of a place where kids that ain't got any mothers and fathers live until somebody adopts them.

JOHNNY

What do you mean, adopts?

56

THE BOY

Somebody who wants a boy or girl comes to the orphanage and looks everybody over and goes away with whoever they like. If they pick you, you go and stay with them.

JOHNNY

Do you like that?

THE BOY

It's all right.
>   (THE BOY *puts away the ball*)

JOHNNY

What's your name?

THE BOY

Henry. What's yours?

JOHNNY

Johnny.

THE BOY

Do you want a paper? There's a War in Europe.

JOHNNY

I haven't got any money. We aren't rich. We don't work. My father writes poetry.

THE BOY

>   (*Giving* JOHNNY *the extra*)
Oh, that's all right. Don't you *ever* have any money?

JOHNNY

Sometimes. I found a quarter once. It was lying on the sidewalk, right in front of me. Once my father got a check for ten dollars from New York, too. We bought a chicken and a lot of stamps and paper and envelopes. The chicken wouldn't lay eggs, though, so my grandmother killed it and cooked it for us. Did you ever eat chicken?

THE BOY

Sure. I guess I've eaten chicken six or seven times.

JOHNNY

What are you going to do when you grow up?

THE BOY

Shucks. I don't know. I don't know what I'll do.

JOHNNY

(Proudly)

I'm going to be a poet, like my father. He said so.

THE BOY

I guess I'll carry a paper route for a while.
(He moves to go)
Well. So long.

JOHNNY

Won't you come here again?

THE BOY

I go by here every morning about this time. I ain't never seen you up before, though.

JOHNNY

(Smiling)

I had a dream and then I woke up and didn't want to sleep any more. I wanted to get up and come out here. I saw my mother.

THE BOY

Maybe I'll see you again some morning when you can't sleep.

58

JOHNNY

I hope so. So long.

THE BOY

So long. Just keep trying and you'll be whistling before you know it.

JOHNNY

Thanks.

> (THE BOY *goes, whistling.* JOHNNY *tosses the folded paper up on the porch, and sits down again on the steps.*
>
> *His* GRANDMOTHER *comes out on the porch with a broom and begins to sweep*)

JOHNNY'S GRANDMOTHER

> (*In Armenian, which is the only language she speaks, with the exception of Turkish, Kurdish, and a little Arabic, which nobody around seems to know*)

How are you, my heart?

JOHNNY

> (*Who understands Armenian, but hardly ever speaks it; in English*)

Fine.

JOHNNY'S GRANDMOTHER

How's your Papa?

JOHNNY

I don't know.

> (*Calling loudly to his father*)

Oh, Pa. How are you?

> (*Pause. Louder*)

59

Pa.

>   (*Pause. Silence*)

I guess he's sleeping.

JOHNNY'S GRANDMOTHER

Is there any money?

JOHNNY

Money?

>   (*Shaking his head*)

No.

JOHNNY'S FATHER

>   (*From inside the house*)

Johnny?

JOHNNY

>   (*Jumping to his feet*)

Pa?

JOHNNY'S FATHER

Did you call?

JOHNNY

Yeah. How are you?

JOHNNY'S FATHER

Fine, Johnny. How are you?

JOHNNY

Fine, Pa.

JOHNNY'S FATHER

Is that all you woke me up for?

JOHNNY

>   (*To his* GRANDMOTHER)

He's fine.

> (*Louder to his* FATHER)
> The old lady wanted to know.

JOHNNY'S FATHER
> (*In Armenian, to the old lady*)
> Good light, Ma.
> (*To* JOHNNY, *in English*)
> What do you mean, old? She's not so old.

JOHNNY
> I don't mean old. You know what I mean.

> > (JOHNNY'S FATHER *comes out on the porch, button-*
> > *ing his shirt, nods to the old lady, looks out of the*
> > *corner of his eye at the sun, exactly the same way*
> > JOHNNY *did, smiling the same way, stretches all*
> > *over, faces the sun, leaps down the steps and turns*
> > *one somersault, not so good. The somersault leaves*
> > *him flat on his back*)

JOHNNY
> You ought to get a little more exercise, Pa. You're always
> sitting down.

JOHNNY'S FATHER
> (*On his back*)
> Johnny, your father is a great poet. I may not be able to
> turn a somersault as well as you, but if you want to know
> what kind of an athlete I am, just read the poetry I wrote
> yesterday.

JOHNNY
> Is it really good, Pa?

JOHNNY'S FATHER
> Good?

(He leaps to his feet, like an acrobat)
It's great. I'm going to send it to *The Atlantic Monthly*,
too.

JOHNNY

Oh, I forgot, Pa. There's a paper on the porch.

JOHNNY'S FATHER
(Going up to the porch)
You mean a morning paper, Johnny?

JOHNNY

Yeah.

JOHNNY'S FATHER

Well, that's a pleasant surprise. Where in the world did
you get it?

JOHNNY

Henry gave it to me.

JOHNNY'S FATHER

Henry? Who's Henry?

JOHNNY

He's a boy who hasn't got a mother or a *father*, either.
He sure can whistle, too.

JOHNNY'S FATHER
(Picking up the paper, opening it)
That was certainly nice of him.
(He loses himself in the headlines)

JOHNNY'S GRANDMOTHER
(To both of them, to herself, and to the world)
Where's that man?

62

JOHNNY'S FATHER

(*Deep in the news*)

Hmmm?

JOHNNY

Who?

JOHNNY'S GRANDMOTHER

You know. That old man who blew the horn.

(*She pantomimes the blowing of a horn*)

JOHNNY

Oh. Mr. MacGregor? They took him back to the Old
People's Home.

JOHNNY'S FATHER

(*Reading the paper*)

Austria. Germany. France. England. Russia. Zeppelins.
Submarines. Tanks. Machine guns. Bombs.

(*Shaking his head*)

They've gone crazy again.

JOHNNY'S GRANDMOTHER

(*To* JOHNNY, *reproachfully*)

Why don't you speak Armenian, boy?

JOHNNY

I can't talk Armenian.

JOHNNY'S FATHER

(*To* JOHNNY)

What's the matter?

JOHNNY

She wants to know about Mr. MacGregor.

63

JOHNNY'S GRANDMOTHER

(To JOHNNY'S FATHER)

Where is he?

JOHNNY'S FATHER

(In Armenian)

He's back in the Old People's Home.

JOHNNY'S GRANDMOTHER

(Shaking her head sadly)

Ahkh, ahkh, the poor old prisoner.

JOHNNY

Is it like a prison, Pa?

JOHNNY'S FATHER

I don't know for sure, Johnny.

JOHNNY'S GRANDMOTHER

(Furiously, the way her son and grandson speak when they are irritated)

Why doesn't he come back and stay here where he belongs?

(She goes into the house)

JOHNNY

That's right, Pa. Why doesn't Mr. MacGregor come back and stay here? Does he have to stay in that place?

JOHNNY'S FATHER

If you're an old, old man, Johnny, and haven't got any people, and no money, I guess you do.

JOHNNY

I sure get lonesome for him sometimes. Don't you, Pa?

JOHNNY'S FATHER

To tell you the truth, Johnny, I do.

JOHNNY

I'm always remembering him, especially the music. And the way he drinks water.

JOHNNY'S FATHER

He's a great man.

JOHNNY

Is his heart really in the highlands like he said, Pa?

JOHNNY'S FATHER

Not exactly.

JOHNNY

Is he really five thousand miles from home, too?

JOHNNY'S FATHER

At least that many.

JOHNNY

Do you think he'll ever get home again some day?

JOHNNY'S FATHER

He's an old man, Johnny. He will.

JOHNNY

You mean he'll take a train and a boat and get back where the highlands are?

JOHNNY'S FATHER

Not that, Johnny. It's a little different from that. He'll *die.*

JOHNNY

Is that the only way a man gets home?

65

JOHNNY'S FATHER

That's the only way.

(*All this time, of course,* JOHNNY'S FATHER *has been turning the pages of the morning paper, and* JOHNNY *has been going through various kinds of acrobatics, walking on the porch railing, leaping down, turning somersaults, standing on his head, and so forth. Some of his questions have been asked while he has been standing on his head.*

A sharp whistle is heard in the distance.)

JOHNNY

(Eagerly)
It's Mr. Wiley, the mailman, Pa.

(JOHNNY'S FATHER *jumps to his feet, dropping the paper*)

JOHNNY

Do you think maybe we'll get a letter from New York with a check in it maybe?

JOHNNY'S FATHER

I don't know, Johnny.

(MR. WILEY, *riding a bicycle, arrives. He is almost knocked off the bicycle by* JOHNNY *and* JOHNNY'S FATHER)

MR. WILEY

(Getting off the bicycle as if it were a horse)
Good morning, Mr. Alexander.

JOHNNY'S FATHER

Good morning, Mr. Wiley.

66

JOHNNY

Any mail for us, Mr. Wiley?

MR. WILEY

(*Bringing a packet of letters from his bag, loosening the strap, and looking them over*)

Well, now, let me see, Johnny. I think I've got something here for your father.

JOHNNY

Is it from New York?

MR. WILEY

(*Holding a flat envelope*)

Yes, it is, Johnny. Well, Mr. Alexander, it looks like Winter's coming again. The geese were flying this morning.

JOHNNY'S FATHER

(*Excited, tense, yet eager to be casual*)

Yes, I know.

(*To himself*)

I know. I know.

JOHNNY

If *I* ever get a letter from New York I'm going to save it up.

MR. WILEY

(*He wants to talk*)

How are things, Mr. Alexander?

JOHNNY'S FATHER

I've been lucky in my work, thank you, Mr. Wiley.

JOHNNY

My father was in New York once. Weren't you, Pa?

JOHNNY'S FATHER

Yes, I was, Johnny. How is your family, Mr. Wiley?

MR. WILEY

All fine, except the littlest one, Joe. He's always crying.
That's one thing I can't stand either, a baby crying all the
time. I don't know what it does to me, but it makes me
lose all faith in everything. When Joe cries I say to myself,
Aw, what's the use?

JOHNNY

I guess I'll reach New York some day before I die.

JOHNNY'S FATHER

It's nothing, Mr. Wiley. He'll stop crying after a while.

MR. WILEY

Well, I hope so, and the sooner the better.
    (*He goes off with the envelope*)
Good-by, Mr. Alexander. Good-by, Johnny.

JOHNNY'S FATHER

Mr. Wiley.

    (MR. WILEY *hands over the envelope. They say
    good-by, and* MR. WILEY *rides off.* JOHNNY'S FATHER
    *holds the envelope before him, obviously eager to
    open it, yet fearful to do so*)

JOHNNY

    (*Impatient*)
All right, Pa. Go ahead; open it. What are you waiting
for?

JOHNNY'S FATHER

    (Angry; roaring)

Johnny, I'm scared. I can't understand how I, your father, can be so scared.

JOHNNY

You don't sound scared, Pa. Who's it from?

JOHNNY'S FATHER

It's from *The Atlantic Monthly* all right. You remember them poems I wrote after Mr. MacGregor was here?

JOHNNY

Maybe they've bought the poems.

JOHNNY'S FATHER

Bought them, my eye. They don't buy *poetry*, Johnny. They *scare* you to death.

    (Reading *his name and address with great solemnity, awful fearfulness and terrible rage*)

Ben Alexander, 2226 San Benito Avenue, Fresno, California.

JOHNNY

It's for you all right, Pa. Why don't you open it?

JOHNNY'S FATHER

    (Roaring)

I'm scared, I tell you. I'm scared and ashamed. *Those poems were great.* How can it be that I'm scared?

JOHNNY

    (Also defiant)

Don't be scared, Pa.

69

JOHNNY'S FATHER

>(Angry)

Why do they clamor for all things but the best? Why do
they destroy themselves running after things of death, and
thrust aside all things of life? I can't understand it. There's
no hope for anybody.

JOHNNY

Sure there is, Pa.

>(Furiously)

Who the hell is The Atlantic Monthly?

JOHNNY'S FATHER

>(Angry)

Johnny, go away. Go away. Please go away.

JOHNNY

>(Angry, too)

All right, Pa.

>(JOHNNY goes around the house, reappears, looks
>at his father a moment, and then knows he must
>stay out of the way)

>(It is obvious that JOHNNY'S FATHER knows The
>Atlantic Monthly has sent back the poems. It is
>equally obvious that he can't believe the poems
>have come back. It is obvious too that the poems
>are great, because the man is. He paces about like a
>tiger. He seems to be speaking to the world, even
>though his lips are set. At last he tears the envelope
>open, in a fury. The envelope falls. He unfolds the
>manuscript of poems. A slip of white, heavy paper
>falls to the floor of the porch. He stands, very tall,

and very proud, and reads the poems to himself, turning the pages swiftly)

JOHNNY'S FATHER

(Furiously)

Ah, you crazy, miserable fools.

(He sits on the steps of the porch and buries his face in his hands. The manuscript of poems is on the steps.

After several minutes he kicks the poems off the steps of the porch onto the ground and takes up the morning paper again, looking at the headlines)

(Quietly, with deep fury, his voice mounting in intensity)

Go ahead, kill everybody. Declare War on one another. Take the people by the thousands and mangle them. Their poor hearts and their poor spirits and their poor bodies. Give them ugliness. Pollute their dreams. Horrify them. Distort them with hatred for one another. Befoul the legend of the living, you maniacs whose greatness is measured by the number you destroy.

(JOHNNY appears at the side of the house, unseen)

(He stands in a trance, listening to his father)

(The sky begins to darken)

You frauds of the world. You wretched and ungodly.

(He stands and points a finger, as if across the world)

Go ahead. Fire your feeble guns. You won't kill anything.

(Quietly, smiling)

There will always be poets in the world.

(Lightning flashes silently)

71

The house. The sky is dark, as at the beginning of a storm. An occasional deep and faraway roar of thunder is heard, and a flash of lightning is seen. JOHNNY'S FATHER *is on the steps of the porch, smiling: a foolish, tragic, desolate, lonely smile. Everything is the same; the manuscript of poems is on the ground; the envelope is on the porch. The newspaper too. It is several hours later.*

JOHNNY'S FATHER
> (*Shaking his head foolishly, unable to accept the truth*)

Johnny.
> (*Pause. A little louder*)

Johnny.
> (*Pause, softer this time*)

Johnny.
> (*Roaring*)

Johnny.

> (*The boy comes around the house shyly and stands before his father*)

> (*His father looks up, fire in his eye, defiant, bitter, stubborn, powerful*)

JOHNNY'S FATHER
> (*Tenderly, but with tremendous power*)

Have you had your breakfast?

JOHNNY
> (*Shyly*)

I'm not hungry, Pa.

72

JOHNNY'S FATHER

You go on inside now and eat.

JOHNNY

I'm not hungry.

JOHNNY'S FATHER

You do what I tell you.

JOHNNY

I won't eat unless you do.

JOHNNY'S FATHER

You do what I *tell* you.

JOHNNY

I won't eat unless you do.

JOHNNY'S FATHER

I'm not hungry.

JOHNNY

I'll go down to Mr. Kosak's and see if I can get something.

JOHNNY'S FATHER

(*Humiliated. Taking the boy's arm*)

No, Johnny.

(*He pauses, obviously trying to find words with
which to explain about themselves and the grocer*)

Johnny? I thought we'd be getting some money. I didn't
think it would be this way. Now, go on inside and eat.

JOHNNY

(*Going up the stairs*)

You got to eat, too.

(*He goes into the house*)

(*There is a silent flash of lightning*)

(A MAN *in a business suit, and a young* HUSBAND *and* WIFE *with a* BABY *in the mother's arms, come up*)

THE REAL ESTATE MAN

This is the house. The rent's six dollars a month. It's not exactly fancy, but it'll keep out the rain and cold.

(JOHNNY'S FATHER *has been staring at the people, his vision frozen*)

THE REAL ESTATE MAN

(*Coming up to* JOHNNY'S FATHER, *extending his hand, while the others stand back in a group*)
Remember me? I put up the "For Rent" sign.

JOHNNY'S FATHER

(*Rising*)
I remember. How do you do.

THE REAL ESTATE MAN

(*Embarrassed*)
Well. Mr. Corey, the owner of the house, is out of town, and these people are looking for a house. Right away.

JOHNNY'S FATHER

Of course. I can leave any time. Have they furniture?

THE REAL ESTATE MAN

(*Turning to the poor family*)
Have you furniture?

THE HUSBAND

No.

74

JOHNNY'S FATHER

(*To the family*)

You can have my furniture. There isn't much of it, but it'll do. There's a pretty good stove.

THE WIFE

(*With the dignity of the poor*)

We wouldn't want to take your furniture.

JOHNNY'S FATHER

That's all right. I haven't paid rent for three months. I'll leave the furniture for the rent.

(THE REAL ESTATE MAN *tries to speak*)

JOHNNY'S FATHER

It's all right. I'm sorry I haven't the $18. The furniture's worth about that much. You can let these people have it till Mr. Corey gets back.

(*To the family*)

Do you want to go through the house?

THE HUSBAND

It looks all right.

THE REAL ESTATE MAN

(*Going*)

Then that's settled.

(*To the people*)

The rent's six dollars a month. We pay the water.

JOHNNY'S FATHER

(*To the people*)

You can move in any time.

75

THE HUSBAND

Thank you very much. We'll be back this afternoon or tomorrow.

> (*They are going as* JOHNNY *comes out with a plate containing two slices of bread and a small bunch of grapes*)

JOHNNY

Who were those people?

JOHNNY'S FATHER

Just some people walking by.

JOHNNY

What were you talking about?

JOHNNY'S FATHER

Just talking, Johnny.

JOHNNY

> (*Shouting; very angry*)

Don't feel bad, Pa.

JOHNNY'S FATHER

> (*Turning and looking at the boy with love, amazement, admiration, and delight, laughing suddenly*)

I don't feel bad, Johnny. Let the world be the world, and God love everyone.

JOHNNY

> (*Bantering*)

All right then. Let's eat.

> (*He puts the plate on the top step and they sit down together and begin to eat.*

They eat in silence, looking at one another, the boy looking at his father out of the corner of his eye as he had looked at the sun; the father looking at the boy the same way. The boy begins to smile. The father begins to smile too)

JOHNNY

Do you like grapes, Pa?

JOHNNY'S FATHER

Of course I like grapes.

JOHNNY

Pa?

JOHNNY'S FATHER

Yes?

JOHNNY

Is it really like a prison?

JOHNNY'S FATHER

Sometimes I'm sure it is. Sometimes I know it never can be.

JOHNNY

What, Pa?

JOHNNY'S FATHER

I guess it's fifty-fifty, Johnny. You know. It's both.

JOHNNY

I mean, do you think he gets homesick sometimes?

JOHNNY'S FATHER

I'm sure he does.

77

JOHNNY

I wish he'd come back.

JOHNNY'S FATHER

I'd like to see him again.

JOHNNY

I remember him all the time.

JOHNNY'S FATHER

I do too. I'll always remember him.

JOHNNY

So will I. Did he *have* to go back, Pa?

JOHNNY'S FATHER

I guess he did.

JOHNNY

He seemed like a nice young man.

JOHNNY'S FATHER

You mean the young man who came and got him?

JOHNNY

Yeah, you know. That young man who talked so sharp,
like he was speaking in front of an audience.

JOHNNY'S FATHER

He was all right.

(There is one more grape on the plate)

JOHNNY

Go ahead, Pa. Take it.

JOHNNY'S FATHER

(Blithely)

No, that's yours, Johnny. I counted.

78

JOHNNY

    All right, Pa.

        (*He takes the last grape and eats it*)

    Is it stealing, Pa?

JOHNNY'S FATHER

        (*Comically*)

    Well, some say it is and some say it isn't.

        (*Dramatically*)

    I say it isn't.

        (*Shouting*)

    You took them off the vines, didn't you?

JOHNNY

    I took them off the vines all right, Pa.

JOHNNY'S FATHER

        (*Comically*)

    Then it couldn't very well be stealing.

JOHNNY

    When would it be stealing?

JOHNNY'S FATHER

        (*Tossing it off like nothing*)

    The way I see it, Johnny, stealing is where there's unnecessary damage or cruelty to an innocent one, so that there may be undeserved profit or power to one who is not innocent.

JOHNNY

    Oh.

        (*Pause*)

    Well, if it isn't stealing, Pa, I guess I'll go get some more.

        (*He gets up*)

They'll be all gone pretty soon.
(Goes off)

JOHNNY'S FATHER
(When the boy is gone, laughing)
My son John. My God, how fortunate I have been. How
grateful I am.
(He picks up the manuscript of poems, puts it
in his coat pocket, and walks down the street)

The inside of Mr. Kosak's Grocery Store. Again
MR. KOSAK is sleeping on his folded arms. The store
looks more poverty-stricken than before. The family
apparently has been eating the stock. JOHNNY'S
FATHER comes into the store quietly, almost shyly.
MR. KOSAK lifts his head, blinks his eyes, stands.

JOHNNY'S FATHER
(Almost guiltily)
I'm Johnny's father.

(The two men stand staring at one another a moment, each of them delighted, embarrassed, impressed, pleased, and angry about the same things
in the world: greed, deceit, unkindliness, dispropor-
tion. They each begin to smile, then shake hands
warmly)

MR. KOSAK
I recognize you. Johnny has told me about you. It is an
honor.

JOHNNY'S FATHER

You are a kind man.

MR. KOSAK

I do not know.

JOHNNY'S FATHER

(*Slowly*)

I have come to say good-by. To apologize. To thank you.

MR. KOSAK

(*Swiftly*)

You're not going away?

JOHNNY'S FATHER

I'm sorry, yes.

MR. KOSAK

We shall all miss Johnny.

JOHNNY'S FATHER

I have no money. I am in debt to you.

MR. KOSAK

It is nothing.

JOHNNY'S FATHER

I may not see you again.

(*He brings the manuscript of poems from his pocket*)

(*Powerfully*)

I am a poet. These are some of my poems.

(*Swiftly*)

I am not offering them to you in place of the money I owe you. Money is another thing.

(*Pleading*)

Will you keep them for your kindness?

81

MR. KOSAK

    (*Sincerely*)

I cannot take your poems.

    (*Pause*)

JOHNNY'S FATHER

 I hope you have been prospering.

MR. KOSAK

The people have no money. I do not know how I am going to put in new stock.

JOHNNY'S FATHER

I'm sorry.

MR. KOSAK

In the Winter it is worse. The packing-houses are closed. There are no jobs. I would give them something if I could, but this Winter I have no money for new stock. I may have to close the store. There is hardly enough for my family.

JOHNNY'S FATHER

    (*Touched and angry*)

These poems. Let me tell you they are the finest I have ever written. I want to leave them with you.

    (*Mr. Kosak's daughter* ESTHER, *a beautiful girl of seven, comes into the store, from the back*)

MR. KOSAK

This is my daughter Esther. Esther, this is Johnny's father.

JOHNNY'S FATHER

Johnny's told me about you.

ESTHER

(*Really pleased, but shy*)

How do you do.

MR. KOSAK

They're going away.

ESTHER

(*Shocked*)

Oh.

JOHNNY'S FATHER

Johnny will miss you.

(*The girl's lips tremble, tears come to her eyes.
She turns and runs out of the store*)

MR. KOSAK

Everything is like that.

JOHNNY'S FATHER

They are children.

MR. KOSAK

Yes, but it's that way from the beginning and it never
changes. Only women never learn to believe it.

JOHNNY'S FATHER

Won't you give her these poems?

MR. KOSAK

Please. It's nothing. She will cry for a while, but it is
nothing.

JOHNNY'S FATHER

Here.

(*Giving* MR. KOSAK *the poems*)

You will be doing me a kindness by keeping them.

(*Loudly, to God and the world*)
Don't you see, poetry must be read to be poetry. It may be that one reader is all that I deserve. If this is so, I want that reader to be you.

MR. KOSAK
Thank you. I am unworthy.

JOHNNY'S FATHER
(*Smiling*)
Good-by.

MR. KOSAK
Good-by.

> (JOHNNY'S FATHER *goes out of the store. The grocer takes his glasses out of his pocket, puts them on, unfolds the manuscript, and standing in the middle of the store, begins to read, softly, to himself, moving his lips. The expression of his face begins to change. Rain begins to fall. His daughter* ESTHER *comes back into the store*)

MR. KOSAK
> (*Reading from one of the poems, in a quiet voice*)
Deep in the bowels of the earth, and far dispersed into the green waters of the sea, and held tight within the hardness of rock, I thee remember, love, remember me.

> (*The* GIRL *begins to sob aloud, and the* FATHER *turns and goes to her*)

84

The living room of the house. Some time later. JOHNNY'S FATHER *is at his table, looking over a stack of manuscripts. It is still raining. Every once in a while he gets up and goes to the window.*

JOHNNY'S FATHER

What the hell's happened to him?

> (*He goes back to his manuscripts and looks over some poems, grows irritated with them, throws them down, and goes to the window again. Then begins to walk back and forth, waiting.*

> *At last* JOHNNY *tears up the front porch stairs, busts into the house, closes the door quickly, and bolts it. He is breathless and scared. You know he is one who has been pursued. He has four medium-sized bunches of purple-red Emperors; a half dozen black figs; and two pomegranates.*)

JOHNNY

> (*Excited and breathless*)

Where shall I hide them, Pa?

JOHNNY'S FATHER

What's the matter, Johnny?

JOHNNY

You said it wasn't stealing, Pa.

JOHNNY'S FATHER

> (*With furious irritation*)

Well, it isn't.

JOHNNY

What about the farmer's dog, then?

JOHNNY'S FATHER

What are you talking about? What farmer's dog?

JOHNNY

The farmer's dog that chased me all the way here.

JOHNNY'S FATHER

(Roaring)

Dog? Do you mean to tell me a dog chased you? What kind of a dog?

JOHNNY

I didn't get a chance to take a good look, but I guess it's a great big one.

JOHNNY'S FATHER

(Very angry at this awful humiliation)

Did the God damn thing try to bite you or anything, Johnny?

JOHNNY

I don't think so, Pa, but I thought it was going to any minute.

JOHNNY'S FATHER

Did it growl at you?

JOHNNY

It wasn't exactly a growl.

JOHNNY'S FATHER

What happened?

JOHNNY

I just ran all the way, with the dog right behind me.

JOHNNY'S FATHER

Where is it now?

86

JOHNNY

It's *outside*, I think, Pa. Are you sure it isn't stealing?

JOHNNY'S FATHER

(*Very angry, eating three or four grapes*)
Of course it isn't stealing. I'll take care of the dog. No man or beast can scare your father, Johnny. Always remember that.
(*He goes cautiously to the window and peeks out*)

JOHNNY

Is it out there, Pa?

JOHNNY'S FATHER

There's a little dog out there, Johnny. It's asleep, I think.

JOHNNY

(*Jumping bitterly*)
I *knew* it. It's the farmer's dog, waiting for me.

JOHNNY'S FATHER

It's not a very big dog, Johnny.

JOHNNY

Yeah, but if it's stealing—if it's the farmer's dog—what about that?

JOHNNY'S FATHER

Why, that little bitty dog doesn't belong to anybody, Johnny. That little dog is looking for a friend, I bet.

JOHNNY

It chased me all the way. Are you sure, Pa?

JOHNNY'S FATHER

Sure I'm sure, Johnny. I'm no poet for nothing. I understand things.

(*The dog begins to growl and bark.* JOHNNY'S
FATHER *jumps back from the window, frightened.*
JOHNNY *grows tense and speechless*)

JOHNNY
(*Whispering*)
What is it, Pa?

JOHNNY'S FATHER
Somebody's coming, I think.

JOHNNY
You see, Pa? *It is stealing.* It's the farmer.
(*He runs to the table and gathers the fruit into his
arms. His* GRANDMOTHER *comes running into the
room*)

JOHNNY'S GRANDMOTHER
(*In Armenian*)
What's all the hullabaloo, in the rain?

JOHNNY'S FATHER
Shhhh.

(JOHNNY *takes the fruit out of the living room;
returns, scared to death. The dog is still growling
and barking.* JOHNNY'S FATHER *is even more scared
than* JOHNNY)

JOHNNY
(*Sore, and now defiant*)
God damn it, Pa. Now look at the mess we're in.

JOHNNY'S FATHER
I wish I had a cigarette.

88

JOHNNY

> (*Now worrying about his father; to his grand-
> mother, in Armenian*)

Are there cigarettes?

> (JOHNNY'S GRANDMOTHER *runs into the next room*)

> (*The dog stops growling*)

JOHNNY

You see, Pa? It's the farmer. Where shall I hide? Don't
open the door.

JOHNNY'S FATHER

Open the door? Help me with this table.

> (*They push the table up against the door, and tip-
> toe back to the center of the room.* JOHNNY'S GRAND-
> MOTHER *runs back with one cigarette and one match
> which she hands to* JOHNNY'S FATHER, *who lights
> the cigarette, inhales deeply, and straightens up*)

JOHNNY'S FATHER

> (*Dramatically*)

I am the one who took the fruit, understand, Johnny?

JOHNNY

Don't open the door, Pa.

> (JOHNNY'S FATHER *picks up a small stool, takes it
> quietly to the table up against the door, places it on
> the table, to make it heavier*)

> (JOHNNY *picks up a chair and puts it on the table.
> The* OLD LADY *puts a vase on the table.* JOHNNY'S
> FATHER *adds three books to the barricade. In fact,*

89

as the knocks continue, the family little by little
puts all the household goods up against the door)

JOHNNY'S FATHER

Don't be afraid, Johnny.

JOHNNY

He can't get in, can he, Pa?

JOHNNY'S FATHER

I don't think so.

> (The GRANDMOTHER, the FATHER and the SON stand
> together in the bare room, defying the world.
>
> There is a long pause, full of a mingling of awful
> fear and furious defiance.
>
> After half a minute the silence is broken.
>
> It is a solo on the bugle: "My Heart's in the High-
> lands."
>
> The sun comes out)

JOHNNY

> (Shouting)

It's Mr. MacGregor.

JOHNNY'S FATHER

> (Running to the window, lifting it, and shouting
> out to MAC GREGOR)

Welcome, Mr. MacGregor. Johnny, rearrange the furniture.

> (JOHNNY'S FATHER returns to the barricade and helps
> JOHNNY and his GRANDMOTHER rearrange the furni-
> ture. At last everything is out of the way. JOHNNY'S

90

FATHER *swings open the door.* JASPER MAC GREGOR, *still playing the solo, preceded by the dog, which is a very small street dog, comes in. The dog runs around playfully, all excited.* MAC GREGOR'S *eyes are full of grief and joy.* JOHNNY *begins making trips to the kitchen, returning with the fruit, on a plate, and a pitcher of water.* MAC GREGOR *finishes the solo. There is a moment when everybody stands stock-still, including the dog.* JOHNNY *offers* MAC GREGOR *the pitcher of water)*

MAC GREGOR
(*Weary*)
Not this time, Johnny.

JOHNNY'S FATHER
Welcome, my friend.

MAC GREGOR
I've run away. They're after me now, but I won't go back. They stole my bugle. They tried to keep me in bed. They said I was sick. I'm not sick; I'm old. I know my days on earth are numbered. I want them to be with you. Don't let them take me back.

JOHNNY'S FATHER
I won't.
(*He draws out a chair for the old man*)
Please sit down.

(*They all sit down.* MAC GREGOR *looks around at everybody*)

MAC GREGOR
It's good to see you again.

91

JOHNNY

Is your heart still in the highlands?

MAC GREGOR

(Nodding)

In the highlands, son.

JOHNNY'S FATHER

(Angry)

Johnny.

JOHNNY

(Sore, too)

What?

JOHNNY'S FATHER

Shut up.

JOHNNY

Why?

JOHNNY'S FATHER

Why? What do you get so dumb for every once in a while?
Can't you see Mr. MacGregor is weary?

JOHNNY

(To MAC GREGOR)

Are you?

MAC GREGOR

(Nods)

But where's your mother, son?

JOHNNY

She's dead.

MAC GREGOR

(Almost to himself)

Not dead, Johnny.
> (*He shakes his head*)

In the highlands.

JOHNNY'S GRANDMOTHER
> (*To his father*)

What's he saying?

JOHNNY'S FATHER
> (*Shaking his head*)

Nothing.
> (*To* MAC GREGOR)

Won't you eat?

MAC GREGOR
> (*Looking at the plate*)

One grape. No more.
> (*He plucks a grape off a bunch, puts it in his mouth.*
> *Suddenly turns, startled*)

Are they coming?

JOHNNY'S FATHER

Don't be afraid, my friend. Lie down and rest.
> (JOHNNY'S FATHER *takes the* OLD MAN *to the couch.*
> *The* OLD MAN *stretches out, face up.* JOHNNY'S
> FATHER *returns to the table. Nobody is eating. The*
> OLD MAN *jumps up suddenly. It's nothing again.*
> *He gets up and returns to the table*)

MAC GREGOR

You won't let them take me back, will you?

JOHNNY'S FATHER

No.

93

(*He breaks open a pomegranate and hands* MAC-
GREGOR *half*)
Try to eat something.

MAC GREGOR

Thank you, my friend.
(*He eats some of the pomegranate*)

(*There is a knock on the door,* MAC GREGOR *leaps to
his feet, furiously*)

MAC GREGOR

(*Roaring*)
You'll not take me back. I warn you. I'll fall down and
die. I belong here, with these people.

JOHNNY'S FATHER

(*Scared*)
Shall we open the door?

JOHNNY

(*Also scared*)
Shall we?

MAC GREGOR

(*Powerful*)
Of course we'll open the door.
(*He goes to the door, opens it. It is* RUFE APLEY,
the carpenter, who is a little shaken up by MAC-
GREGOR'S *fury*)

RUFE APLEY

Hello, Mr. MacGregor.

JOHNNY

Who is it?

94

RUFE APLEY

It's Rufe Apley.

MAC GREGOR

How do you do, Rufe.

JOHNNY'S FATHER

(At the door)
Come in, Rufe.

(RUFE comes in. He has a loaf of bread, a sausage and two eggs in his hands)

RUFE

I was sitting home doing nothing when I heard that song again. I was sure it was Mr. MacGregor.

MAC GREGOR

I'm delighted you remembered.

RUFE

Nobody could ever forget that song, Mr. MacGregor. I brought these few things.

MAC GREGOR

(Taking them and putting them on the table)
Thank you, my friend, thank you.

(There is another knock at the door. It is SAM WALLACE; he is a lineman, in full regalia: overalls, tools hanging all over him, tape, straps around his calves, spikes, everything. He has cheese and tomatoes and radishes with him)

WALLACE

I knew it was Mr. MacGregor. I said to myself, I'll go over with a few little things to eat.

95

MAC GREGOR

This is indeed a pleasant surprise.

RUFE

      (*Obviously trying hard to say something*)
Ah, Mr. MacGregor?

MAC GREGOR

Yes, my friend? Speak up. I'm a plain man, no different in any way from yourself.

RUFE

My wife's sister and her family are outside. I know they'd like to hear you play again. There are some other people.

MAC GREGOR

      (*Flattered*)
Of course I'll play. I'm over eighty and not long for this world. Before I go I'd like to become a part of you who shall live after I am dead. Are there children out there too?

RUFE

Seven. My wife's sister's kids.

      (*Three or four more neighbors come in, bringing food.* MAC GREGOR *takes up his bugle. Everybody follows him out of the room to the porch, except* JOHNNY'S FATHER. MAC GREGOR *begins to play the solo again. This time he's too old and weak to really play, but he finishes the solo as well as he is able to.*

      JOHNNY'S FATHER *paces about the room, smiling, frowning, loving the place. The door to the kitchen*

96

opens quietly and ESTHER KOSAK *stands in the door-way.* JOHNNY'S FATHER *turns and sees her. She is no longer crying. She has something clutched in her fist*)

JOHNNY'S FATHER
    (Quietly)
Hello, Esther.

ESTHER
Where's Johnny?

JOHNNY'S FATHER
I'll go get him.
    (He goes out on the porch)

(The GIRL *stands alone in terrible sadness and lone-liness. After a moment* JOHNNY *comes rushing in, all excited, but calms down quickly when he begins to feel the mood of the girl*)

JOHNNY
Hello, Esther.

ESTHER
Hello, Johnny.

JOHNNY
What's the matter?

ESTHER
My father read me the poems.

JOHNNY
What?

97

ESTHER

(Holding out her hand)

Here. This is all I've got.

(JOHNNY takes a handful of coins)

I've been saving up for Christmas.

(She begins to cry, turns, and runs out of the house)

JOHNNY

(Deeply touched and furious, sensing something profound and beautiful and terrible)

Holy Moses.

(His face takes on boyhood's tragic expression of grief, and he begins to cry. He throws the coins against the wall and falls down, sobbing)

Who the hell wants that stuff?

(JOHNNY'S FATHER comes back)

JOHNNY'S FATHER

Johnny.

(Going closer)

Johnny?

JOHNNY

(Sobbing and angry)

She brought me money.

JOHNNY'S FATHER

It's no use crying, Johnny.

JOHNNY

(Jumping up)

Who's crying?

(He cries harder than ever)

98

JOHNNY'S FATHER

Go wash your face. It's nothing.

JOHNNY

(Going)

Something's wrong somewhere.

(MAC GREGOR finishes the solo, the people are silent with awe and the knowledge that something is wrong. MAC GREGOR'S VOICE is heard for a moment in a speech)

MAC GREGOR

(Wearily)

The years, my friends. I have walked to the end of them. I'm sorry I can no longer play for you. Thank you. Thank you.

(JOHNNY'S FATHER walks back and forth in the room. He sits down at the table and looks at the food. MAC GREGOR and JOHNNY'S GRANDMOTHER return and sit at the table. The dog lies down in a corner)

MAC GREGOR

(He lifts the water pitcher, drinks a little)

They wouldn't let me play.

(He drinks a little more)

They stole my bugle.

(He drinks a little more)

They said I was sick.

(He drinks a little more)

I'm as strong as a bull. If they come to take me back, I shall pretend that I am dying. I shall play the death scene from "King Lear." I shall play all the death scenes.

99

(JOHNNY *returns solemnly. They are all at the*
table. Nobody can eat but the OLD LADY. *There is*
a long silence. The OLD LADY *stops eating*)

JOHNNY'S GRANDMOTHER
What's the matter? Why this terrible gloom?

(MAC GREGOR *rises*)

MAC GREGOR
(*Reciting, remembering lines from Shakespeare,*
and inventing a few of his own)
Blow, winds, and crack your cheeks!
Rage! blow!
You cataracts and hurricanes, spout
Till you have drenched our steeples,
    drowned the cocks!
You sulphurous and thought-executing fires,
Singe my white head!
Humble thy belly-full, spit fire, spout rain!
I never gave you kingdom, call'd you children.
Here I stand, your slave,
A poor infirm, weak and despised old man.

To be or not to be . . .
    (*Tragically*)
To be— To be—
What? A fool? A man mocked by destiny?
Turned away from home and fire and love?
I am a man more sinned against than sinning.
Arms! Arms! Sword! Fire!
Corruption in the place! The little dogs and all,
Tray, Blanche, Sweetheart. See? They bark at me.

100

O, that way madness lies—no more of that—
Let me shun that. My wits begin to turn.

(JOHNNY *goes to him, and kneels*)

Come on, my boy, how dost my boy? Art cold?
Let me alone! Wilt break my heart?
And my poor fool is hang'd.
No, no, no life!
Why should a dog, a horse, a rat have life
And thou no life at all?
Thou'lt come no more,
Never, never, never, never!
Pray you undo this button—thank you, sir—
(*Holds the bugle before him*)
Do you see this? Look on her. Look.
Look there, look there!!

(*While* MAC GREGOR *is acting* JOHNNY *returns to the
coins on the floor and picks them up one by one
and looks at them.*

*The room is in absolute silence. A horse and wagon
in the street is heard; then steps on the front porch;
then a knock at the door.* JOHNNY'S FATHER *goes to
the door. It is* PHILIP CARMICHAEL *and two guards
from the Old People's Home. The guards stand at
attention at the door*)

CARMICHAEL
We heard him playing. He's very sick. We've come to
take him back.

JOHNNY'S FATHER
Please come in.

(*He enters*)

(*To* MAC GREGOR)

Mr. MacGregor.

(*There is no answer*)

JOHNNY'S FATHER
(*Louder*)
Mr. MacGregor.
(*Goes closer*)
Mr. MacGregor. Mr. Mac—

(CARMICHAEL *hurries over to* MAC GREGOR *and examines him*)

CARMICHAEL
He's dead.

JOHNNY
No, he isn't. He was acting.

JOHNNY'S FATHER
By God, he was the greatest Shakespearean actor of our day.

CARMICHAEL
I'm sorry this had to happen here.

JOHNNY'S FATHER
Why not? Why not here? This is where he wanted it to be.

JOHNNY
He was acting, Pa. He isn't dead.
(*He goes to* MAC GREGOR)
Are you, Mr. MacGregor?

(*There is no answer, of course*)

102

CARMICHAEL

We'll take him back.

JOHNNY'S FATHER

Here's his bugle. Keep it with him.

(JOHNNY'S FATHER lifts MAC GREGOR and carries him out. The guards carry him up the street.

The light of the afternoon sun increases to the same intensity as at the beginning of the play.

The horse and wagon goes off. There is a moment of strange silence, and the faint far-away sound of the bugle solo. A knock at the door. JOHNNY'S FATHER opens the door. It's the young HUSBAND and WIFE. The BABY is crying. They come in)

THE WIFE

The kid is tired and sleepy.

JOHNNY'S FATHER

The house is ready.

(To JOHNNY)

Get your stuff.

(To the OLD LADY, in Armenian)

We're going.

(He gets a straw suitcase from under the couch and throws his poems, books, envelopes, one loaf of bread, and a few of the other items of food into it. The OLD LADY puts a shawl around her head and shoulders. JOHNNY leaves all his junk; takes only the handful of coins. The BABY stops crying. The dog follows JOHNNY around. The music increases in intensity)

103

THE HUSBAND
   Thank you very much.

THE WIFE
   Have you some place to go?

JOHNNY'S FATHER
   Yes, we have. Good-by.

THE HUSBAND AND WIFE
   Good-by.

         (*They go out of the house to the street.*)

JOHNNY
   Where the hell do we think we're going, Pa?

JOHNNY'S FATHER
   Never mind, Johnny. You just follow me.

JOHNNY
   I'm not mentioning any names, Pa, but something's wrong
somewhere.

         (*The music grows louder. They walk up the street*)

HOW THE PLAY WAS RECEIVED
IN NEW YORK

These reviews of "My Heart's in the Highlands" by the drama critics of the New York dailies and the principal national weeklies are reprinted here for the student and for the record. I wish to express my sincere thanks to each of the critics.

BURNS MANTLE, *New York Daily News:*

So far as this reviewer is concerned there is an incompleted sentence in the program giving the production details of "My Heart's in the Highlands" at the Guild Theatre.

"The play will be performed without an intermission," reads the sentence. "And without reason" should have been added.

But do not let me discourage you, if you happen to be an admirer of that flashing young Armenian, William Saroyan, poet and story writer, who wrote the play.

Because all meaning, sense or excuse for "My Heart's in the Highlands" eluded me it does not follow that you might not get something for your money, and possibly something for your mind, by attendance upon it.

It is a fantastic drama about a poor poet and his loyal son. About the starving they do, and the neighbors they have, and a crazed ancient who believes he is a great actor.

Together they play out a single scene during which the poet bites his nails, and his son wheedles groceries from a trusting grocer, and the old actor plays songs on his trumpet and the neighbors are drawn as children to a Pied Piper.

They bring vegetables, too, but do not throw them. And that, I suspect, is a symbol of forbearance.

I left the theatre feeling as Mr. Saroyan did after he had had an adventure at the movies (*Time*, March 2, 1936):

". . . but, God Almighty, it didn't seem funny to me and I sat in the darkness trying to laugh, but kept thinking, 'Why are they wasting everything, why are they making all these mistakes, why is everybody so awkward and mean, what is the God damn meaning of this stuff?' "

Philip Loeb played the poet, and a young boy, Sidney Lumet, was very good as his son. The settings, by Herbert Andrews, were attractively lighted, and the music by Paul Bowles was probably good, too, being a little weird.

The Group Theatre made the production by way of testing the popularity of the play. They expect to repeat it for another four performances.

JOHN ANDERSON, *New York Journal American*:

Though Mr. Saroyan has leaped through no store windows with a shy bathtub, he is, I suspect, the Salvador Dali of the drama, a surrealist playwright whose "My Heart's in the Highlands" at the Guild Theatre last night could be compared favorably with a fur-lined teacup. If you squint your eyes and try to understand it, it doesn't make any sense at all, but if you let it alone and let it pry around in the gizzard, it will very likely tug your heart strings. People seemed to find themselves weeping without knowing what the hell was the matter with them and—if this doesn't make sense you may take it up with Mr. Saroyan. He may be addressed from now on, I hope, in care of the Group Theatre, which sponsored last night's special performance. It will be repeated four times.

In any search for literal meaning in the play one man's guess is as good as another's. When I read the play in its original shorter form a couple of years ago in *One-Act Play Magazine* I set up a mild clamor for its production because it seemed a fascinating experiment.

Saroyan takes a penniless poet, his small son, and the boy's grandmother living in jovial poverty in a vague dwelling in Fresno. To them comes a white-whiskered old actor, escaped with his trumpet from an old folks' home, and he plays the music to Bobbie Burns's "My Heart's in the Highlands" with such plaintive beauty that the neighbors all bring in things to eat. The guards take the old man away but he escapes again, and finally dies while the little boy, looking on, thinks he is just playing "Lear."

That is, so help me Heaven, all there is to it, if you want it in so many words, no plot, no elaborate build-up of entrances and exits, no careful analysis of character. Saroyan simply glimpses a few human beings, and evokes from them moods and situations of compelling emotion. He manipulates the theatre as frankly as a musician pulling out the sobstops on the Music Hall organ, and if he leaves you knowing only that you have given in to some mechanical exercises he proves, at least, that they're effective.

From vague hints in the dialogue the playlet, which is an hour and a half long, and all in one piece, might be taken as a parable of beauty—the unearthly longing of people for a place that the heart knows. Or, more directly, there is a hint of social thesis in a line or two about the dispossessed poet who cries out, in momentary bitterness at the injustice of a world which values things in money.

I do not profess to know what Saroyan means. This is guesswork. I know only that he conjures up passages of poignant sadness as definite as music can be, and as inexplicable. He can impart swift mischief to a line, and make it smile across the play as if it were a streak of bright paint, done for the effect. His people talk with a simplicity that belies the extraordinary sophistication of the writing, and in the structure of a scene he can fuse these qualities so powerfully that he holds his audience fascinated.

The Group's production is superbly done. It meets the play on its own level, and enhances its theatrical values enormously, not only in the amusing scene designs by Herbert Andrews, but in Robert Lewis's direction, which achieves the startling effect now and then of making all the performances resemble Mr. Lewis, and capturing in gesture an accent which Mr. Andrews gets, in one instance, in dressing the boy and his father exactly alike.

The performances are excellent, notably Philip Loeb as the poet, Art Smith as the bewhiskered old man whose heart is in the highlands, and William Hansen, who gives a meticulous portrait of a storekeeper. Sidney Lumet, the boy actor who gave a memorable performance in "The Eternal Road," plays the child, and again assumes an important part without once distracting attention from the play itself, which is no small feat.

Thus it may be said that the Group has brought to Broadway its most peculiar play, a one-piece drama that is baffling, funny, tender and probably not entirely right in the head. But it is a fascinating crackpot, full of hokum and beauty and the sort of compelling unreality that is real only on the stage. Good grief! Saroyan got me doing it.

SIDNEY B. WHIPPLE, *New York World-Telegram:*

The Group Theater has gone in for surrealist drama. It presented, last night, the first of five performances of William Saroyan's crackpot comedy called "My Heart's in the Highlands" and, for something like an hour and a half, held an audience that didn't know whether to titter or weep.

If Mr. Saroyan means anything at all, which is doubtful, it is entirely lost in a welter of incongruous lines, impossible situations and humor that demands the immediate attention of pathologists. My own impression is that Mr. Saroyan, who must have a brain else he would not have given us the lucid works for which he is noted, is, as the British say so neatly, having us on. He is indulging in a bit of nose-thumbing.

When William Kozlenko, the astute and exceptionally sane editor of the *One-Act Play Magazine*, first printed Mr. Saroyan's nonsense, I was shocked beyond measure. I thought that it was a stenographic report of a drunken conversation at Mr. Bleeck's bar, and that Mr. Saroyan would presently sue Mr. Kozlenko for reporting an off-the-record literary transaction. To my horror, I discovered that both Mr. Saroyan and Mr. Kozlenko were in earnest. At least they pretended to be in earnest, and what's more, Mr. Saroyan threatened to write another act as an added insult to the intelligence of Mr. Kozlenko's readers.

The additional act was, unfortunately, written, and the Group Theater, with the sly connivance of Philip Loeb, staged it as an "experimental dramatic work."

You will search in vain for any trace of truth, beauty or moral in it. It is as obscure as James Joyce, although it has the happy quality of brevity, which Mr. Joyce never had, and something of the character of Philip Barry when he goes mystical on us. In the form in which it was staged last night it reminded me of Jimmy Savo trying to interpret Gertrude Stein.

It is impossible to escape the feeling, however, that all this painful experiment was conducted for one purpose—to test the I.Q. of the public and the critics. It was comparable, in the field of art, to the painter who enlisted the services of a cow's tail to create a work of art that won a first prize as a perfect example of cubist perfection.

Far worse than the impossibility of the play was its capacity for boring an audience. Even insanity can be forgiven if it is bright and moving, but this was not.

I do not need to say that Mr. Loeb, with a consummate appreciation for subtle comedy, makes the most of the ridiculous situation. It may be added that Sidney Lumet's name must be affixed to the rapidly growing roster of children who have endeared themselves to the public this season. And that Art Smith, made up almost as horribly as his namesake, Kent, in "Jeremiah," turns in a workmanlike performance.

But, at the risk of being called a pickle-puss, I would request the Group Theater to pay no further attention to Mr. Saroyan's babbling.

JOHN MASON BROWN, New York Post:

That seeing is believing is an adage we have all been brought up to respect. That is one of our limitations—and

110

one of the limitations of our theatre, too. It holds our stage down to the literal and the superficial. All too frequently it forces it to function as a realm of verifiable but flat reality where everything aims at being rational, and no more than that, and where there is no such thing as a line, a character, a scene, or a plot that does not possess a meaning which can be easily explained.

That other world, that world of unprecise meanings and yet genuine emotions which the musicians have long ago invaded and into which the *surrealists* have strayed, is not one to which humdrum Broadway often leads us. But last night, when it turned to William Saroyan's "My Heart's in the Highlands" for a series of extremely interesting experimental performances at the Guild, the Group Theatre did succeed in making playgoers realize that there can be more to seeing than believing, that seeing can mean feeling, too, even when you do not understand exactly what you have seen.

Far be it from me to pretend that I understand precisely what Mr. Saroyan is up to. But what he is saying with deliberate vagueness, and what the Group Theatre has staged with a formalism that turns its back skillfully on everyday reality, interested and moved me more than most of the productions I have seen this winter. That much I do know. And I surmise from those around me who had tears in their eyes that they were no less touched than I was by what is poignant, charming, and yet indefinable in "My Heart's in the Highlands."

To try to reduce Mr. Saroyan's drama to a synopsis is as futile as it would be to claim to have captured the quality of an opera's score by relating its plot. What is important about his fable is not that it tells a story but that it strikes several chords. Its formlessness is intentional. Yet it does

111

things to you in its wanderings which a host of dramas that follow a straight and narrow path cannot pretend to do.

My guess is (for I am certain about nothing that has to do with "My Heart's in the Highlands" except my pleasure in its really distinguished moments and its power to move me) that in telling how a starving poet and his son are visited to the delight of their poor neighbors by a great, gray-bearded old Shakespearean actor who plays beguilingly on a golden bugle, Mr. Saroyan is writing an allegory of sociological significance.

I presume he is leading us among the gay dispossessed to tell us, without naming names, that something is radically wrong with the world. I gather, too, that his heroes are a father and son who are one and the same person; that he is showing how starved, yet constant, is mankind's love for beauty; and that he is urging us to realize that the great people of the earth are not the "big" men whose greatness is measured by the numbers they have slain but the little men who rise to greatness by the gallantry with which they meet their privations and sustain their dreams.

Personally, I wish Mr. Saroyan had been surer in the writing of some of his single scenes. I regret that he chose to kill off his venerable bugler with the ineffectual jumble of Shakespearean speeches he assigned to him. But hazy as the meaning of this or that scene may be, and elusive as is the whole play's concrete significance, I congratulate Mr. Saroyan upon having employed his symbols so that all of them combine to establish a mood and evoke emotions, even when they defy exact comprehension.

For without being freakish or objectionably arty, Mr. Saroyan has managed to widen the theatre's horizons by escaping from facts and reason and making the unintelligible seem intelligible. In doing this he has been abundantly aided by the Group, by Herbert Andrews's admirable *surrealist* settings, by Robert Lewis's inventive direction, and the heart-warming performances of Philip Loeb, Sidney Lumet, William Hansen, and Art Smith.

Mr. Saroyan's play is frankly an experiment. But it is an experiment of which not only the Group but all genuinely adventurous theatre lovers should be proud. It throws open some welcome windows, even if it opens them upon a fog. The air it admits may be cloudy, but it is moving and fresh, and a pleasure to inhale.

WOLCOTT GIBBS, *The New Yorker:*

Young William Saroyan, who is not so very much unlike a character in a play himself, made his bow at the Guild last week with a fantasy called "My Heart's in the Highlands." This collision between the most completely undisciplined talent in American letters and the actors of the Group Theatre bored me nearly to distraction and I would advise you to stay away from it (there is a good chance it won't be around to stay away from by the time this comes out) unless you are especially fond of being badgered in the name of the experimental drama. Mr. Saroyan's work deals, in a cloudy and agitated way, with the fundamental human yearning for food, affection, music, and some faraway, ineffable home where the heart can be at rest. It also says, to quote the author himself, that "it is better to be poor and alive than to be rich and dead." This is a considerable message for one play, but Mr. Saroyan is no man to be disconcerted by mere magnitude and would, I feel sure, undertake a biography of

God without the slightest feeling of doubt or embarrassment. It is my opinion that the singular hodgepodge of geometrical scenery, trumpet playing, crêpe hair, and tangled prose on exhibition in Fifty-second Street conveys no rational message to anybody, including the actors who play in it, and I think we'd better forget all about it as soon as possible.

BROOKS ATKINSON, *New York Times:*

For further proof of the Group Theatre's courage and acting skill, see William Saroyan's "My Heart's in the Highlands," which had the first of five performances at the Guild Theatre last evening. As a bit of virtuoso scribbling and acting, it is the finest new play the Group has put on the stage this season. Probably it would be wise not to inquire too earnestly into the exact meaning of Mr. Saroyan's free-hand drawing on a fantasy screen. He is no rationalist and rational minds had best stay away. But his capricious imagination, his delight in mad people with a sane talent for living and his frank pleasure in sheer expression have resulted in an amusing, tender, whimsical poem which the Group Theatre has translated into the lightest sort of beauty. "Experiment" is what we used to call this sort of guileless fooling when the theatre was young and joyful. That is a word the Group Theatre has now restored to honorable usage.

Just suppose that the greatest unknown poet in the world were living happily in California with a son he loved and a grimy Armenian mother who can speak no English. Just suppose it, for it never happened. But once you suppose it you immediately perceive that a little star-dust is more fruitful than a settled living. For this is the madcap saga of a poet who cannot get money for his poems and can get food only by theft or cozenage, but who takes delight in living among people naturally. Although the editors do not understand him, his neighbors do. In the end he is defeated. "There's something wrong somewhere," his little boy sadly declares when the little family takes to the road again. But they trudge off into the world with honor and dignity, a little puzzled by the indifference of society, but still free and honest.

This hurried report takes no account of the old actor who has escaped from the old people's home and wants merely to play tunes on a golden trumpet and live with folks who understand him. Nor does it include the newsboy who can whistle in three styles, the garrulous postman and the compassionate grocer who is easily touched by goodness and friendship. But Mr. Saroyan writes with so much artless spontaneity, like a trumpeter improvising, that his pattern is loose and impulsive. And perhaps it is only important that he has created some lovable wandering characters and given an impression of joy, hospitality, loyalty and sadness. A storyteller seated on a mat at a street corner might spin a yarn as innocently delightful as this one.

He needs a director with as exultant an imagination as his and the ability to capture a dream in stage dimensions. Let Robert Lewis take a bow here. He has conquered the awkward transitions; he has found the rhythms for the evanescent moods. He has also collected a cast of remarkable actors who can dance on Mr. Saroyan's moonbeams without stubbing their toes. Score a hundred for Art Smith's bewhiskered old tragedian with a grand manner before impromptu audiences. Score about the same for Philip Loeb's uncorrupted poet who cannot understand why the world ignores him; and save a nice red apple for young Sidney Lumet, who plays the part of the son with wholesome, filial affection.

The settings and costumes by Herbert Andrews wonderfully convey the vagrant spirit of the fable, and Paul Bowles' music notably sweetens the occasion. Your correspondent does not know nor greatly care what Mr. Saroyan means. To your correspondent "My Heart's in the Highlands" is wholly enchanting.

Time:

"My Heart's in the Highlands" is the first play of William Saroyan, literary jackanapes and self-styled genius. Originally slated for only five performances, "My Heart's in the Highlands" was warmly praised by several critics, now plans an indefinite run.

Most of the critics, whether they liked the play or not, ostentatiously confessed ignorance of what it meant. A long, amorphous one-acter, it tells of an unsuccessful poet and his little son who live, not always even from hand-to-mouth, in a California town. Upon them stumbles an aged Shakespearean ham actor (Art Smith), a runaway from the Old Folks' Home, whose playing on a trumpet delights his hosts and the townsfolk. The old actor finally dies spouting King Lear, and the poet and his son are evicted from their little house, take bravely to the road.

The point made by "My Heart's in the Highlands" is the old anti-Philistine insistence: that worldly success means nothing, that artistic failure means nothing, that what alone matters is man's vaulting imagination, his perdurable dream, the spiritual geography of his heart. On this theme Saroyan has composed the freest of fantasias, introducing rumbling chords of social protest, screwy dissonances, gaudy trills, touching pianissimos, mushy rubatos.

Violently anti-intellectual in his first play, as in most of his stories, Saroyan relies not on ordered thought but on a kind of surrealist association of words and moods. If his play is sometimes picturesque and tender, it is far too often soft, like a slushy Chopin nocturne: seeking to evoke something, never mind what; to bring tears to the eyes, never mind why.

GEORGE JEAN NATHAN, *Newsweek*:

For the second time in two years a playwriting novice has come out of the California that isn't Hollywood and showed up most of his theoretical professional masters. Last year it was John Steinbeck with "Of Mice and Men." This year it is William Saroyan with "My Heart's in the Highlands," as bonny, imaginative, and utterly fascinating a sentimental lark as has come the way of the local stage in a long spell. Lit with the gleam of a smiling fancy and stirred with a humorous compassion, this loose and gently jovial mixture of almost everything from fantasy to nuts simultaneously squeezes the laughter and tears out of you with some of the seemingly most carefree playwriting it has been my surprised pleasure to have experienced. The fable of a tenth-rate poet whose protective little boy worships him as a genius and of the twain's machinations against an unappreciative world, embellished as it is with half a dozen other characters rich in a joint tenderness and jocosity, is one of the season's few treasures, and a further lift to the eminence of the finely adventurous Group Theater.

The majority of the reviewers, while praising the play, complained bitterly that they couldn't discern any clear meaning in it. Which struck some of the rest of us like complaining bitterly over the absence of any clear meaning in Brahms's solo scherzo in E flat minor, the Black Forest in the early morning sunlight, a good hamburger with onions, or human life itself.

OTIS FERGUSON, *The New Republic:*

"My Heart's in the Highlands" is one of those frank evasions of the demand that a play be made like a play which tact rushes in to cover with the term Experimental Theatre. For all that, there is more human pressure per square foot than in from three to six acres of Mr. Behrman's neat parquet. It is an expansion of one of William Saroyan's two or three very best stories—indeed one of the lovely things among all short stories. With a miracle-play simplicity of setting and development (miracle-play, that is, via "The Living Newspaper," "Our Town" and other modern trick pieces), it makes a pleasant experience because of its sunny stretches of life among nice people.

The play shoots off at some vague cosmic angles in its later sections, and in this padding of the original idea has muffled its clear effect without adding anything (the old Saroyan trick of making his meaning high and inscrutable when he hasn't any). But the relations among the different kids are unstrained, the idea of an old and broken ham playing his bugle songs like a new pied piper is touching, and the father-and-son motive is as open and fine as it has ever been shown. Part of this is due to the sense, to the unaffected

118

feeling and wisdom and humor behind the words; part of the credit goes to Philip Loeb and Sidney Lumet, who have brought out this sense and feeling in their father and son on the stage. Others too: Art Smith, William Hansen, Phil Brown and Mae Grimes, who is the world's own homely girl in pigtails.

The scenes ran about average and the music (Paul Bowles) was just the right music (though why they should have fostered that hollow attitude of the old man holding his prop auto horn for minutes while a thin trumpet played on the wrong side offstage, is hard to see). This evening is remembered not for how good the play was, but for the play's balm of simple human sweetness.

RICHARD WATTS, JR., *New York Herald Tribune:*

Mr. Saroyan, the antic Armenian, is a strange mixture of nonsense and talent. For all his posturing and his studied eccentricities, however, he is essentially a literary artist of genuine distinction, a man important enough to make one put up with his outbursts of foolishness. Now he turns to the theatre in his expanded one-act play, "My Heart's in the Highlands," and, as usual, his propensity for combining affectation with humor, imagination and honest tenderness is strongly in evidence. As is his custom, also, the merits of his work fortunately outweigh the arrant defects. In its original version the play accented the humor and fantasy of the story he had to tell. As enlarged, "My Heart's in the Highlands" leans rather too heavily on its pathos, its whimsically and its much-too-forced "social significance," and I cannot say that the changes are, on the whole, for the better. Nevertheless,

Mr. Saroyan's brief contribution to the season's drama is a work of originality and imagination, indelibly stamped by the mark of his strange personality, and given a splendid production by the distinguished Group Theater under Robert Lewis's fine direction.

It grows increasingly evident that this is the Group's year in the theatre, just as last season belonged to the meteoric Mercury. "My Heart's in the Highlands" is being put on for a series of five experimental performances, and it is just the sort of work that such an organization as the Group Theater, after a successful theatrical year, should be doing. The play is neither sturdy enough nor, to tell you the truth, satisfying enough to warrant production in the ordinary commercial theatre, which can't afford such chances. But for an experimental presentation by an up-and-coming theatrical organization interested in provocative modern work in writing, acting and direction, it is a fine laboratory exercise. Fortunately, the production accorded it shows the Group at its best. The settings of Herbert Andrews are handsome and imaginative, the music by Paul Bowles is evocative and effective, and the acting is of typical Group excellence. Real dramatic imagination has gone into every phase of the presentation, and the Group Theater should once more be congratulated.

As for the play itself, I do wish that Mr. Saroyan had been content to keep it in the fantastically humorous mold in which it was first cast. Now he often grows excessively sentimental and from time to time he hurls forth shouts of social protest that have an unfortunate way of seeming an afterthought. For all that, however, "My Heart's in the Highlands" is a curiously entertaining little play, with a strange eloquence and tenderness all its own. In the manner of a wistful memory of affectionately recalled youth, the author seems to be setting down in slightly fantastic form his recollection of a sensitive but sturdy boy; the father who was a poet in his heart although he could never write verses of importance, and the poor old Scotsman, fugitive from the poorhouse, who played to them and brought them glimpses of beauty and freedom. It is a play filled with affection for small people, for the innocents of this world who long dimly for a beauty they but vaguely understand. For all its moments of affection, there is an essential decency, sweetness and fine human sympathy about the little play.

Among the fine things about "My Heart's in the Highlands" is that it brings to the Group Theater for the first time that excellent actor, Philip Loeb, who plays the father with humor, sympathy and understanding. Mr. Loeb is a player of fine skill and it is a pleasure to see him with an organization that should keep him wisely employed. Art Smith, that admirable and seldom properly appreciated Group veteran, has his fattest part as the trumpet-playing Scotsman with his heart in the Highlands, and he manages it with the skill that anyone who has watched him would expect. It is a genuinely touching performance. That good child actor, Sidney Lumet, is admirable as the boy of the fable, and the minor roles are excellently managed. There is, for example, a fine bit by Phil Brown as an orphaned newsboy. The best tribute I can think of to pay the Group at the moment is to say that after seeing it at work in the Saroyan play one can understand why those who have once played with it never seem happy until they return to its fold.

The Time of Your Life

To George Jean Nathan

NOTE

"The Time of Your Life" was produced by Eddie Dowling in conjunction with The Theatre Guild, and directed by Mr. Dowling and myself. It was first performed in New Haven at the Shubert Theatre, Saturday evening, October 7, 1939. From New Haven it moved to the Plymouth Theatre in Boston for a run of two weeks. It opened in New York at the Booth Theatre on Wednesday, October 25.

This is the cast which opened the play:

The Newsboy	ROSS BAGDASARIAN
The Drunkard	JOHN FARRELL
Willie	WILL LEE
Joe	EDDIE DOWLING
Nick	CHARLES DE SHEIM
Tom	EDWARD ANDREWS
Kitty Duval	JULIE HAYDON
Dudley	CURT CONWAY
Harry	GENE KELLY
Wesley	REGINALD BEANE
Lorene	NENE VIBBER
Blick	GROVER BURGESS
Arab	HOUSELEY STEVENS, SR.
Mary L.	CELESTE HOLME
Krupp	WILLIAM BENDIX
McCarthy	TOM TULLY
Kit Carson	LEN DOYLE
Nick's Ma	MICHELETTE BURANI
Sailor	RANDOLPH WADE

3

Elsie	CATHIE BAILEY
A Killer	EVELYN GELLER
Her Side Kick	MARY CHEFFEY
A Society Lady	EVA LEONARD BOYNE
A Society Gentleman	AINSWORTH ARNOLD
First Cop	RANDOLPH WADE
Second Cop	JOHN FARRELL

I wish to express my sincere gratitude to each member of the cast.

William Bendix, who plays Krupp, contributed an excellent line to his part, as well as a delightful piece of business, for which I thank him.

The play would not be what it is without the piano-playing, and presence, of Reginald Beane, who plays Wesley; Gene Kelly's hoofing and monologue-reciting as Harry; Manuel Tolegian's off-stage harmonica-playing, for the Arab. My sincere thanks to each of these fine artists.

Charles de Sheim, as Nick, and Edward Andrews, as Tom, improved some of my lines, and Len Doyle, as Kit Carson, introduced pleasant business into his part. My sincere thanks.

My greatest debt of gratitude is to Mr. Dowling, whose great experience in the theater improved the playing of the play throughout.

I must thank Miss Julie Haydon for her splendid portrayal of Kitty Duval. I feel that no other actress in America could give this part the quality Miss Haydon gives it, and the quality which I feel the part should have.

John Farrell, as The Drunkard, made a small role into something, which to me at least, shall always be unforgettable, and Ross Bagdasarian, as The Newsboy, brought youth and foreign-American vigor to another small, but important, part. These two parts were written into the play in Boston, and were expertly performed by these two players

4

almost immediately after the parts were written. My sincere thanks.

The character of Anna, Nick's daughter, although in the play long before the New York opening, was omitted from the cast when the play opened, owing to the fact that in Boston children are not allowed to act on the stage, and there wasn't time enough in New York before the opening to rehearse someone. The part will undoubtedly be in the play by the time this book is published.

There was a good deal of hard work for me to do in getting this play ready for its opening. Even so, because the players were all so capable and enthusiastic, the work was pleasant. I am grateful to everybody.

w. s.

New York.
November 1, 1939.

PREFACE

Statistics

The first draft was written in six days, in New York, beginning Monday, May 8, 1939, and ending Saturday, May 13. The first title was "The Light Fantastic." There were to have been six acts, one for each day of work. It turned out that the number of acts was five instead of six. Five or six, however, the idea was to write the play in six days. In the number of days of any worker's week. Writers are workers.

George Jean Nathan read the play, liked it and wrote about it in *Newsweek*. Eddie Dowling bought the play.

The writing of the play was, in great part, the consequence of the encouragement of George Jean Nathan and John Mason Brown who voted for "My Heart's in the Highlands," my first play, as the play of the 1938-1939 season; which, in turn, landed me as a guest at the Drama Critics' Circle Dinner at The Algonquin; which, in another turn, enabled me to meet all the critics who are members of the circle, as well as Mr. Dowling, who sat across the table from me, and along about ten o'clock at night said, "Any play you write, I'll buy sight unseen." This is the kind of American talk I respect. I asked Mr. Dowling if he was on the level and he assured me that he was. I asked him why, and he told me he believed in my future as a playwright. I felt fine and pretty sure I would have a good play for him very soon, so

7

I began to brag about myself to John Anderson and Tallu-lah Bankhead and any other critic or actress or playwright who happened to be near by and unable to get away swiftly.

I didn't begin to write the play the next morning because at the time I was living a social life. I began not living a social life the next day, and by Monday, May 8th, I was ready to be a writer again. I began to write.

The idea was also to find out why a writer can't write in New York. What's to stop him? The answer is, of course, nothing. A writer can write anywhere, under any circum-stance or complication of circumstances, and nothing's to stop him. He can write well, and he can do it as swiftly as the work involved needs to be done swiftly. In the case of this play it needed to be done very swiftly. The weather was muggy. My room at The Great Northern Hotel had no view, little ventilation, and as soon as possible I wanted to go to Ireland for a long-delayed visit. I also needed money urgently and knew I couldn't earn any unless I had a play to offer Mr. Dowling.

The play was written on a rented Royal Portable Type-writer, which I later bought for $30 from Miss Sophe Rab-son, manager of Rabson's, which was across the street from The Great Northern on 56th Street, but is now in a new building, on 52nd Street, and where Miss Rabson graciously allowed me to listen to any phonograph record I cared to listen to, without any obligation; and where a young clerk named Bill was always ready to listen to me on the theme of human nature and so on; and where Miss Rabson's brothers, numbering, I believe, seven, were always pleased to let me watch their television sets and inquire two or three times a day about the cost of new and used Cape-harts.

8

The cigarettes smoked were Chesterfields. The cigars were panatelas. I have forgotten the name of the brand, but they were ten cents straight. The food was Automat food, mainly chicken pie, and occasionally a late supper at the Golden Horn, after which I would sleep an hour or so. The liquor was Scotch.

The play was written night and day. The work did me good. The social life makes me feel ridiculous after a while. Six days of hard work is all I need to restore me to the pride and dignity of the worker, however.

This work was the first substantial work I had ever done in New York. It was also the longest work I had ever done, anywhere. I felt very good about it. Even if it was a bad play (and I had no reason to believe that it was not a good play), there was nothing lost, nothing to lose, and if the worst came to the worst I was simply broke and would have to borrow money somewhere and go back to San Francisco, instead of visiting Dublin.

Nathan, as I've said, liked the play and Dowling drew up a contract with me and advanced me an enormous sum of money. The title by that time was "The Time of Your Life." I studied the play every now and then and made certain changes in it. I considered other titles, inasmuch as I wasn't sure people wouldn't imagine the play wasn't some fluffy drawing-room comedy. Mr. Nathan's "Sunset Sonata" didn't seem quite right. Certain things were lifted out of the play. New things were put into it. I went to Dublin.

As I write these notes, the play has been revised four or five times, and is still likely to be revised. Even now, there are certain changes I would like to make in my first play, "My Heart's in the Highlands." Everything is there of course, as everything is in a child of three, or a man of

9

thirty, or a man of sixty, but there is always room for refinement.

The World of a Play

Like "My Heart's in the Highlands," "The Time of Your Life" will very likely take an important place in the development of the new American theater. I know why, but I am going to leave the full details to the critics, as I believe in the right of every profession to function. In one dimension I shall probably always understand the play better than anybody else, but in another I shall certainly never understand it as fully as critics, professional or amateur. Every performance of a play varies, if ever so little. Every audience beholding a play varies, if ever so little. Every individual in every audience varies, if ever so little. A play is a world, with its own inhabitants and its own laws and its own values. Although the real world is always essentially the same, it is actually never the same from one hour to another, never exactly the same, so that the same thing today as yesterday, is a different thing, nevertheless. One world furnishes itself to us every morning, and we furnish ourselves to a new world every morning. The world never changes and is always changing, and we in turn never change and are always changing. The world of a play is slightly more secure because considerably less complex, since a play consists of isolation, whereas the world has nothing to be isolated from. The writer of a play himself varies, if ever so little. The parts in a play vary, greatly or less greatly. The people taken from the world and placed in a play vary, greatly superficially, only very little deeply. The players in a play, as themselves, vary considerably.

10

Unlike the poem, essay, story, or novel, a play is not fully created in itself, as a play. It is not an affair, finally, between one man and one man: the writer and the reader. It becomes fully created only through the deliberate and cultivated functioning of a considerable number of people rehearsed to behave harmoniously and on schedule, so that a desired meaning and message will be conveyed to each individual beholding the play, a meaning which more or less should be the same to all the individuals in the audience.

"The Time of Your Life" is a play of our time. The people in the play are people you are likely to see any day in almost any part of America, certainly at least in certain kinds of American places. Most of the critics said they didn't understand my first play. After a while a few of them turned around and said they did, but on the whole the critics appeared not to like the play because they didn't know why they liked it. I predict that fewer critics this time will need to imagine that they cannot understand this play. I know a few critics won't like it at all, and that many critics will not like all of it.

I don't want this state of affairs to change.

WILLIAM SAROYAN

San Francisco

THE TIME OF YOUR LIFE

IN the time of your life, live—so that in that good time there shall be no ugliness or death for yourself or for any life your life touches. Seek goodness everywhere, and when it is found, bring it out of its hiding-place and let it be free and unashamed. Place in matter and in flesh the least of the values, for these are the things that hold death and must pass away. Discover in all things that which shines and is beyond corruption. Encourage virtue in whatever heart it may have been driven into secrecy and sorrow by the shame and terror of the world. Ignore the obvious, for it is unworthy of the clear eye and the kindly heart. Be the inferior of no man, nor of any man be the superior. Remember that every man is a variation of yourself. No man's guilt is not yours, nor is any man's innocence a thing apart. Despise evil and ungodliness, but not men of ungodliness or evil. These, understand. Have no shame in being kindly and gentle, but if the time comes in the time of your life to kill, kill and have no regret. In the time of your life, live—so that in that wondrous time you shall not add to the misery and sorrow of the world, but shall smile to the infinite delight and mystery of it.

THE PEOPLE

JOE, *a young loafer with money and a good heart*

TOM, *his admirer, disciple, errand boy, stooge and friend*

KITTY DUVAL, *a young woman with memories*

NICK, *owner of Nick's Pacific Street Saloon, Restaurant, and Entertainment Palace*

ARAB, *an Eastern philosopher and harmonica-player*

KIT CARSON, *an old Indian-fighter*

MC CARTHY, *an intelligent and well-read longshoreman*

KRUPP, *his boyhood friend, a waterfront cop who hates his job but doesn't know what else to do instead*

HARRY, *a natural-born hoofer who wants to make people laugh but can't*

WESLEY, *a colored boy who plays a mean and melancholy boogie-woogie piano*

DUDLEY, *a young man in love*

ELSIE, *a nurse, the girl he loves*

LORENE, *an unattractive woman*

MARY L., *an unhappy woman of quality and great beauty*

WILLIE, *a marble-game maniac*

BLICK, *a heel*

MA, *Nick's mother*

A KILLER

HER SIDE KICK

A COP

ANOTHER COP

A SAILOR

A SOCIETY GENTLEMAN

A SOCIETY LADY

THE DRUNKARD

THE NEWSBOY

ANNA, Nick's daughter

THE PLACE

Nick's Pacific Street Saloon, Restaurant, and Entertainment Palace at the foot of Embarcadero, in San Francisco. A suggestion of room 21 at The New York Hotel, upstairs, around the corner.

THE TIME

Afternoon and night of a day in October, 1939.

18

ACT ONE

Nick's is an American place: a San Francisco water-front honky-tonk.

At a table, JOE: always calm, always quiet, always thinking, always eager, always bored, always superior. His expensive clothes are casually and youthfully worn and give him an almost boyish appearance. He is thinking.

Behind the bar, NICK: a big red-headed young Italian-American with an enormous naked woman tattooed in red on the inside of his right arm. He is studying The Racing Form.

The ARAB, at his place at the end of the bar. He is a lean old man with a rather ferocious old-country mustache, with the ends twisted up. Between the thumb and forefinger of his left hand is the Mohammedan tattoo indicating that he has been to Mecca. He is sipping a glass of beer.

It is about eleven-thirty in the morning. SAM is sweeping out. We see only his back. He disappears into the kitchen. The SAILOR at the bar finishes his drink and leaves, moving thoughtfully, as though he were trying very hard to discover how to live.

The NEWSBOY comes in.

NEWSBOY

(*Cheerfully*)
Good-morning, everybody.

19

>(No answer. To NICK)

Paper, Mister?

>NICK shakes his head, no. The NEWSBOY goes to JOE.

Paper, Mister?

>JOE shakes his head, no. The NEWSBOY walks away, counting papers.

JOE

>(Noticing him)

How many you got?

NEWSBOY

Five.

>JOE gives him a quarter, takes all the papers, glances at the headlines with irritation, throws them away.

>The NEWSBOY watches carefully, then goes.

ARAB

>(Picks up paper, looks at headlines, shakes head as if rejecting everything else a man might say about the world)

No foundation. All the way down the line.

>The DRUNK comes in. Walks to the telephone, looks for a nickel in the chute, sits down at JOE's table.

>NICK takes the DRUNK out. The DRUNK returns.

DRUNK

>(Champion of the Bill of Rights)

This is a free country, ain't it?

>WILLIE, the marble-game maniac, explodes through the swinging doors and lifts the forefinger of his right hand comically, indicating one beer. He is a

very young man, not more than twenty. *He is
wearing heavy shoes, a pair of old and dirty cordu-
roys, a light green turtle-neck jersey with a large
letter "F" on the chest, an oversize two-button
tweed coat, and a green hat, with the brim up.*
NICK *sets out a glass of beer for him, he drinks it,
straightens up vigorously, saying Aaah, makes a
solemn face, gives* NICK *a one-finger salute of adieu,
and begins to leave, refreshed and restored in spirit.
He walks by the marble game, halts suddenly,
turns, studies the contraption, gestures as if to say,
Oh, no. Turns to go, stops, returns to the machine,
studies it, takes a handful of small coins out of his
pants pocket, lifts a nickel, indicates with a gesture,
One game, no more. Puts the nickel in the slot,
pushes in the slide, making an interesting noise.*

NICK

You can't beat that machine.

WILLIE

Oh, yeah?

*The marbles fall, roll, and take their place. He
pushes down the lever, placing one marble in position. Takes a very deep breath, walks in a small
circle, excited at the beginning of great drama.
Stands straight and pious before the contest. Himself vs. the machine. Willie vs. Destiny. His
skill and daring vs. the cunning and trickery of
the novelty industry of America, and the whole
challenging world. He is the last of the American
pioneers, with nothing more to fight but the ma-*

21

chine, with no other reward than lights going on and off, and six nickels for one. Before him is the last champion, the machine. He is the last challenger, the young man with nothing to do in the world. WILLIE grips the knob delicately, studies the situation carefully, draws the knob back, holds it a moment, and then releases it. The first marble rolls out among the hazards, and the contest is on. At the very beginning of the play "The Missouri Waltz" is coming from the phonograph. The music ends here.

This is the signal for the beginning of the play. JOE suddenly comes out of his reverie. He whistles the way people do who are calling a cab that's about a block away, only he does it quietly. WILLIE turns around, but JOE gestures for him to return to his work. NICK looks up from The Racing Form.

JOE

    (Calling)

Tom.

    (To himself)

Where the hell is he, every time I need him?

    (He looks around calmly: the nickel-in-the-slot phonograph in the corner; the open public telephone; the stage; the marble-game; the bar; and so on. He calls again, this time very loud)

Hey, Tom.

NICK

    (With morning irritation)

What do you want?

JOE

    (*Without thinking*)
I want the boy to get me a watermelon, that's what *I* want. What do you want? Money, or love, or fame, or what? You won't get them studying The Racing Form.

NICK

I like to keep abreast of the times.

        TOM *comes hurrying in. He is a great big man of about thirty or so who appears to be much younger because of the childlike expression of his face: handsome, dumb, innocent, troubled, and a little bewildered by everything. He is obviously adult in years, but it seems as if by all rights he should still be a boy. He is defensive as clumsy, self-conscious, overgrown boys are. He is wearing a flashy cheap suit.* JOE *leans back and studies him with casual disapproval.* TOM *slackens his pace and becomes clumsy and embarrassed, waiting for the bawling-out he's pretty sure he's going to get.*

JOE

    (*Objectively, severely, but a little amused*)
Who saved your life?

TOM

    (*Sincerely*)
You did, Joe. Thanks.

JOE

    (*Interested*)
How'd I do it?

23

TOM

    (Confused)
What?

JOE

    (Even more interested)
How'd I do it?

TOM

    Joe, you know how you did it.

JOE

    (Softly)
I want you to answer me. How'd I save your life? I've
forgotten.

TOM

    (Remembering, with a big sorrowful smile)
You made me eat all that chicken soup three years ago
when I was sick and hungry.

JOE

    (Fascinated)
Chicken soup?

TOM

    (Eagerly)
Yeah.

JOE

    Three years? Is it that long?

TOM

    (Delighted to have the information)
Yeah, sure. 1937. 1938. 1939. This is 1939, Joe.

24

JOE

(Amused)
Never mind what year it is. Tell me the whole story.

TOM

You took me to the doctor. You gave me money for food and clothes, and paid my room rent. Aw, Joe, you know all the different things you did.

JOE *nods, turning away from* TOM *after each question.*

JOE
You in good health now?

TOM
Yeah, Joe.

JOE
You got clothes?

TOM
Yeah, Joe.

JOE
You eat three times a day. Sometimes four?

TOM
Yeah, Joe. Sometimes five.

JOE
You got a place to sleep?

TOM
Yeah, Joe.

JOE *nods. Pauses. Studies* TOM *carefully.*

25

JOE

Then, where the hell have you been?

TOM

(Humbly)

Joe, I was out in the street listening to the boys. They're talking about the trouble down here on the waterfront.

JOE

(Sharply)

I want you to be around when I need you.

TOM

(Pleased that the bawling-out is over)

I won't do it again. Joe, one guy out there says there's got to be a revolution before anything will ever be all right.

JOE

(Impatient)

I know all about it. Now, here. Take this money. Go up to the Emporium. You know where the Emporium is?

TOM

Yeah, sure, Joe.

JOE

All right. Take the elevator and go up to the fourth floor. Walk around to the back, to the toy department. Buy me a couple of dollars' worth of toys and bring them here.

TOM

(Amazed)

Toys? What kind of toys, Joe?

JOE

Any kind of toys. Little ones that I can put on this table.

26

TOM

What do you want toys for, Joe?

JOE

(Mildly angry)
What?

TOM

All right, all right. You don't have to get sore at *every-thing*. What'll people think, a big guy like me buying toys?

JOE

What people?

TOM

Aw, Joe, you're always making me do crazy things for you, and *I'm* the guy that gets embarrassed. You just sit in this place and make me do all the dirty work.

JOE

(Looking away)
Do what I tell you.

TOM

O.K., but I wish I knew why.
He makes to go.

JOE

Wait a minute. Here's a nickel. Put it in the phonograph. Number seven. I want to hear that waltz again.

TOM

Boy, I'm glad *I* don't have to stay and listen to it. Joe, what do you hear in that song anyway? We listen to that song ten times a day. Why can't we hear number six, or two, or nine? There are a lot of other numbers.

27

JOE

    (*Emphatically*)
Put the nickel in the phonograph.
    (*Pause*)
Sit down and wait till the music's over. Then go get me some toys.

TOM

    O.K. O.K.

JOE

    (*Loudly*)
Never mind being a martyr about it either. The cause isn't worth it.

        TOM *puts the nickel into the machine, with a ritual of impatient and efficient movement which plainly shows his lack of sympathy or enthusiasm. His manner also reveals, however, that his lack of sympathy is spurious and exaggerated. Actually, he is fascinated by the music, but is so confused by it that he pretends he dislikes it.*

        The music begins. It is another variation of "The Missouri Waltz," played dreamily and softly, with perfect orchestral form, and with a theme of weeping in the horns repeated a number of times.

        At first TOM *listens with something close to irritation, since he can't understand what is so attractive in the music to* JOE, *and what is so painful and confusing in it to himself. Very soon, however, he is carried away by the melancholy story of grief and nostalgia of the song.*

28

He stands, troubled by the poetry and confusion in himself.

JOE, on the other hand, listens as if he were not listening, indifferent and unmoved. What he's interested in is TOM. He turns and glances at TOM.

KITTY DUVAL, who lives in a room in The New York Hotel, around the corner, comes beyond the swinging doors quietly, and walks slowly to the bar, her reality and rhythm a perfect accompaniment to the sorrowful American music, which is her music, as it is Tom's. Which the world drove out of her, putting in its place brokenness and all manner of spiritually crippled forms. She seems to understand this, and is angry. Angry with herself, full of hate for the poor world, and full of pity and contempt for its tragic, unbelievable, confounded people. She is a small powerful girl, with that kind of delicate and rugged beauty which no circumstance of evil or ugly reality can destroy. This beauty is that element of the immortal which is in the seed of good and common people, and which is kept alive in some of the female of our kind, no matter how accidentally or pointlessly they may have entered the world. KITTY DUVAL is somebody. There is an angry purity, and a fierce pride, in her.

In her stance, and way of walking, there is grace and arrogance. JOE recognizes her as a great person immediately. She goes to the bar.

29

KITTY

Beer.

NICK *places a glass of beer before her mechanically.*

She swallows half the drink, and listens to the music again.

TOM *turns and sees her. He becomes dead to everything in the world but her. He stands like a lump, fascinated and undone by his almost religious adoration for her.* JOE *notices* TOM.

JOE

(Gently)

Tom.

TOM *begins to move toward the bar, where* KITTY *is standing.*

(Loudly)

Tom.

TOM *halts, then turns, and* JOE *motions to him to come over to the table.* TOM *goes over.*

(Quietly)

Have you got everything straight?

TOM

(Out of the world)

What?

JOE

What do you mean, what? I just gave you some instructions.

30

TOM

(*Pathetically*)
What do you want, Joe?

JOE

I want you to come to your senses.

He stands up quietly and knocks Tom's hat off.
TOM *picks up his hat quickly.*

TOM

I got it, Joe. I got it. The Emporium. Fourth floor. In
the back. The toy department. Two dollars' worth of toys.
That you can put on a table.

KITTY

(*To herself*)
Who the hell is he to push a big man like that around?

JOE

I'll expect you back in a half hour. Don't get side-tracked
anywhere. Just do what I tell you.

TOM

(*Pleading*)
Joe? Can't I bet four bits on a horse race? There's a long
shot—Precious Time—that's going to win by ten lengths.
I got to have money.

JOE *points to the street.* TOM *goes out.* NICK *is comb-
ing his hair, looking in the mirror.*

NICK

I thought you wanted him to get you a watermelon.

JOE

I forgot.

31

(*He watches* KITTY *a moment. To* KITTY, *clearly,
slowly, with great compassion*)
What's the dream?

KITTY

(*Moving to* JOE, *coming to*)
What?

JOE

(*Holding the dream for her*)
What's the dream, *now*?

KITTY

(*Coming still closer*)
What dream?

JOE

What dream! The dream you're dreaming.

NICK

Suppose he did bring you a watermelon? What the hell
would you do with it?

JOE

(*Irritated*)
I'd put it on this table. I'd look at it. Then I'd eat it.
What do you *think* I'd do with it, sell it for a profit?

NICK

How should I know what you'd do with *anything*? What
I'd like to know is, where do you get your money from?
What work do you do?

JOE

(*Looking at* KITTY)
Bring us a bottle of champagne.

32

KITTY

Champagne?

JOE

(*Simply*)
Would you rather have something else?

KITTY

What's the big idea?

JOE

I thought you might like some champagne. I myself am
very fond of it.

KITTY

Yeah, but what's the big idea? You can't push me around.

JOE

(*Gently but severely*)
It's not in my nature to be unkind to another human
being. I have only contempt for wit. Otherwise I might
say something obvious, therefore cruel, and perhaps un-
true.

KITTY

You be careful what you think about me.

JOE

(*Slowly, not looking at her*)
I have only the noblest thoughts for both your person,
and your spirit.

NICK

(*Having listened carefully and not being able to
make it out*)
What are you talking about?

33

KITTY

You shut up. You—

JOE

He owns this place. He's an important man. All kinds of
people come to him looking for work. Comedians. Singers.
Dancers.

KITTY

I don't care. He can't call me names.

NICK

All right, sister. I know how it is with a two-dollar whore
in the morning.

KITTY

(Furiously)

Don't you dare call me names. I used to be in burlesque.

NICK

If you were ever in burlesque, I used to be Charlie Chap-
lin.

KITTY

(Angry and a little pathetic)

I was in burlesque. I played the burlesque circuit from
coast to coast. I've had flowers sent to me by European
royalty. I've had dinner with young men of wealth and
social position.

NICK

You're dreaming.

KITTY

(To JOE)

I was in burlesque. Kitty Duval. That was my name. Life-

34

size photographs of me in costume in front of burlesque
theaters all over the country.

JOE

(Gently, coaxingly)
I believe you. Have some champagne.

NICK

(Going to table, with champagne bottle and glasses)
There he goes again.

JOE

Miss Duval?

KITTY

(Sincerely, going over)
That's not my real name. That's my stage name.

JOE

I'll call you by your stage name.

NICK

(Pouring)
All right, sister, make up your mind. Are you going to
have champagne with him, or not?

JOE

Pour the lady some wine.

NICK

O.K., Professor. Why you come to this joint instead of
one of the high-class dumps uptown is more than I can
understand. Why don't you have champagne at the St.
Francis? Why don't you drink with a lady?

KITTY

(Furiously)
Don't you call me names—you dentist.

JOE
    Dentist?

NICK

        (Amazed, loudly)
What kind of cussing is that?
        (Pause. Looking at KITTY, then at JOE, bewildered)
This guy doesn't belong here. The only reason I've got
champagne is because he keeps ordering it all the time.
        (To KITTY)
Don't think you're the only one he drinks champagne
with. He drinks with all of them.
        (Pause)
He's crazy. Or something.

JOE

        (Confidentially)
Nick, I think you're going to be all right in a couple of
centuries.

NICK

I'm sorry, I don't understand your English.

        JOE lifts his glass.
        KITTY slowly lifts hers, not quite sure of what's
        going on.

JOE

        (Sincerely)
To the spirit, Kitty Duval.

KITTY

        (Beginning to understand, and very grateful, look-
        ing at him)
Thank you.

36

They drink.

JOE

  (Calling)

 Nick.

NICK

 Yeah?

JOE

 Would you mind putting a nickel in the machine again?
Number—

NICK

 Seven. I know. I know. I don't mind at all, Your High-
ness, although, personally, I'm not a lover of music.

  (Going to the machine)

As a matter of fact I think Tchaikowsky was a dope.

JOE

 Tchaikowsky? Where'd you ever hear of Tchaikowsky?

NICK

 He was a dope.

JOE

 Yeah. Why?

NICK

 They talked about him on the radio one Sunday morning.
He was a sucker. He let a woman drive him crazy.

JOE

 I see.

NICK

 I stood behind that bar listening to the God damn stuff

37

and cried like a baby. *None but the lonely heart!* He was a dope.

JOE

What made you cry?

NICK

What?

JOE

(*Sternly*)
What made you cry, Nick?

NICK

(*Angry with himself*)
I don't know.

JOE

I've been underestimating you, Nick. Play number seven.

NICK

They get everybody worked up. They give everybody stuff they shouldn't have.

> NICK *puts the nickel into the machine and the Waltz begins again. He listens to the music. Then studies The Racing Form.*

KITTY

(*To herself, dreaming*)
I like champagne, and everything that goes with it. Big houses with big porches, and big rooms with big windows, and big lawns, and big trees, and flowers growing everywhere, and big shepherd dogs sleeping in the shade.

38

NICK

I'm going next door to Frankie's to make a bet. I'll be right back.

JOE

Make one for me.

NICK

(Going to JOE)

Who do you like?

JOE

(Giving him money)

Precious Time.

NICK

Ten dollars? Across the board?

JOE

No. On the nose.

NICK

O.K.

(He goes)

DUDLEY R. BOSTWICK, as he calls himself, breaks through the swinging doors, and practically flings himself upon the open telephone beside the phonograph.

DUDLEY is a young man of about twenty-four or twenty-five, ordinary and yet extraordinary. He is smallish, as the saying is, neatly dressed in bargain clothes, over-worked and irritated by the routine and dullness and monotony of his life, apparently

39

nobody and nothing, but in reality a great personality. The swindled young man. Educated, but without the least real understanding. A brave, dumb, salmon-spirit struggling for life in weary, stupefied flesh, dueling ferociously with a banal mind which has been only irritated by what it has been taught. He is a great personality because, against all these handicaps, what he wants is simple and basic: a woman. This urgent and violent need, common yet miraculous enough in itself, considering the unhappy environment of the animal, is the force which elevates him from nothingness to greatness. A ridiculous greatness, but in the nature of things beautiful to behold. All that he has been taught, and everything he believes, is phony, and yet he himself is real, almost super-real, because of this indestructible force in himself. His face is ridiculous. His personal rhythm is tense and jittery. His speech is shrill and violent. His gestures are wild. His ego is disjointed and epileptic. And yet deeply he possesses the same wholeness of spirit, and directness of energy, that is in all species of animals. There is little innate or cultivated spirit in him, but there is no absence of innocent animal force. He is a young man who has been taught that he has a chance, as a person, and believes it. As a matter of fact, he hasn't a chance in the world, and should have been told by somebody, or should not have had his natural and valuable ignorance spoiled by education, ruining an otherwise perfectly good and charming member of the human race.

At the telephone he immediately begins to dial furiously, hesitates, changes his mind, stops dialing, hangs up furiously, and suddenly begins again.

Not more than half a minute after the firecracker arrival of DUDLEY R. BOSTWICK, occurs the polka-and-waltz arrival of HARRY.

HARRY is another story.

He comes in timidly, turning about uncertainly, awkward, out of place everywhere, embarrassed and encumbered by the contemporary costume, sick at heart, but determined to fit in somewhere. His arrival constitutes a dance.

His clothes don't fit. The pants are a little too large. The coat, which doesn't match, is also a little too large, and loose.

He is a dumb young fellow, but he has ideas. A philosophy, in fact. His philosophy is simple and beautiful. The world is sorrowful. The world needs laughter. HARRY is funny. The world needs HARRY. HARRY will make the world laugh.

He has probably had a year or two of high school. He has also listened to the boys at the pool room.

He's looking for Nick. He goes to the ARAB, and says, Are you Nick? The ARAB shakes his head. He stands at the bar, waiting. He waits very busily.

HARRY
    (As NICK returns)
You Nick?

41

NICK

(Very loudly)

I am Nick.

HARRY

(Acting)

Can you use a great comedian?

NICK

(Behind the bar)

Who, for instance?

HARRY

(Almost angry)

Me.

NICK

You? What's funny about you?

> DUDLEY *at the telephone, is dialing. Because of some defect in the apparatus the dialing is very loud.*

DUDLEY

Hello. Sunset 7349? May I speak to Miss Elsie Mandelspiegel?

(Pause)

HARRY

(With spirit and noise, dancing)

I dance and do gags and stuff.

NICK

In costume? Or are you wearing your costume?

DUDLEY

All I need is a cigar.

42

KITTY

    (*Continuing the dream of grace*)

I'd walk out of the house, and stand on the porch, and look at the trees, and smell the flowers, and run across the lawn, and lie down under a tree, and read a book.

    (*Pause*)

A book of poems, maybe.

DUDLEY

    (*Very, very clearly*)

Elsie Mandelspiegel.

    (*Impatiently*)

She has a room on the fourth floor. She's a nurse at the Southern Pacific Hospital. Elsie Mandelspiegel. She works at night. Elsie. Yes.

    He begins waiting again.

    WESLEY, *a colored boy, comes to the bar and stands near* HARRY, *waiting.*

NICK

Beer?

WESLEY

No, sir. I'd like to talk to you.

NICK

    (*To* HARRY)

All right. Get funny.

HARRY

    (*Getting funny, an altogether different person, an actor with great energy, both in power of voice, and in force and speed of physical gesture*)

Now, I'm standing on the corner of Third and Market. I'm looking around. I'm figuring it out. There it is. Right

43

in front of me. The whole city. The whole world. People going by. They're going somewhere. I don't know where, but they're going. I ain't going anywhere. Where the hell can you go? I'm figuring it out. All right, I'm a citizen. A fat guy bumps his stomach into the face of an old lady. They were in a hurry. Fat and old. *They bumped.* Boom. I don't know. It may mean war. War. Germany. England. Russia. I don't know for sure.

(*Loudly, dramatically, he salutes, about faces, presents arms, aims, and fires*)

WAAAAAR.

He blows a call to arms. NICK *gets sick of this, indicates with a gesture that* HARRY *should hold it, and goes to* WESLEY.

NICK

What's on your mind?

WESLEY

(*Confused*)

Well—

NICK

Come on. Speak up. Are you hungry, or what?

WESLEY

Honest to God, I ain't hungry. All I want is a job. I don't want no charity.

NICK

Well, what can you do, and how good are you?

WESLEY

I can run errands, clean up, wash dishes, anything.

44

DUDLEY

(*On the telephone, very eagerly*)

Elsie? Elsie, this is Dudley. Elsie, I'll jump in the bay if you don't marry me. Life isn't worth living without you. I can't sleep. I can't think of anything but you. All the time. Day and night and night and day. Elsie, I love you. I love you. What?

(*Burning up*)

Is this Sunset 7-3-4-9?

(*Pause*)

7943?

(*Calmly, while* WILLIE *begins making a small racket*)

Well, what's your name? Lorene? Lorene Smith? I thought you were Elsie Mandelspiegel. What? Dudley. Yeah. Dudley R. Bostwick. Yeah. R. It stands for Raoul, but I never spell it out. I'm pleased to meet you, too. What? There's a lot of noise around here.

WILLIE *stops hitting the marble-game.*

Where am I? At Nick's, on Pacific Street. I work at the S. P. I told them I was sick and they gave me the afternoon off. Wait a minute. I'll ask them. I'd like to meet you, too. Sure. I'll ask them.

(*Turns around to* NICK)

What's this address?

NICK

Number 3 Pacific Street, you cad.

DUDLEY

Cad? You don't know how I've been suffering on account of Elsie. I take things too ceremoniously. I've got to be more lackadaisical.

45

(*Into telephone*)

Hello, Elenore? I mean, Lorene. It's number 3 Pacific Street. Yeah. Sure. I'll wait for you. How'll you know me? You'll know me. I'll recognize you. Good-by, now.

(*He hangs up*)

HARRY

(*Continuing his monologue, with gestures, movements, and so on*)

I'm standing there. I didn't do anything to anybody. Why should I be a soldier?

(*Sincerely, insanely*)

BOOOOOOOOOM. WAR! O.K. War. I retreat. I hate war. I move to Sacramento.

NICK

(*Shouting*)

All right, Comedian. Lay off a minute.

HARRY

(*Broken-hearted, going to* WILLIE)

Nobody's got a sense of humor any more. The world's dying for comedy like never before, but nobody knows how to *laugh*.

NICK

(*To* WESLEY)

Do you belong to the union?

WESLEY

What union?

NICK

For the love of Mike, where've you been? Don't you know you can't come into a place and ask for a job and get one

46

and go to work, just like that. You've got to belong to
one of the unions.

WESLEY

I didn't know. I got to have a job. Real soon.

NICK

Well, you've got to belong to a union.

WESLEY

I don't want any favors. All I want is a chance to earn a
living.

NICK

Go on into the kitchen and tell Sam to give you some
lunch.

WESLEY

Honest, I ain't hungry.

DUDLEY

(Shouting)
What I've gone through for Elsie.

HARRY

I've got all kinds of funny ideas in my head to help make
the world happy again.

NICK

(Holding WESLEY)
No, he isn't hungry.

WESLEY almost faints from hunger. NICK catches
him just in time. The ARAB and NICK go off with
WESLEY into the kitchen.

HARRY

(To WILLIE)

47

See if you think this is funny. It's my own idea. I created
this dance myself. It comes after the monologue.

> HARRY *begins to dance.* WILLIE *watches a moment,
> and then goes back to the game. It's a goofy dance,
> which* HARRY *does with great sorrow, but much
> energy.*

DUDLEY

Elsie. Aw, gee, Elsie. What the hell do I want to see
Lorene Smith for? Some girl I don't know.

> JOE *and* KITTY *have been drinking in silence. There
> is no sound now except the soft shoe shuffling of*
> HARRY, *the Comedian.*

JOE

What's the dream now, Kitty Duval?

KITTY

(*Dreaming the words and pictures*)
I dream of home. Christ, I always dream of home. I've
no home. I've no place. But I always dream of all of us
together again. We had a farm in Ohio. There was nothing good about it. It was always sad. There was always
trouble. But I always dream about it as if I could go back
and Papa would be there and Mamma and Louie and
my little brother Stephen and my sister Mary. I'm Polish.
Duval! My name isn't Duval, it's Koranovsky. Katerina
Koranovsky. We lost everything. The house, the farm,
the trees, the horses, the cows, the chickens. Papa died.
He was old. He was thirteen years older than Mamma.
We moved to Chicago. We tried to work. We tried to
stay together. Louie got in trouble. The fellows he was

with killed him for something. I don't know what. Stephen ran away from home. Seventeen years old. I don't know where he is. Then Mamma died.

(*Pause*)

What's the dream? I dream of home.

NICK *comes out of the kitchen with* WESLEY.

NICK

Here. Sit down here and rest. That'll hold you for a while. Why didn't you tell me you were hungry? You all right now?

WESLEY

(*Sitting down in the chair at the piano*)

Yes, I am. Thank you. I didn't know I was that hungry.

NICK

Fine.

(*To* HARRY *who is dancing*)

Hey. What the hell do you think you're doing?

HARRY

(*Stopping*)

That's my own idea. I'm a natural-born dancer and comedian.

WESLEY *begins slowly, one note, one chord at a time, to play the piano.*

NICK

You're no good. Why don't you try some other kind of work? Why don't you get a job in a store, selling something? What do you want to be a comedian for?

49

HARRY

I've got something for the world and they haven't got sense enough to let me give it to them. Nobody knows me.

DUDLEY

Elsie. Now I'm waiting for some dame I've never seen before. Lorene Smith. Never saw her in my life. Just happened to get the wrong number. She turns on the personality, and I'm a cooked Indian. Give me a beer, please.

HARRY

Nick, you've got to see my act. It's the greatest thing of its kind in America. All I want is a chance. No salary to begin. Let me try it out tonight. If I don't wow 'em, O.K., I'll go home. If vaudeville wasn't dead, a guy like me would have a chance.

NICK

You're not funny. You're a sad young punk. What the hell do you want to try to be funny for? You'll break everybody's heart. What's there for you to be funny about? You've been poor all your life, haven't you?

HARRY

I've been poor all right, but don't forget that some things count more than some other things.

NICK

What counts more, for instance, than what else, for instance?

HARRY

Talent, for instance, counts more than money, for instance, that's what, and I've got talent. I get new ideas night and day. Everything comes natural to me. I've got style, but it'll take me a little time to round it out. That's all.

> By now WESLEY is playing something of his own which is very good and out of the world. He plays about half a minute, after which HARRY begins to dance.

NICK

(Watching)

I run the lousiest dive in Frisco, and a guy arrives and makes me stock up with champagne. The whores come in and holler at me that they're ladies. Talent comes in and begs me for a chance to show itself. Even society people come here once in a while. I don't know what for. Maybe it's liquor. Maybe it's the location. Maybe it's my personality. Maybe it's the crazy personality of the joint. The old honky-tonk.

(Pause)

Maybe they can't feel at home anywhere else.

> By now WESLEY is really playing, and HARRY is going through a new routine. DUDLEY grows sadder and sadder.

KITTY

Please dance with me.

JOE

(Loudly)

I never learned to dance.

KITTY

Anybody can dance. Just hold me in your arms.

JOE

I'm very fond of you. I'm *sorry*. I can't dance. I wish to God I could.

KITTY

Oh, please.

JOE

Forgive me. I'd like to very much.

> KITTY *dances alone.* TOM *comes in with a package. He sees* KITTY *and goes ga-ga again. He comes out of the trance and puts the bundle on the table in front of* JOE.

JOE

(*Taking the package*)
What'd you get?

TOM

Two dollars' worth of toys. That's what you sent me for. The girl asked me what I wanted with toys. I didn't know what to tell her.
(*He stares at* KITTY, *then back at* JOE)
Joe? I've got to have some money. After all you've done for me, I'll do anything in the world for you, but, Joe, you got to give me some money once in a while.

JOE

What do you want it for?

> TOM *turns and stares at* KITTY *dancing.*

JOE

(*Noticing*)
Sure. Here. Here's five.

52

(*Shouting*)
Can you dance?

TOM

    (*Proudly*)
I got second prize at the Palomar in Sacramento five years ago.

JOE

    (*Loudly, opening package*)
O.K., dance with her.

TOM

You mean *her?*

JOE

    (*Loudly*)
I mean Kitty Duval, the burlesque queen. I mean the queen of the world burlesque. Dance with her. She wants to dance.

TOM

    (*Worshiping the name Kitty Duval, helplessly*)
Joe, can I tell you something?

JOE

    (*He brings out a toy and winds it*)
You don't have to. I know. You love her. You *really* love her. I'm not blind. I know. But take care of yourself. Don't get sick that way again.

NICK

    (*Looking at and listening to* WESLEY *with amazement*)

53

Comes in here and wants to be a dish-washer. Faints from hunger. And then sits down and plays better than Heifetz.

JOE

Heifetz plays the violin.

NICK

All right, don't get careful. He's good, ain't he?

TOM

(To KITTY)

Kitty.

JOE

(He lets the toy go, loudly)

Don't talk. Just dance.

TOM and KITTY dance. NICK is at the bar, watching everything. HARRY is dancing. DUDLEY is grieving into his beer. LORENE SMITH, about thirty-seven, very overbearing and funny-looking, comes to the bar.

NICK

What'll it be, lady?

LORENE

(Looking about and scaring all the young men)

I'm looking for the young man I talked to on the telephone. Dudley R. Bostwick.

DUDLEY

(Jumping, running to her, stopping, shocked)

Dudley R.

(Slowly)

54

Bostwick? Oh, yeah. He left here ten minutes ago. You
mean Dudley Bostwick, that poor man on crutches?

LORENE

Crutches?

DUDLEY

Yeah. Dudley Bostwick. That's what he said his name was.
He said to tell you not to wait.

LORENE

Well.
(She begins to go, turns around)
Are you sure you're not Dudley Bostwick?

DUDLEY

Who—me?
(Grandly)
My name is Roger Tenefrancia. I'm a French-Canadian.
I never saw the poor fellow before.

LORENE

It seems to me your voice is like the voice I heard over
the telephone.

DUDLEY

A coincidence. An accident. A quirk of fate. One of those
things. Dismiss the thought. That poor cripple hobbled
out of here ten minutes ago.

LORENE

He said he was going to commit suicide. I only wanted to
be of help.
(She goes)

DUDLEY

Be of help? What kind of help could she be, of?

55

DUDLEY *runs to the telephone in the corner.*

Gee whiz, Elsie. Gee whiz. I'll never leave you again.

He turns the pages of a little address book.

Why do I always forget the number? I've tried to get her on the phone a hundred times this week and I still forget the number. She won't come to the phone, but I keep trying anyway. She's out. She's not in. She's working. I get the wrong number. Everything goes haywire. I can't sleep.

(*Defiantly*)

She'll come to the phone one of these days. If there's anything to true love at all, she'll come to the phone. Sunset 7349.

He dials the number, as JOE *goes on studying the toys. They are one big mechanical toy, whistles, and a music box.* JOE *blows into the whistles, quickly, by way of getting casually acquainted with them.*

TOM *and* KITTY *stop dancing.* TOM *stares at her.*

DUDLEY

Hello. Is this Sunset 7349? May I speak to Elsie? Yes.

(*Emphatically, and bitterly*)

No, this is *not* Dudley Bostwick. This is Roger Tenefrancia of Montreal, Canada. I'm a childhood friend of Miss Mandelspiegel. We went to kindergarten together.

(*Hand over phone*)

God damn it. (*Into phone*) Yes. I'll wait, thank you.

TOM

I love you.

56

KITTY

You want to go to my room?
(TOM *can't answer*)
Have you got two dollars?

TOM

(*Shaking his head with confusion*)
I've got *five* dollars, but I *love* you.

KITTY

(*Looking at him*)
You want to spend *all* that money?

TOM *embraces her. They go.* JOE *watches. Goes back to the toy.*

JOE

Where's that longshoreman, McCarthy?

NICK

He'll be around.

JOE

What do you think he'll have to say today?

NICK

Plenty, as usual. I'm going next door to see who won that third race at Laurel.

JOE

Precious Time won it.

NICK

That's what you think.
(*He goes*)

57

JOE

    (To himself)
A horse named McCarthy is running in the sixth race today.

DUDLEY

    (On the phone)
Hello. Hello, Elsie? Elsie?

    (His voice weakens; also his limbs)
My God. She's come to the phone. Elsie, I'm at Nick's on Pacific Street. You've got to come here and talk to me. Hello. Hello, Elsie?

    (Amazed)
Did she hang up? Or was I disconnected?

    He hangs up and goes to bar.

        WESLEY *is still playing the piano.* HARRY *is still dancing.* JOE *has wound up the big mechanical toy and is watching it work.*

        NICK *returns.*

NICK

    (Watching the toy)
Say. That's some gadget.

JOE

How much did I win?

NICK

How do you know you won?

JOE

Don't be silly. He said Precious Time was going to win by ten lengths, didn't he? He's in love, isn't he?

58

NICK

O.K. I don't know why, but Precious Time won. You got eighty for ten. How do you do it?

JOE

(Roaring)
Faith. Faith. How'd he win?

NICK

By a nose. Look him up in The Racing Form. The slowest, the cheapest, the worst horse in the race, and the worse jockey. What's the matter with my luck?

JOE

How much did you lose?

NICK

Fifty cents.

JOE

You should never gamble.

NICK

Why not?

JOE

You always bet fifty cents. You've got no more faith than a flea, that's why.

HARRY

(Shouting)
How do you like this, Nick?
He is really busy now, all legs and arms.

NICK

(Turning and watching)
Not bad. Hang around. You can wait table.

59

(*To* WESLEY)
Hey. Wesley. Can you play that again tonight?

WESLEY
(*Turning, but still playing the piano*)
I don't know for sure, Mr. Nick. I can play *something*.

NICK
Good. You hang around, too.
He goes behind the bar.

The atmosphere is now one of warm, natural, American ease; every man innocent and good; each doing what he believes he should do, or what he must do. There is deep American naïveté and faith in the behavior of each person. No one is competing with anyone else. No one hates anyone else. Every man is living, and letting live. Each man is following his destiny as he feels it should be followed; or is abandoning it as he feels it must, by now, be abandoned; or is forgetting it for the moment as he feels he should forget it. Although everyone is dead serious, there is unmistakable smiling and humor in the scene; a sense of the human body and spirit emerging from the world-imposed state of stress and fretfulness, fear and awkwardness, to the more natural state of casualness and grace. Each person belongs to the environment, in his own person, as himself: WESLEY is playing better than ever. HARRY is hoofing better than ever. NICK is behind the bar shining glasses. JOE is smiling at the toy and studying it. DUDLEY, although still troubled, is at least calm now and

60

full of melancholy poise. WILLIE, at the marble-game, is happy. The ARAB is deep in his memories, where he wants to be.

Into this scene and atmosphere comes BLICK.

BLICK is the sort of human being you dislike at sight. He is no different from anybody else physically. His face is an ordinary face. There is nothing obviously wrong with him, and yet you know that it is impossible, even by the most generous expansion of understanding, to accept him as a human being. He is the strong man without strength—strong only among the weak—the weakling who uses force on the weaker.

BLICK enters casually, as if he were a customer, and immediately HARRY begins slowing down.

BLICK
(Oily, and with mock-friendliness)
Hello, Nick.

NICK
(Stopping his work and leaning across the bar)
What do you want to come here for? You're too big a man for a little honky-tonk.

BLICK
(Flattered)
Now, Nick.

NICK
Important people never come here. Here. Have a drink.
(Whiskey bottle)

61

Thanks, I don't drink.

NICK

     (Drinking the drink himself)
Well, why don't you?

BLICK

I have responsibilities.

NICK

You're head of the lousy Vice Squad. There's no vice here.

BLICK

     (Sharply)
Street-walkers are working out of this place.

NICK

     (Angry)
What do you want?

BLICK

     (Loudly)
I just want you to know that it's got to stop.

> *The music stops. The mechanical toy runs down.
> There is absolute silence, and a strange fearfulness
> and disharmony in the atmosphere now.* HARRY
> *doesn't know what to do with his hands or feet.*
> WESLEY's *arms hang at his sides.* JOE *quietly pushes
> the toy to one side of the table eager to study
> what is happening.* WILLIE *stops playing the marble-
> game, turns around and begins to wait.* DUDLEY
> *straightens up very, very vigorously, as if to say:
> "Nothing can scare me. I know love is the only
> thing." The* ARAB *is the same as ever, but watchful.*

62

NICK *is arrogantly aloof. There is a moment of this silence and tension, as though* BLICK *were waiting for everybody to acknowledge his presence. He is obviously flattered by the acknowledgment of Harry, Dudley, Wesley, and Willie, but a little irritated by Nick's aloofness and unfriendliness.*

NICK

Don't look at me. I can't tell a street-walker from a lady. You married?

BLICK

You're not asking *me* questions. *I'm* telling you.

NICK

(*Interrupting*)
You're a man of about forty-five or so. You *ought* to know better.

BLICK

(*Angry*)
Street-walkers are working out of this place.

NICK

(*Beginning to shout*)
Now, don't start any trouble with me. People come here to drink and loaf around. I don't care who they are.

BLICK

Well, I do.

NICK

The only way to find out if a lady is a street-walker is to walk the streets with her, go to bed, and make sure. You wouldn't want to do that. You'd *like* to, of course.

63

BLICK

Any more of it, and I'll have your joint closed.

NICK

(*Very casually, without ill-will*)

Listen. I've got no use for you, or anybody like you. You're out to change the world from something bad to something worse. Something like yourself.

BLICK

(*Furious pause, and contempt*)

I'll be back tonight.

He begins to go.

NICK

(*Very angry but very calm*)

Do yourself a big favor and don't come back tonight. Send somebody else. I don't like your personality.

BLICK

(*Casually, but with contempt*)

Don't break any laws. I don't like yours, either.

He looks the place over, and goes.

There is a moment of silence. Then WILLIE *turns and puts a new nickel in the slot and starts a new game.* WESLEY *turns to the piano and rather falteringly begins to play. His heart really isn't in it.* HARRY *walks about, unable to dance.* DUDLEY *lapses into his customary melancholy, at a table.* NICK *whistles a little: suddenly stops.* JOE *winds the toy.*

JOE

(*Comically*)

Nick. You going to kill that man?

NICK

I'm disgusted.

JOE

Yeah? Why?

NICK

Why should I get worked up over a guy like that? Why should I hate *him*? He's nothing. He's nobody. He's a mouse. But every time he comes into this place I get burned up. He doesn't want to drink. He doesn't want to sit down. He doesn't want to take things easy. Tell me one thing?

JOE

Do my best.

NICK

What's a punk like *that* want to go out and try to change the world for?

JOE

(Amazed)

Does *he* want to change the world, too?

NICK

(Irritated)

You know what I mean. What's he want to bother people for? He's *sick*.

JOE

(Almost to himself, reflecting on the fact that Blick too wants to change the world)

I guess he wants to change the world at that.

65

NICK

So I go to work and hate him.

JOE

It's not him, Nick. It's everything.

NICK

Yeah, *I* know. But I've still got no use for him. He's no
good. You know what I mean? He hurts little people.
(*Confused*)
One of the girls tried to commit suicide on account of
him.
(*Furiously*)
I'll break his head if he hurts anybody around here. This
is my joint.
(*Afterthought*)
Or anybody's *feelings*, either.

JOE

He may not be so bad, deep down underneath.

NICK

I know all about him. He's no good.

> *During this talk* WESLEY *has really begun to play
> the piano, the toy is rattling again, and little by
> little* HARRY *has begun to dance.* NICK *has come
> around the bar, and now, very much like a child
> —forgetting all his anger—is watching the toy work.
> He begins to smile at everything: turns and listens
> to* WESLEY: *watches* HARRY: *nods at the* ARAB: *shakes
> his head at* DUDLEY: *and gestures amiably about*
> WILLIE. *It's his joint all right.*

66

*It's a good, low-down, honky-tonk American place
that lets people alone.*

NICK

I've got a good joint. There's nothing wrong here. Hey.
Comedian. Stick to the dancing tonight. I think you're
O.K. Wesley? Do some more of that tonight. That's fine!

HARRY

Thanks, Nick. Gosh, I'm on my way at last.
   (*On telephone*)
Hello, Ma? Is that you, Ma? Harry. I got the job.
   He hangs up and walks around, smiling.

NICK

   (*Watching the toy all this time*)
Say, that really is something. What is that, anyway?

   MARY L. *comes in.*

JOE

   (*Holding it toward* NICK, *and* MARY L.)
Nick, this is a toy. A contraption devised by the cunning
of man to drive boredom, or grief, or anger out of children. A noble gadget. A gadget, I might say, infinitely
nobler than any other I can think of at the moment.

   *Everybody gathers around Joe's table to look at
   the toy. The toy stops working.* JOE *winds the
   music box. Lifts a whistle: blows it, making a very
   strange, funny and sorrowful sound.*

Delightful. Tragic, but delightful.

   WESLEY *plays the music-box theme on the piano.*
   MARY L. *takes a table.*

67

Joe. That girl, Kitty. What's she mean, calling me a dentist? I wouldn't hurt anybody, let alone a tooth.

NICK *goes to* Mary L.'s *table.* HARRY *imitates the toy. Dances. The piano music comes up, the light dims slowly, while the piano solo continues.*

CURTAIN

ACT TWO

An hour later. All the people who were at Nick's
when the curtain came down are still there. JOE at
his table, quietly shuffling and turning a deck of
cards, and at the same time watching the face of
the woman, and looking at the initials on her
handbag, as though they were the symbols of the
lost glory of the world. The WOMAN, in turn, very
casually regards JOE occasionally. Or rather senses
him; has sensed him in fact the whole hour. She
is mildly tight on beer, and JOE himself is tight,
but as always completely under control; simply
sharper. The others are about, at tables, and so on.

JOE

Is it Madge—Laubowitz?

MARY

Is what what?

JOE

Is the name Mabel Lepescu?

MARY

What name?

JOE

The name the initials M. L. stand for. The initials on
your bag.

69

MARY

No.

JOE

(After a long pause, thinking deeply what the
name might be, turning a card, looking into the
beautiful face of the woman)

Margie Longworthy?

MARY

(All this is very natural and sincere, no comedy on
the part of the people involved: they are both
solemn, being drunk)

No.

JOE

(His voice higher-pitched, as though he were growing a little alarmed)

Midge Laurie?

(MARY shakes her head)

My initials are J. T.

MARY

(Pause)

John?

JOE

No.

(Pause)

Martha Lancaster?

MARY

No.

70

(*Slight pause*)
Joseph?

MARY

JOE

Well, not exactly. That's my first name, but everybody calls me Joe. The last name is the tough one. I'll help you a little. I'm Irish.
(*Pause*)
Is it just plain Mary?

MARY

Yes, it is. I'm Irish, too. At least on my father's side. English on my mother's side.

JOE

I'm Irish on both sides. Mary's one of my favorite names. I guess that's why I didn't think of it. I met a girl in Mexico City named Mary once. She was an American from Philadelphia. She got married there. In Mexico City, I mean. While I was there. We were in love, too. At least I was. You never know about anyone else. They were engaged, you see, and her mother was with her, so they went through with it. Must have been six or seven years ago. She's probably got three or four children by this time.

MARY

Are you still in love with her?

JOE

Well—no. To tell you the truth, I'm not sure. I guess I am. I didn't even know she was engaged until a couple of days before they got married. I thought I was going to marry her. I kept thinking all the time about the kind of kids we would be likely to have. My favorite was the

71

third one. The first two were fine. Handsome and fine and
intelligent, but that third one was different. Dumb and
goofy-looking. I liked *him* a lot. When she told me she
was going to be married, I didn't feel so bad about the
first two, it was that dumb one.

MARY

(*After a pause of some few seconds*)
What do you do?

JOE

Do? To tell you the truth, nothing.

MARY

Do you always drink a great deal?

JOE

(*Scientifically*)
Not *always*. Only when I'm awake. I sleep seven or eight
hours every night, you know.

MARY

How nice. I mean to drink when you're awake.

JOE

(*Thoughtfully*)
It's a privilege.

MARY

Do you really *like* to drink?

JOE

(*Positively*)
As much as I like to *breathe*.

72

MARY

    (*Beautifully*)

Why?

JOE

    (*Dramatically*)

Why do I like to drink?

    (*Pause*)

Because I don't like to be gypped. Because I don't like
to be dead most of the time and just a little alive every
once in a long while.

    (*Pause*)

If I don't drink, I become fascinated by unimportant
things—like everybody else. I get busy. Do things. All
kinds of little stupid things, for all kinds of little stupid
reasons. Proud, selfish, *ordinary* things. I've done them.
Now I don't do anything. *I live all the time.* Then I go
to sleep.

    (*Pause*)

MARY

Do you sleep well?

JOE

    (*Taking it for granted*)

Of course.

MARY

    (*Quietly, almost with tenderness*)

What are your plans?

JOE

    (*Loudly, but also tenderly*)

Plans? I haven't got any. *I just get up.*

73

MARY

    (Beginning to understand everything)
Oh, yes. Yes, of course.

    DUDLEY *puts a nickel in the phonograph.*

JOE

    (Thoughtfully)
Why do I drink?
    (Pause, while he thinks about it. The thinking appears to be profound and complex, and has the effect of giving his face a very comical and naive expression)
That question calls for a pretty complicated answer.
    (He smiles abstractly)

MARY

    Oh, I didn't mean—

JOE

    (Swiftly, gallantly)
No. No. I *insist.* I *know* why. It's just a matter of finding words. Little ones.

MARY

    It really doesn't matter.

JOE

    (Seriously)
Oh, yes, it does.
    (Clinically)
Now, why do I drink?
    (Scientifically)
No. Why does anybody drink?
    (Working it out)
Every day has twenty-four hours.

74

MARY

(Sadly, but brightly)
Yes, that's true.

JOE

Twenty-four hours. Out of the twenty-four hours at *least*
twenty-three and a half are—my God, I don't know why—
dull, dead, boring, empty, and murderous. Minutes on the
clock, *not time of living*. It doesn't make any difference
who you are or what you do, twenty-three and a half
hours of the twenty-four are spent *waiting*.

MARY

Waiting?

JOE

(Gesturing, loudly)
And the more you wait, the less there is to wait *for*.

MARY

(Attentively, beautifully his student)
Oh?

JOE

(Continuing)
That goes on for days and days, and weeks and months
and years, and years, and the first thing you know all the
years are dead. All the minutes are dead. You yourself
are dead. There's nothing to wait for any more. Nothing
except *minutes* on the *clock*. No time of life. Nothing
but minutes, and idiocy. Beautiful, bright, intelligent
idiocy.

(Pause)

75

Does that answer your question?

MARY

(Earnestly)

I'm afraid it does. Thank you. You shouldn't have gone
to all the trouble.

JOE

No trouble at all.

(Pause)

You have children?

MARY

Yes. Two. A son and a daughter.

JOE

(Delighted)

How swell. Do they look like you?

MARY

Yes.

JOE

Then why are you sad?

MARY

I was always sad. It's just that after I was married I was
allowed to drink.

JOE

(Eagerly)

Who are you waiting for?

MARY

No one.

76

JOE

(*Smiling*)
I'm not waiting for anybody, either.

MARY

My husband, of course.

JOE

Oh, sure.

MARY

He's a lawyer.

JOE

(*Standing, leaning on the table*)
He's a great guy. I like him. I'm very fond of him.

MARY

(*Listening*)
You have responsibilities?

JOE

(*Loudly*)
One, and *thousands*. As a matter of fact, I feel responsible to everybody. At least to everybody I meet. I've been trying for three years to find out if it's possible to live what I think is a civilized life. I mean a life that can't hurt any other life.

MARY

You're famous?

JOE

Very. Utterly unknown, but very famous. Would you like to dance?

77

MARY

All right.

JOE

(Loudly)
I'm sorry. I don't dance. I didn't think you'd like to.

MARY

To tell you the truth, I don't like to dance at all.

JOE

(Proudly. Commentator)
I can hardly walk.

MARY

You mean you're tight?

JOE

(Smiling)
No. I mean all the time.

MARY

(Looking at him closely)
Were you ever in Paris?

JOE

In 1929, and again in 1934.

MARY

What month of 1934?

JOE

Most of April, all of May, and a little of June.

MARY

I was there in November and December that year.

78

JOE

We were there almost at the same time. You were married?

MARY

Engaged.

> (They are silent a moment, looking at one another. Quietly and with great charm)

Are you really in love with me?

JOE

Yes.

MARY

Is it the champagne?

JOE

Yes. Partly, at least.

> (He sits down)

MARY

If you don't see me again, will you be very unhappy?

JOE

Very.

MARY

> (Getting up)

I'm so pleased.

> JOE is deeply grieved that she is going. In fact, he is almost panic-stricken about it, getting up in a way that is full of furious sorrow and regret.

I must go now. Please don't get up.

> JOE is up, staring at her with amazement.

79

Good-by.

JOE

(Simply)
Good-by.

The WOMAN stands looking at him a moment, then turns and goes. JOE stands staring after her for a long time. Just as he is slowly sitting down again, the NEWSBOY enters, and goes to Joe's table.

NEWSBOY

Paper, Mister?

JOE

How many you got this time?

NEWSBOY

Eleven.

JOE buys them all, looks at the lousy headlines, throws them away.

The NEWSBOY looks at JOE, amazed. He walks over to NICK at the bar.

NEWSBOY

(Troubled)
Hey, Mister, do you own this place?

NICK

(Casually but emphatically)
I own this place.

NEWSBOY

Can you use a great lyric tenor?

80

NICK

    (Almost to himself)
Great lyric tenor?
    (Loudly)
Who?

NEWSBOY

    (Loud and the least bit angry)
Me. I'm getting too big to sell papers. I don't want to
holler headlines all the time. I want to *sing*. You can use
a great lyric tenor, can't you?

NICK

What's lyric about you?

NEWSBOY

    (Voice high-pitched, confused)
My voice.

NICK

Oh.
    (Slight pause, giving in)
All right, then—sing!

    The NEWSBOY *breaks into swift and beautiful song:*
    "When Irish Eyes Are Smiling." NICK *and* JOE
    listen carefully: NICK *with wonder,* JOE *with amaze-*
    ment and delight.

NEWSBOY

    (Singing)
When Irish eyes are smiling,
Sure 'tis like a morn in Spring.
In the lilt of Irish laughter,
You can hear the angels sing.

81

When Irish hearts are happy,
All the world seems bright and gay.
But when Irish eyes are smiling—

NICK

> (Loudly, swiftly)

Are you Irish?

NEWSBOY

> (Speaking swiftly, loudly, a little impatient with
> the irrelevant question)

No. I'm Greek.

> (He finishes the song, singing louder than ever)

Sure they steal your heart away.

> He turns to NICK dramatically, like a vaudeville
> singer begging his audience for applause. NICK stud-
> ies the boy eagerly. JOE gets to his feet and leans
> toward the BOY and NICK.

NICK

Not bad. Let me hear you again about a year from now.

NEWSBOY

> (Thrilled)

Honest?

NICK

Yeah. Along about November 7th, 1940.

NEWSBOY

> (Happier than ever before in his life, running over
> to JOE)

Did you hear it too, Mister?

JOE

Yes, and it's great. What part of Greece?

82

NEWSBOY

Salonica. Gosh, Mister. Thanks.

JOE

Don't wait a year. Come back with some papers a little later. You're a great singer.

NEWSBOY

(Thrilled and excited)
Aw, thanks, Mister. So long.
(Running, to NICK)
Thanks, Mister.
He runs out. JOE and NICK look at the swinging doors. JOE sits down. NICK laughs.

NICK

Joe, people are so wonderful. Look at that kid.

JOE

Of course they're wonderful. Every one of them is wonderful.

MC CARTHY and KRUPP come in, talking.

MC CARTHY is a big man in work clothes, which make him seem very young. He is wearing black jeans, and a blue workman's shirt. No tie. No hat. He has broad shoulders, a lean intelligent face, thick black hair. In his right back pocket is the longshore-man's hook. His arms are long and hairy. His sleeves are rolled up to just below his elbows. He is a casual man, easy-going in movement, sharp in per-ception, swift in appreciation of charm or inno-

83

cence or comedy, and gentle in spirit. *His speech
is clear and full of warmth. His voice is powerful,
but modulated. He enjoys the world, in spite of
the mess it is, and he is fond of people, in spite of
the mess they are.*

KRUPP *is not quite as tall or broad-shouldered as*
MC CARTHY. *He is physically encumbered by his uniform, club, pistol, belt, and cap. And he is plainly
not at home in the role of policeman. His movement is stiff and unintentionally pompous. He is a
naive man, essentially good. His understanding is
less than McCarthy's, but he is honest and he
doesn't try to bluff.*

KRUPP

You don't understand what I mean. Hi-ya, Joe.

JOE

Hello, Krupp.

MC CARTHY

Hi-ya, Joe.

JOE

Hello, McCarthy.

KRUPP

Two beers, Nick.

(*To* MC CARTHY)

All I do is carry out orders, carry out orders. I don't know
what the idea is behind the order. Who it's for, or who
it's against, or why. All I do is carry it out.

NICK *gives them beer.*

84

MC CARTHY

You don't read enough.

KRUPP

I do read. I read *The Examiner* every morning. *The Call-Bulletin* every night.

MC CARTHY

And carry out orders. What are the orders now?

KRUPP

To keep the peace down here on the waterfront.

MC CARTHY

Keep it for who?
  (*To* JOE)
Right?

JOE
  (*Sorrowfully*)
Right.

KRUPP

How do I know for who? The peace. Just keep it.

MC CARTHY

It's got to be kept for somebody. Who would you suspect it's kept for?

KRUPP

For citizens!

MC CARTHY

I'm a citizen!

KRUPP

All right, I'm keeping it for you.

MC CARTHY

By hitting me over the head with a club?
(*To* JOE)
Right?

JOE

(*Melancholy, with remembrance*)
I don't know.

KRUPP

Mac, you know I never hit you over the head with a club.

MC CARTHY

But you will if you're on duty at the time and happen to stand on the opposite side of myself, on duty.

KRUPP

We went to Mission High together. We were always good friends. The only time we ever fought was that time over Alma Haggerty. Did you marry Alma Haggerty?
(*To* JOE)
Right?

JOE

Everything's right.

MC CARTHY

No. Did you?
(*To* JOE)
Joe, are you with me or against me?

JOE

I'm with everybody. One at a time.

KRUPP

No. And that's just what I mean.

86

MC CARTHY

You mean neither one of us is going to marry the thing
we're fighting for?

KRUPP

I don't even know what it is.

MC CARTHY

You don't read enough, I tell you.

KRUPP

Mac, you don't know what you're fighting for, either.

MC CARTHY

It's so simple, it's fantastic.

KRUPP

All right, what are you fighting for?

MC CARTHY

For the rights of the inferior. Right?

JOE

Something like that.

KRUPP

The who?

MC CARTHY

The inferior. The world full of Mahoneys who haven't
got what it takes to make monkeys out of everybody else,
near by. The men who were created equal. Remember?

KRUPP

Mac, you're not inferior.

MC CARTHY

I'm a longshoreman. And an idealist. I'm a man with too

87

much brawn to be an intellectual, exclusively. I married a small, sensitive, cultured woman so that my kids would be sissies instead of suckers. A strong man with any sensibility has no choice in this world but to be a heel, or a worker. I haven't the heart to be a heel, so I'm a worker. I've got a son in high school who's already thinking of being a writer.

KRUPP

I wanted to be a writer once.

JOE

Wonderful.

> *He puts down the paper, looks at* KRUPP *and* MC-CARTHY.

MC CARTHY

They *all* wanted to be writers. Every maniac in the world that ever brought about the murder of people through war started out in an attic or a basement writing poetry. It stank. So they got even by becoming important heels. And it's still going on.

KRUPP

Is it really, Joe?

JOE

Look at today's paper.

MC CARTHY

Right now on Telegraph Hill is some punk who is trying to be Shakespeare. Ten years from now he'll be a senator. Or a communist.

KRUPP

Somebody ought to do something about it.

MC CARTHY

(*Mischievously, with laughter in his voice*)

The thing to do is to have more magazines. Hundreds of them. *Thousands.* Print everything they write, so they'll believe they're immortal. That way keep them from going haywire.

KRUPP

Mac, you ought to be a writer yourself.

MC CARTHY

I hate the tribe. They're mischief-makers. Right?

JOE

(*Swiftly*)

Everything's right. Right and wrong.

KRUPP

Then why do you read?

MC CARTHY

(*Laughing*)

It's relaxing. It's soothing.

(*Pause*)

The lousiest people born into the world are writers. Language is all right. It's the people who use language that are lousy.

The ARAB *has moved a little closer, and is listening carefully.*

(*To the* ARAB)

What do you think, Brother?

ARAB

(*After making many faces, thinking very deeply*)

89

No foundation. All the way down the line. What. What-not. Nothing. I go walk and look at sky.

>   (He goes)

KRUPP

>   What? What-not?
>   >   (TO JOE)
>   What's that mean?

JOE

>   >   (Slowly, thinking, remembering)
>   What? What-not? That means this side, that side. Inhale, exhale. What: birth. What-not: death. The inevitable, the astounding, the magnificent seed of growth and decay in all things. Beginning, and end. That man, in his own way, is a prophet. He is one who, with the help of beer, is able to reach that state of deep understanding in which what and what-not, the reasonable and the unreasonable, are one.

MC CARTHY

>   Right.

KRUPP

>   If you can understand that kind of talk, how can you be a longshoreman?

MC CARTHY

>   I come from a long line of McCarthys who never married or slept with anything but the most powerful and quarrelsome flesh.

>   >   He drinks beer.

KRUPP

>   I could listen to you two guys for hours, but I'll be damned if I know what the hell you're talking about.

90

MC CARTHY

The consequence is that all the McCarthys are too great and too strong to be heroes. Only the weak and unsure perform the heroic. They've *got* to. The more heroes you have, the worse the history of the world becomes. Right?

JOE

Go outside and look at it.

KRUPP

You sure can philos—philosoph— Boy, you can talk.

MC CARTHY

I wouldn't talk this way to anyone but a man in uniform, and a man who couldn't understand a word of what I was saying. The party I'm speaking of, my friend, is YOU.

> *The phone rings.*

> HARRY *gets up from his table suddenly and begins a new dance.*

KRUPP

> (*Noticing him, with great authority*)

Here. Here. What do you think you're doing?

HARRY

> (*Stopping*)

I just got an idea for a new dance. I'm trying it out. Nick. Nick, the phone's ringing.

KRUPP

> (*To* MC CARTHY)

Has he got a right to do that?

MC CARTHY

The living have danced from the beginning of time. I

91

might even say, the dance and the life have moved along together, until now we have—

(To HARRY)

Go into your dance, son, and show us what we have.

HARRY

I haven't got it worked out *completely* yet, but it starts out like this.

He dances.

NICK

(On phone)

Nick's Pacific Street Restaurant, Saloon, and Entertainment Palace. Good afternoon. Nick speaking.

(Listens)

Who?

(Turns around)

Is there a Dudley Bostwick in the joint?

DUDLEY *jumps to his feet and goes to phone.*

DUDLEY

(On phone)

Hello. Elsie?

(Listens)

You're coming down?

(Elated. To the saloon)

She's coming down.

(Pause)

No. I won't drink. Aw, gosh, Elsie.

He hangs up, looks about him strangely, as if he were just born, walks around touching things, putting chairs in place, and so on.

92

MC CARTHY
(*To* HARRY)
Splendid. Splendid.

HARRY
Then I go into this little routine.
(*He demonstrates*)

KRUPP
Is that good, Mac?

MC CARTHY
It's awful, but it's honest and ambitious, like everything
else in this great country.

HARRY
Then I work along into this.
(*He demonstrates*)
And this is where I really get going.
(*He finishes the dance*)

MC CARTHY
Excellent. A most satisfying demonstration of the present
state of the American body and soul. Son, you're a genius.

HARRY
(*Delighted, shaking hands with* MC CARTHY)
I go on in front of an audience for the first time in my
life tonight.

MC CARTHY
They'll be delighted. Where'd you learn to dance?

HARRY
Never took a lesson in my life. I'm a natural-born dancer.
And comedian, too.

93

MC CARTHY

(Astounded)
You can make people *laugh?*

HARRY

(Dumbly)
I can be funny, but they won't laugh.

MC CARTHY

That's odd. Why not?

HARRY

I don't know. They just won't laugh.

MC CARTHY

Would you care to be funny now?

HARRY

I'd like to try out a new monologue I've been thinking about.

MC CARTHY

Please do. I promise you if it's funny I shall *roar* with laughter.

HARRY

This is it.
(Goes into the act, with much energy)
I'm up at Sharkey's on Turk Street. It's a quarter to nine, daylight saving. Wednesday, the eleventh. What I've got is a headache and a 1918 nickel. What I *want* is a cup of coffee. If I buy a cup of coffee with the nickel, I've got to walk home. I've got an eight-ball problem. George the Greek is shooting a game of snooker with Pedro the Filipino. *I'm in rags.* They're wearing thirty-five dollar suits, made to order. I haven't got a cigarette. They're smoking

94

Bobby Burns panatelas. I'm thinking it over, like I always do. George the Greek is in a tough spot. If I buy a cup of coffee, I'll want another cup. What happens? My ear aches! My ear. George the Greek takes the cue. Chalks it. Studies the table. Touches the cue-ball delicately. Tick. What happens? He makes the three-ball! What do I do? I get confused. *I go out and buy a morning paper.* What the hell do I want with a morning paper? What I *want* is a cup of coffee, and a good used car. I go out and buy a morning paper. Thursday, the twelfth. Maybe the head-line's about me. I take a quick look. No. *The headline is not about me.* It's about Hitler. Seven thousand miles away. I'm here. Who the hell is Hitler? Who's behind the eight-ball? I turn around. *Everybody's behind the eight-ball!*

> Pause. KRUPP *moves toward* HARRY *as if to make an important arrest.* HARRY *moves to the swinging doors.* MC CARTHY *stops* KRUPP.

MC CARTHY

(*To* HARRY)
It's the funniest thing I've ever heard. Or *seen*, for that matter.

HARRY

(*Coming back to* MC CARTHY)
Then, why don't you laugh?

MC CARTHY

I don't know, yet.

HARRY

I'm always getting funny ideas that nobody will laugh at.

95

MC CARTHY

 (Thoughtfully)

It may be that you've stumbled headlong into a new kind of comedy.

HARRY

Well, what good is it if it doesn't make anybody laugh?

MC CARTHY

There are *kinds* of laughter, son. I must say, in all truth, that I *am* laughing, although not out *loud*.

HARRY

I want to *hear* people laugh. *Out loud.* That's why I keep thinking of funny things to say.

MC CARTHY

Well. They may catch on in time. Let's go, Krupp. So long, Joe.

  MC CARTHY *and* KRUPP *go.*

JOE

So long.

 (After a moment's pause)

Hey, Nick.

NICK

Yeah.

JOE

Bet McCarthy in the last race.

NICK

You're crazy. That horse is a double-crossing, no-good—

JOE

Bet everything you've got on McCarthy.

96

NICK

I'm not betting a nickel on him. You bet everything you've got on McCarthy.

JOE

I don't need money.

NICK

What makes you think McCarthy's going to win?

JOE

McCarthy's name's McCarthy, isn't it?

NICK

Yeah. So what?

JOE

The horse named McCarthy is going to win, that's all. Today.

NICK

Why?

JOE

You do what I tell you, and everything will be all right.

NICK

McCarthy likes to talk, that's all.
   (Pause)
Where's Tom?

JOE

He'll be around. He'll be miserable, but he'll be around. Five or ten minutes more.

NICK

You don't believe that Kitty, do you? About being in burlesque?

JOE

(Very clearly)

I believe dreams sooner than statistics.

NICK

(Remembering)

She sure is somebody. Called me a dentist.

TOM, turning about, confused, troubled, comes in, and hurries to Joe's table.

JOE

What's the matter?

TOM

Here's your five, Joe. I'm in trouble again.

JOE

If it's not organic, it'll cure itself. If it is organic, science will cure it. What is it, organic or non-organic?

TOM

Joe, I don't know—

(He seems to be completely broken-down)

JOE

What's eating you? I want you to go on an errand for me.

TOM

It's Kitty.

JOE

What about her?

TOM

She's up in her room, crying.

98

JOE

Crying?

TOM

Yeah, she's been crying for over an hour. I been talking to her all this time, but she won't stop.

JOE

What's she crying about?

TOM

I don't know. I couldn't understand anything. She kept crying and telling me about a big house and collie dogs all around and flowers and one of her brother's dead and the other one lost somewhere. Joe, I can't stand Kitty crying.

JOE

You want to marry the girl?

TOM

(Nodding)
Yeah.

JOE

(Curious and sincere)
Why?

TOM

I don't know why, exactly, Joe.
(Pause)
Joe, I don't like to think of Kitty out in the streets. I guess I love her, that's all.

JOE

She's a nice girl.

99

TOM

She's like an angel. She's not like those other street-walkers.

JOE

(Swiftly)

Here. Take all this money and run next door to Frankie's and bet it on the nose of McCarthy.

TOM

(Swiftly)

All this money, Joe? McCarthy?

JOE

Yeah. Hurry.

TOM

(Going)

Ah, Joe. If McCarthy wins we'll be rich.

JOE

Get going, will you?

> TOM *runs out and nearly knocks over the* ARAB *coming back in.* NICK *fills him a beer without a word.*

ARAB

No foundation, anywhere. Whole world. No foundation. All the way down the line.

NICK

(Angry)

McCarthy! Just because you got a little lucky this morning, you have to go to work and throw away eighty bucks.

JOE

He wants to marry her.

100

NICK

Suppose she doesn't want to marry *him?*

JOE

   (Amazed)
Oh, yeah.
   (Thinking)
Now, why wouldn't she want to marry a nice guy like Tom?

NICK

She's been in burlesque. She's had flowers sent to her by European royalty. She's dined with young men of quality and social position. She's above Tom.

   TOM *comes running in.*

TOM

   (Disgusted)
They were running when I got there. Frankie wouldn't take the bet. McCarthy didn't get a call till the stretch. I thought we were going to save all this money. Then McCarthy won by two lengths.

JOE

What'd he pay, fifteen to one?

TOM

Better, but Frankie wouldn't take the bet.

NICK

   (Throwing a dish towel across the room)
Well, for the love of Mike.

JOE

Give me the money.

TOM

(Giving back the money)

We would have had about a thousand five hundred dollars.

JOE

(Bored, casually, inventing)

Go up to Schwabacher-Frey and get me the biggest Rand-McNally map of the nations of Europe they've got. On your way back stop at one of the pawn shops on Third Street, and buy me a good revolver and some cartridges.

TOM

She's up in her room crying, Joe.

JOE

Go get me those things.

NICK

What are you going to do, study the map, and then go out and shoot somebody?

JOE

I want to read the names of some European towns and rivers and valleys and mountains.

NICK

What do you want with the revolver?

JOE

I want to study it. I'm interested in things. Here's twenty dollars, Tom. Now go get them things.

TOM

A big map of Europe. And a revolver.

JOE

Get a good one. Tell the man you don't know anything

102

about firearms and you're trusting him not to fool you. Don't pay more than ten dollars.

TOM

Joe, you got something on your mind. Don't go fool with a revolver.

JOE

Be sure it's a good one.

TOM

Joe.

JOE

   (Irritated)
What, Tom?

TOM

Joe, what do you send me out for crazy things for all the time?

JOE

   (Angry)
They're not crazy, Tom. Now, get going.

TOM

What about Kitty, Joe?

JOE

Let her cry. It'll do her good.

TOM

If she comes in here while I'm gone, talk to her, will you, Joe? Tell her about me.

JOE

O.K. Get going. Don't load that gun. Just buy it and bring it here.

TOM

    (Going)

You won't catch me loading any gun.

JOE

Wait a minute. Take these toys away.

TOM

Where'll I take them?

JOE

Give them to some kid.

    (Pause)

No. Take them up to Kitty. Toys stopped me from crying once. That's the reason I had you buy them. I wanted to see if I could find out *why* they stopped me from crying. I remember they seemed awfully stupid at the time.

TOM

Shall I, Joe? Take them up to Kitty? Do you think they'd stop *her* from crying?

JOE

They might. You get curious about the way they work and you forget whatever it is you're remembering that's making you cry. That's what they're for.

TOM

Yeah. Sure. The girl at the store asked me what I wanted with toys. I'll take them up to Kitty.

    (Tragically)

She's like a little girl.

    (He goes)

WESLEY

Mr. Nick, can I play the piano again?

104

NICK

Sure. Practice all you like—until I tell you to stop.

WESLEY

You going to pay me for playing the piano?

NICK

Sure. I'll give you enough to get by on.

WESLEY

(Amazed and delighted)

Get money for playing the piano?

> *He goes to the piano and begins to play quietly.*
> HARRY *goes up on the little stage and listens to the*
> *music. After a while he begins a soft shoe dance.*

NICK

What were you crying about?

JOE

My mother.

NICK

What about her?

JOE

She was dead. I stopped crying when they gave me the
toys.

> NICK'S MOTHER, *a little old woman of sixty or so,*
> *dressed plainly in black, her face shining, comes in*
> *briskly, chattering loudly in Italian, gesturing.* NICK
> *is delighted to see her.*

NICK'S MOTHER

(In Italian)

Everything all right, Nickie?

NICK

(*In Italian*)
Sure, Mamma.

(NICK'S MOTHER *leaves as gaily and as noisily as she
came, after half a minute of loud Italian family
talk.*)

JOE

Who was that?

NICK

(*To* JOE, *proudly and a little sadly*)
My mother.
(*Still looking at the swinging doors*)

JOE

What'd she say?

NICK

Nothing. Just wanted to see me.
(*Pause*)
What do you want with that gun?

JOE

I study things, Nick.

An old man who looks as if he might have been
Kit Carson at one time walks in importantly, moves
about, and finally stands at Joe's table.

KIT CARSON

Murphy's the name. Just an old trapper. Mind if I sit
down?

JOE

Be delighted. What'll you drink?

106

KIT CARSON

(Sitting down)

Beer. Same as I've been drinking. And thanks.

JOE

(To NICK)

Glass of beer, Nick.

> NICK brings the beer to the table, KIT CARSON swallows it in one swig, wipes his big white mustache with the back of his right hand.

KIT CARSON

(Moving in)

I don't suppose you ever fell in love with a midget weighing thirty-nine pounds?

JOE

(Studying the man)

Can't say I have, but have another beer.

KIT CARSON

(Intimately)

Thanks, thanks. Down in Gallup, twenty years ago. Fellow by the name of Rufus Jenkins came to town with six white horses and two black ones. Said he wanted a man to break the horses for him because his left leg was wood and he couldn't do it. Had a meeting at Parker's Mercantile Store and finally came to blows, me and Henry Walpal. Bashed his head with a brass cuspidor and ran away to Mexico, but he didn't die.

Couldn't speak a word. Took up with a cattle-breeder named Diego, educated in California. Spoke the language better than you and me. Said, Your job, Murph, is to feed them prize bulls. I said, Fine, what'll I feed them? He said, Hay, lettuce, salt, beer, and aspirin.

Came to blows two days later over an accordion he claimed I stole. I had *borrowed* it. During the fight I busted it over his head; ruined one of the finest accordions I ever saw. Grabbed a horse and rode back across the border. Texas. Got to talking with a fellow who looked honest. Turned out to be a Ranger who was looking for me.

JOE

Yeah. You were saying, a thirty-nine-pound midget.

KIT CARSON

Will I ever forget that lady? Will I ever get over that amazon of small proportions?

JOE

Will you?

KIT CARSON

If I live to be sixty.

JOE

Sixty? You look more than sixty now.

KIT CARSON

That's trouble showing in my face. Trouble and complications. I was fifty-eight three months ago.

JOE

That accounts for it, then. Go ahead, tell me more.

KIT CARSON

Told the Texas Ranger my name was Rothstein, mining engineer from Pennsylvania, looking for something worth while. Mentioned two places in Houston. Nearly lost an

108

eye early one morning, going down the stairs. Ran into a six-footer with an iron-claw where his right hand was supposed to be. Said, You broke up my home. Told him I was a stranger in Houston. The girls gathered at the top of the stairs to see a fight. Seven of them. Six feet and an iron claw. That's bad on the nerves. Kicked him in the mouth when he swung for my head with the claw. Would have lost an eye except for quick thinking. He rolled into the gutter and pulled a gun. Fired seven times. I was back upstairs. Left the place an hour later, dressed in silk and feathers, with a hat swung around over my face. Saw him standing on the corner, waiting. Said, Care for a wiggle? Said he didn't. I went on down the street and left town. I don't suppose you ever had to put a dress on to save your skin, did you?

JOE

No, and I never fell in love with a midget weighing thirty-nine pounds. Have another beer?

KIT CARSON

Thanks.
          (Swallows glass of beer)
Ever try to herd cattle on a bicycle?

JOE

No. I never got around to that.

KIT CARSON

Left Houston with sixty cents in my pocket, gift of a girl named Lucinda. Walked fourteen miles in fourteen hours. Big house with barb-wire all around, and big dogs. One thing I never could get around. Walked past the gate, anyway, from hunger and thirst. Dogs jumped up and came for me. Walked right into them, growing older every second. Went up to the door and knocked. Big negress opened the door, closed it quick. Said, On your way, white trash.

Knocked again. Said, On your way. Again. On your way. Again. This time the old man himself opened the door, ninety, if he was a day. Sawed-off shotgun, too.

Said, I ain't looking for trouble, Father. I'm hungry and thirsty, name's Cavanaugh.

Took me in and made mint juleps for the two of us.

Said, Living here alone, Father?

Said, Drink and ask no questions. Maybe I am and maybe I ain't. You saw the lady. Draw your own conclusions.

I'd heard of that, but didn't wink out of tact. If I told you that old Southern gentleman was my grandfather, you wouldn't believe me, would you?

JOE

I might.

KIT CARSON

Well, it so happens he wasn't. Would have been romantic if he had been, though.

JOE

Where did you herd cattle on a bicycle?

KIT CARSON

Toledo, Ohio, 1918.

JOE

Toledo, Ohio? They don't herd cattle in Toledo.

110

They don't anymore. They did in 1918. One fellow did, leastaways. Bookkeeper named Sam Gold. Straight from the East Side, New York. Sombrero, lariats, Bull Durham, two head of cattle and two bicycles. Called his place The Gold Bar Ranch, two acres, just outside the city limits.

That was the year of the War, you'll remember.

JOE

Yeah, I remember, but how about herding them two cows on a bicycle? How'd you do it?

KIT CARSON

Easiest thing in the world. Rode no hands. Had to, otherwise couldn't lasso the cows. Worked for Sam Gold till the cows ran away. Bicycles scared them. They went into Toledo. Never saw hide nor hair of them again. Advertised in every paper, but never got them back. Broke his heart. Sold both bikes and returned to New York.

Took four aces from a deck of red cards and walked to town. Poker. Fellow in the game named Chuck Collins, liked to gamble. Told him with a smile I didn't suppose he'd care to bet a hundred dollars I wouldn't hold four aces the next hand. Called it. My cards were red on the blank side. The other cards were blue. Plumb forgot all about it. Showed him four aces. Ace of spades, ace of clubs, ace of diamonds, ace of hearts. I'll remember them four cards if I live to be sixty. Would have been killed on the spot except for the hurricane that year.

JOE

Hurricane?

111

KIT CARSON

You haven't forgotten the Toledo hurricane of 1918, have you?

JOE

No. There was no hurricane in Toledo in 1918, or any other year.

KIT CARSON

For the love of God, then what do you suppose that commotion was? And how come I came to in Chicago, dream-walking down State Street?

JOE

I guess they scared you.

KIT CARSON

No, that wasn't it. You go back to the papers of November 1918, and I think you'll find there was a hurricane in Toledo. I remember sitting on the roof of a two-story house, floating northwest.

JOE

(Seriously)

Northwest?

KIT CARSON

Now, son, don't tell me you don't believe me, either?

JOE

(Pause. Very seriously, energetically and sharply)

Of course I believe you. Living is an art. It's not bookkeeping. It takes a lot of rehearsing for a man to get to be himself.

112

KIT CARSON

(*Thoughtfully, smiling, and amazed*)
You're the first man I've ever met who believes me.

JOE

(*Seriously*)
Have another beer.

TOM *comes in with the Rand-McNally book, the revolver, and the box of cartridges.* KIT *goes to bar.*

JOE

(To TOM)
Did you give her the toys?

TOM

Yeah, I gave them to her.

JOE

Did she stop crying?

TOM

No. She started crying harder than ever.

JOE

That's funny. I wonder why.

TOM

Joe, if I was a minute earlier, Frankie would have taken the bet and now we'd have about a thousand five hundred dollars. How much of it would you have given me, Joe?

JOE

If she'd marry you—*all* of it.

TOM

Would you, Joe?

113

JOE

(Opening packages, examining book first, and revolver next)

Sure. In this realm there's only one subject, and you're it. It's my duty to see that my subject is happy.

TOM

Joe, do you think we'll ever have eighty dollars for a race sometime again when there's a fifteen-to-one shot that we like, weather good, track fast, they get off to a good start, our horse doesn't get a call till the stretch, we think we're going to lose all that money, and then it wins, by a nose?

JOE

I didn't quite get that.

TOM

You know what I mean.

JOE

You mean the impossible. No, Tom, we won't. We were just a little late, that's all.

TOM

We might, Joe.

JOE

It's not likely.

TOM

Then how am I ever going to make enough money to marry her?

JOE

I don't know, Tom. Maybe you aren't.

114

TOM

Joe, I got to marry Kitty.
(*Shaking his head*)
You ought to see the crazy room she lives in.

JOE

What kind of a room is it?

TOM

It's little. It crowds you in. It's bad, Joe. Kitty don't belong
in a place like that.

JOE

You want to take her away from there?

TOM

Yeah. I want her to live in a house where there's room
enough to live. Kitty ought to have a garden, or something.

JOE

You want to take care of her?

TOM

Yeah, sure, Joe. I ought to take care of somebody good
that makes me feel like *I'm* somebody.

JOE

That means you'll have to get a job. What can you do?

TOM

I finished high school, but I don't know what I can do.

JOE

Sometimes when you think about it, what do you think
you'd like to do?

TOM

Just sit around like you, Joe, and have somebody run errands for me and drink champagne and take things easy and never be broke and never worry about money.

JOE

That's a noble ambition.

NICK

(*To* JOE)
How do you do it?

JOE

I really don't know, but I think you've got to have the full co-operation of the Good Lord.

NICK

I can't understand the way you talk.

TOM

Joe, shall I go back and see if I can get her to stop crying?

JOE

Give me a hand and I'll go with you.

TOM

(Amazed)
What! You're going to get up already?

JOE

She's crying, isn't she?

TOM

She's crying. Worse than ever now.

JOE

I thought the toys would stop her.

116

TOM

I've seen you sit in one place from four in the morning till two the next morning.

JOE

At my best, Tom, I don't travel by foot. That's all. Come on. Give me a hand. I'll find some way to stop her from crying.

TOM

(Helping JOE)

Joe, I never did tell you. You're a different kind of a guy.

JOE

(Swiftly, a little angry)

Don't be silly. I don't understand things. I'm trying to understand them.

JOE is a little drunk. They go out together. The lights go down slowly, while WESLEY plays the piano, and come up slowly on:

ACT THREE

A cheap bed in Nick's to indicate room 21 of The New York Hotel, upstairs, around the corner from Nick's. The bed can be at the center of Nick's, or up on the little stage. Everything in Nick's is the same, except that all the people are silent, immobile and in darkness, except WESLEY who is playing the piano softly and sadly. KITTY DUVAL, in a dress she has carried around with her from the early days in Ohio, is seated on the bed, tying a ribbon in her hair. She looks at herself in a hand mirror. She is deeply grieved at the change she sees in herself. She takes off the ribbon, angry and hurt. She lifts a book from the bed and tries to read. She begins to sob again. She picks up an old picture of herself and looks at it. Sobs harder than ever, falling on the bed and burying her face. There is a knock, as if at the door.

KITTY

(Sobbing)
Who is it?

TOM'S VOICE
Kitty, it's me. Tom. Me and Joe.

JOE, followed by TOM, comes to the bed quietly. JOE is holding a rather large toy carousel. JOE studies KITTY a moment.

119

*He sets the toy carousel on the floor, at the foot
of Kitty's bed.*

TOM

> *(Standing over* KITTY *and bending down close to
> her)*

Don't cry any more, Kitty.

KITTY

> *(Not looking, sobbing)*

I don't like this life.

> JOE *starts the carousel which makes a strange, sor-
> rowful, tinkling music. The music begins slowly,
> becomes swift, gradually slows down, and ends.*
> JOE *himself is interested in the toy, watches and
> listens to it carefully.*

TOM

> *(Eagerly)*

Kitty. Joe got up from his chair at Nick's just to get you
a toy and come here. This one makes music. We rode all
over town in a cab to get it. Listen.

> KITTY *sits up slowly, listening, while* TOM *watches
> her. Everything happens slowly and somberly.*
> KITTY *notices the photograph of herself when she
> was a little girl. Lifts it, and looks at it again.*

TOM

> *(Looking)*

Who's that little girl, Kitty?

KITTY

That's me. When I was seven.

(KITTY *hands the photo to* TOM)

TOM

(*Looking, smiling*)
Gee, you're pretty, Kitty.

JOE *reaches up for the photograph, which* TOM *hands to him.* TOM *returns to* KITTY *whom he finds as pretty now as she was at seven.* JOE *studies the photograph.* KITTY *looks up at* TOM. *There is no doubt that they really love one another.* JOE *looks up at them.*

KITTY

Tom?

TOM

(*Eagerly*)
Yeah, Kitty.

KITTY

Tom, when you were a little boy what did you want to be?

TOM

(*A little bewildered, but eager to please her*)
What, Kitty?

KITTY

Do you remember when you were a little boy?

TOM

(*Thoughtfully*)
Yeah, I remember sometimes, Kitty.

KITTY

What did you want to be?

121

TOM

> (*Looks at* JOE. JOE *holds Tom's eyes a moment.*
> *Then* TOM *is able to speak*)

Sometimes I wanted to be a locomotive engineer. Sometimes I wanted to be a policeman.

KITTY

I wanted to be a great actress.
> (*She looks up into Tom's face*)

Tom, didn't you ever want to be a doctor?

TOM

> (*Looks at* JOE. JOE *holds Tom's eyes again, encouraging Tom by his serious expression to go on talking*)

Yeah, now I remember. Sure, Kitty. I wanted to be a doctor—once.

KITTY

> (*Smiling sadly*)

I'm so glad. Because I wanted to be an actress and have a young doctor come to the theater and see me and fall in love with me and send me flowers.

> (JOE *pantomimes to* TOM, *demanding that he go on talking*)

TOM

I would do that, Kitty.

KITTY

I wouldn't know who it was, and then one day I'd see him in the street and fall in love with him. I wouldn't know *he* was the one who was in love with me. I'd think about him all the time. I'd dream about him. I'd dream of being near him the rest of my life. I'd dream of having children that looked like him. I wouldn't be an actress all the time. Only until I found him and fell in love with him. After that we'd take a train and go to beautiful cities and see the wonderful people everywhere and give money to the poor and whenever people were sick he'd go to them and make them well again.

> TOM *looks at* JOE, *bewildered, confused, and full of sorrow.* KITTY *is deep in memory, almost in a trance.*

JOE
>   (Gently)
Talk to her, Tom. Be the wonderful young doctor she dreamed about and never found. Go ahead. Correct the errors of the world.

TOM
Joe.
>   (Pathetically)
I don't know what to say.

> There is rowdy singing in the hall. A loud young VOICE sings: "Sailing, sailing, over the bounding main."

VOICE
Kitty. Oh, Kitty!

> KITTY *stirs, shocked, coming out of the trance.*

Where the hell are you? Oh, Kitty.

> TOM *jumps up, furiously.*

WOMAN'S VOICE
>   (In the hall)
Who you looking for, Sailor Boy?

VOICE

The most beautiful lay in the world.

WOMAN'S VOICE

Don't go any further.

VOICE

(*With impersonal contempt*)
You? No. Not you. Kitty. You stink.

WOMAN'S VOICE

(*Rasping, angry*)
Don't you dare talk to me that way. You pickpocket.

VOICE

(*Still impersonal, but louder*)
Oh, I see. Want to get tough, hey? Close the door. Go
hide.

WOMAN'S VOICE

You pickpocket. All of you.

The door slams.

VOICE

(*Roaring with laughter which is very sad*)
Oh—Kitty.
Room 21. Where the hell is that room?

TOM

(*To* JOE)
Joe, I'll kill him.

KITTY

(*Fully herself again, terribly frightened*)
Who is it?

124

She looks long and steadily at TOM *and* JOE. TOM
is standing, excited and angry. JOE *is completely
at ease, his expression full of pity.* KITTY *buries her
face in the bed.*

JOE

 (Gently)

Tom. Just take him away.

VOICE

Here it is. Number 21. Three naturals. Heaven. My blue
heaven. The west, a nest, and you. Just Molly and me.
 (Tragically)
Ah, to hell with everything.

 A young SAILOR, *a good-looking boy of no more
 than twenty or so, who is only drunk and lonely,
 comes to the bed, singing sadly.*

SAILOR

Hi-ya, Kitty.

 (Pause)

Oh. Visitors. Sorry. A thousand apologies.

 (To KITTY)

I'll come back later.

TOM

 (Taking him by the shoulders, furiously)

If you do, I'll kill you.

 JOE *holds* TOM. TOM *pushes the frightened boy
 away.*

JOE

 (Somberly)

Tom. You stay here with Kitty. I'm going down to Union

125

Square to hire an automobile. I'll be back in a few minutes. We'll ride out to the ocean and watch the sun go down. Then we'll ride down the Great Highway to Half Moon Bay. We'll have supper down there, and you and Kitty can dance.

TOM

       (*Stupefied, unable to express his amazement and gratitude*)

Joe, you mean you're going to go on an errand for me? You mean you're not going to send me?

JOE

That's right.

       He gestures toward KITTY, *indicating that* TOM *shall talk to her, protect the innocence in her which is in so much danger when* TOM *isn't near, which* TOM *loves so deeply.* JOE *leaves.* TOM *studies* KITTY, *his face becoming child-like and somber. He sets the carousel into motion, listens, watching* KITTY, *who lifts herself slowly, looking only at* TOM. TOM *lifts the turning carousel and moves it slowly toward* KITTY, *as though the toy were his heart. The piano music comes up loudly and the lights go down, while* HARRY *is heard dancing swiftly.*

       BLACKOUT

ACT FOUR

A little later.

WESLEY, the colored boy, is at the piano.

HARRY is on the little stage, dancing.

NICK is behind the bar.

The ARAB is in his place.

KIT CARSON is asleep on his folded arms.

The DRUNKARD comes in. Goes to the telephone for the nickel that might be in the return-chute. NICK comes to take him out. He gestures for NICK to hold on a minute. Then produces a half dollar. NICK goes behind the bar to serve the DRUNKARD whiskey.

THE DRUNKARD

To the old, God bless them.
    (Another)
To the new, God love them.
    (Another)
To—children and small animals, like little dogs that don't bite.
    (Another. Loudly)
To reforestation.
    (Searches for money. Finds some)

127

To—President Taft.

He goes out.

The telephone rings.

KIT CARSON

(*Jumping up, fighting*)
Come on, all of you, if you're looking for trouble. I never asked for quarter and I always gave it.

NICK

(*Reproachfully*)
Hey, Kit Carson.

DUDLEY

(*On the phone*)
Hello. Who? Nick? Yes. He's here.
(*To* NICK)
It's for you. I think it's important.

NICK

(*Going to the phone*)
Important! What's important?

DUDLEY

He sounded like big-shot.

NICK

Big what?
(*To* WESLEY *and* HARRY)
Hey, you. Quiet. I want to hear this important stuff.

WESLEY *stops playing the piano.* HARRY *stops dancing.* KIT CARSON *comes close to* NICK.

KIT CARSON

If there's anything I can do, name it. I'll do it for you.

128

I'm fifty-eight years old; been through three wars; married four times; the father of countless children whose names I don't even know. I've got no money. I live from hand to mouth. But if there's anything I can do, name it. I'll do it.

NICK

(Patiently)

Listen, Pop. For a moment, please sit down and go back to sleep—for me.

KIT CARSON

I can do that, too.

He sits down, folds his arms, and puts his head into them. But not for long. As NICK *begins to talk, he listens carefully, gets to his feet, and then begins to express in pantomime the moods of each of Nick's remarks.*

NICK

(On phone)

Yeah?

(Pause)

Who? Oh, I see.

(Listens)

Why don't you leave them alone?

(Listens)

The church-people? Well, to hell with the church-people. I'm a Catholic myself.

(Listens)

All right. I'll send them away. I'll tell them to lay low for a couple of days. Yeah, I know how it is.

129

Nick's daughter ANNA *comes in shyly, looking at her father, and stands unnoticed by the piano.*

What?

(Very angry)

Listen. I don't like that Blick. He was here this morning, and I told him not to come back. I'll keep the girls out of here. You keep Blick out of here.

(Listens)

I know his brother-in-law is important, but I don't want him to come down here. He looks for trouble everywhere, and he always finds it. I don't break any laws. I've got a dive in the lousiest part of town. Five years nobody's been robbed, murdered, or gypped. I leave people alone. Your swanky joints uptown make trouble for you every night.

(NICK *gestures to* WESLEY—*keeps listening on the phone—puts his hand over the mouthpiece. To* WESLEY *and* HARRY.)

Start playing again. My ears have got a headache. Go into your dance, son.

(WESLEY *begins to play again.* HARRY *begins to dance.* NICK, *into mouthpiece.*)

Yeah. I'll keep them out. Just see that Blick doesn't come around and start something.

(Pause)

O.K.

(He hangs up)

KIT CARSON

Trouble coming?

NICK

That lousy Vice Squad again. It's that gorilla Blick.

130

KIT CARSON

Anybody at all. You can count on me. What kind of a gorilla is this gorilla Blick?

NICK

Very dignified. Toenails on his fingers.

ANNA

(*To* KIT CARSON, *with great, warm, beautiful pride, pointing at* NICK)

That's my father.

KIT CARSON

(*Leaping with amazement at the beautiful voice, the wondrous face, the magnificent event*)

Well, bless your heart, child. Bless your lovely heart. I had a little daughter point me out in a crowd once.

NICK

(*Surprised*)

Anna. What the hell are you doing here? Get back home where you belong and help Grandma cook me some supper.

ANNA *smiles at her father, understanding him, knowing that his words are words of love. She turns and goes, looking at him all the way out, as much as to say that she would cook for him the rest of her life.* NICK *stares at the swinging doors.* KIT CARSON *moves toward them, two or three steps.* ANNA *pushes open one of the doors and peeks in, to look at her father again. She waves to him. Turns and runs.* NICK *is very sad. He doesn't know what to do. He gets a glass and a bottle. Pours*

131

himself a drink. Swallows some. It isn't enough,
so he pours more and swallows the whole drink.

(*To himself*)
My beautiful, beautiful baby. Anna, she is you again.
(*He brings out a handkerchief, touches his eyes,
and blows his nose.* KIT CARSON *moves close to*
NICK, *watching Nick's face.* NICK *looks at him.
Loudly, almost making* KIT *jump*)
You're broke, aren't you?

KIT CARSON

Always. Always.

NICK

All right. Go into the kitchen and give Sam a hand. Eat
some food and when you come back you can have a couple
of beers.

KIT CARSON

(*Studying* NICK)
Anything at all. I know a good man when I see one.
(*He goes*)

ELSIE MANDELSPIEGEL comes into Nick's. She is a
beautiful, dark girl, with a sorrowful, wise, dreaming face, almost on the verge of tears, and full of
pity. There is an aura of dream about her. She
moves softly and gently, as if everything around
her were unreal and pathetic. DUDLEY doesn't notice
her for a moment or two. When he does finally
see her, he is so amazed, he can barely move or
speak. Her presence has the effect of changing him
completely. He gets up from his chair, as if in a
trance, and walks toward her, smiling sadly.

132

ELSIE

    (*Looking at him*)

Hello, Dudley.

DUDLEY

    (*Broken-hearted*)

Elsie.

ELSIE

I'm sorry.

    (*Explaining*)

So many people are sick. Last night a little boy died. I
love you, but—

    She gestures, trying to indicate how hopeless love
    is. They sit down.

DUDLEY

    (*Staring at her, stunned and quieted*)

Elsie. You'll never know how glad I am to see you. Just
to see you.

    (*Pathetically*)

I was afraid I'd never see you again. It was driving me
crazy. I didn't want to live. Honest.

    (*He shakes his head mournfully, with dumb and*
    beautiful affection. TWO STREETWALKERS *come in,*
    and pause near DUDLEY, *at the bar*)

I know. You told me before, but I can't help it, Elsie.
I love you.

ELSIE

    (*Quietly, somberly, gently, with great compassion*)

I know you love me, and I love you, but don't you see
love is impossible in this world?

133

DUDLEY

Maybe it isn't, Elsie.

ELSIE

Love is for birds. They have wings to fly away on when it's time for flying. For tigers in the jungle because they don't know their end. We know our end. Every night I watch over poor, dying men. I hear them breathing, crying, talking in their sleep. Crying for air and water and love, for mother and field and sunlight. We can never know love or greatness. We *should* know both.

DUDLEY

(*Deeply moved by her words*)
Elsie, I love you.

ELSIE

You want to live. I want to live, too, but where? Where can we escape our poor world?

DUDLEY

Elsie, we'll find a place.

ELSIE

(*Smiling at him*)
All right. We'll try again. We'll go together to a room in a cheap hotel, and dream that the world is beautiful, and that living is full of love and greatness. But in the morning, can we forget debts, and duties, and the cost of ridiculous things?

DUDLEY

(*With blind faith*)
Sure, we can, Elsie.

134

ELSIE

All right, Dudley. Of course. Come on. The time for the new pathetic war has come. Let's hurry, before they dress you, stand you in line, hand you a gun, and have you kill and be killed.

> ELSIE *looks at him gently, and takes his hand.* DUDLEY *embraces her shyly, as if he might hurt her. They go, as if they were a couple of young animals. There is a moment of silence. One of the* STREETWALKERS *bursts out laughing.*

KILLER

Nick, what the hell kind of a joint are you running?

NICK

Well, it's not out of the world. It's on a street in a city, and people come and go. They bring whatever they've got with them and they say what they must say.

THE OTHER STREETWALKER

It's floozies like her that raise hell with our racket.

NICK

(Remembering)

Oh, yeah. Finnegan telephoned.

KILLER

That mouse in elephant's body?

THE OTHER STREETWALKER

What the hell does *he* want?

NICK

Spend your time at the movies for the next couple of days.

KILLER

They're all lousy.
(*Mocking*)
All about love.

NICK

Lousy or not lousy, for a couple of days the flat-foots are going to be romancing you, so stay out of here, and lay low.

KILLER

I always was a pushover for a man in uniform, with a badge, a club and a gun.

KRUPP comes into the place. The girls put down their drinks.

NICK

O.K., get going.

The GIRLS begin to leave and meet KRUPP.

THE OTHER STREETWALKER

We was just going.

KILLER

We was formerly models at Magnin's.

They go.

KRUPP

(*At the bar*)
The strike isn't enough, so they've got to put us on the tails of the girls, too. I don't know. I wish to God I was back in the Sunset holding the hands of kids going home from school, where I belong. I don't like trouble. Give me a beer.

NICK *gives him a beer. He drinks some.*

Right now, McCarthy, my best friend, is with sixty strikers who want to stop the finks who are going to try to unload the *Mary Luckenbach* tonight. Why the hell Mc-Carthy ever became a longshoreman instead of a professor of some kind is something I'll never know.

NICK

Cowboys and Indians, cops and robbers, longshoremen and finks.

KRUPP

They're all guys who are trying to be happy; trying to make a living; support a family; bring up children; enjoy sleep. Go to a movie; take a drive on Sunday. They're all good guys, so out of nowhere, comes trouble. All they want is a chance to get out of debt and relax in front of a radio while Amos and Andy go through their act. What the hell do they always want to make trouble for? I been thinking everything over, Nick, and you know what I think?

NICK

No. What?

KRUPP

I think we're all crazy. It came to me while I was on my way to Pier 27. All of a sudden it hit me like a ton of bricks. A thing like that never happened to me before. Here we are in this wonderful world, full of all the wonderful things—here we are—all of us, and look at us. Just look at us. We're crazy. We're nuts. We've got everything, but we always feel lousy and dissatisfied just the same.

137

NICK

Of course we're crazy. Even so, we've got to go on living together.

(*He waves at the people in his joint*)

KRUPP

There's no hope. I don't suppose it's right for an officer of the law to feel the way I feel, but, by God, right or not right, that's how I feel. Why are we all so lousy? This is a good world. It's wonderful to get up in the morning and go out for a little walk and smell the trees and see the streets and the kids going to school and the clouds in the sky. It's wonderful just to be able to move around and whistle a song if you feel like it, or maybe try to sing one. This is a nice world. So why do they make all the trouble?

NICK

I don't know. Why?

KRUPP

We're crazy, that's why. We're no good any more. All the corruption everywhere. The poor kids selling themselves. A couple of years ago they were in grammar school. Everybody trying to get a lot of money in a hurry. Everybody betting the horses. Nobody going quietly for a little walk to the ocean. Nobody taking things easy and not wanting to make some kind of a killing. Nick, I'm going to quit being a cop. Let somebody else keep law and order. The stuff I hear about at headquarters. I'm thirty-seven years old, and I still can't get used to it. The only trouble is, the wife'll raise hell.

138

NICK

Ah, the wife.

KRUPP

She's a wonderful woman, Nick. We've got two of the swellest boys in the world. Twelve and seven years old. *The* ARAB *gets up and moves closer to listen.*

NICK

I didn't know that.

KRUPP

Sure. But what'll I do? I've wanted to quit for seven years. I wanted to quit the day they began putting me through the school. I didn't quit. What'll I do if I quit? Where's money going to be coming in from?

NICK

That's one of the reasons we're all crazy. We don't know where it's going to be coming in from, except from wherever it happens to be coming in from at the time, which we don't usually like.

KRUPP

Every once in a while I catch myself being mean, hating people just because they're down and out, broke and hungry, sick or drunk. And then when I'm with the stuffed shirts at headquarters, all of a sudden I'm nice to them, trying to make an impression. On who? People I don't like. And I feel disgusted.

(*With finality*)

I'm going to quit. That's all. Quit. Out. I'm going to give them back the uniform and the gadgets that go with it. I don't want any part of it. This is a good world. What do they want to make all the trouble for all the time?

139 .

ARAB

> (*Quietly, gently, with great understanding*)
No foundation. All the way down the line.

KRUPP

What?

ARAB

No foundation. No foundation.

KRUPP

I'll say there's no foundation.

ARAB

All the way down the line.

KRUPP

> (*To* NICK)
Is that all he ever says?

NICK

That's all he's been saying this week.

KRUPP

What is he, anyway?

NICK

He's an Arab, or something like that.

KRUPP

No, I mean what's he do for a living?

NICK

> (*To* ARAB)
What do you do for a living, brother?

ARAB

Work. Work all my life. All my life, work. From small

140

boy to old man, work. In old country, work. In new country, work. In New York. Pittsburgh. Detroit. Chicago. Imperial Valley. San Francisco. Work. No beg. Work. For what? Nothing. Three boys in old country. Twenty years, not see. Lost. Dead. Who knows? What. What-not. No foundation. All the way down the line.

KRUPP

What'd he say last week?

NICK

Didn't say anything. Played the harmonica.

ARAB

Old country song, I play.
He brings a harmonica from his back pocket.

KRUPP

Seems like a nice guy.

NICK

Nicest guy in the world.

KRUPP

(*Bitterly*)
But crazy. Just like all the rest of us. Stark raving mad.

WESLEY *and* HARRY *long ago stopped playing and dancing. They sat at a table together and talked for a while; then began playing casino or rummy. When the* ARAB *begins his solo on the harmonica, they stop their game to listen.*

WESLEY

You hear that?

141

HARRY

That's something.

WESLEY

That's crying. That's crying.

HARRY

I want to make people laugh.

WESLEY

That's deep, deep crying. That's crying a long time ago. That's crying a thousand years ago. Some place five thousand miles away.

HARRY

Do you think you can play to that?

WESLEY

I want to sing to that, but I can't sing.

HARRY

You try and play to that. I'll try to dance.

> WESLEY goes to the piano, and after closer listening, he begins to accompany the harmonica solo. HARRY goes to the little stage and after a few efforts begins to dance to the song. This keeps up quietly for some time.
>
> KRUPP and NICK have been silent, and deeply moved.

KRUPP

(Softly)
Well, anyhow, Nick.

NICK

Hmmmmmmm?

142

KRUPP

What I said. Forget it.

NICK

Sure.

KRUPP

It gets me down once in a while.

NICK

No harm in talking.

KRUPP

(The POLICEMAN again, loudly)

Keep the girls out of here.

NICK

(Loud and friendly)

Take it easy.

The music and dancing are now at their height.

CURTAIN

ACT FIVE

> *That evening. Fog-horns are heard throughout the scene. A man in evening clothes and a top hat, and his woman, also in evening clothes, are entering.*

> WILLIE *is still at the marble game.* NICK *is behind the bar.* JOE *is at his table, looking at the book of maps of the countries of Europe. The box containing the revolver and the box containing the cartridges are on the table, beside his glass. He is at peace, his hat tilted back on his head, a calm expression on his face.* TOM *is leaning against the bar, dreaming of love and Kitty. The* ARAB *is gone.* WESLEY *and* HARRY *are gone.* KIT CARSON *is watching the boy at the marble game.*

LADY

Oh, come on, please.

> *The gentleman follows miserably.*

> *The* SOCIETY MAN *and* WIFE *take a table.* NICK *gives them a menu.*

> *Outside, in the street, the Salvation Army people are playing a song. Big drum, tambourines, cornet and singing. They are singing "The Blood of the Lamb." The music and words come into the place*

faintly and comically. This is followed by an old
sinner testifying. It is the DRUNKARD. *His words*
are not intelligible, but his message is unmistakable.
He is saved. He wants to sin no more. And so on.

DRUNKARD

(*Testifying, unmistakably drunk*)
Brothers and sisters. I was a sinner. I chewed tobacco and
chased women. Oh, I sinned, brothers and sisters. And
then I was saved. Saved by the Salvation Army, God forgive me.

JOE

Let's see now. Here's a city. Pribor. Czecho-slovakia.
Little, lovely, lonely Czecho-slovakia. I wonder what kind
of a place Pribor was?
(*Calling*)
Pribor! *Pribor!*

(TOM *leaps*)

LADY

What's the matter with him?

MAN

(*Crossing his legs, as if he ought to go to the
men's room*)
Drunk.

TOM

Who you calling, Joe?

JOE

Pribor.

TOM

Who's Pribor?

146

JOE

He's a Czech. And a Slav. A Czecho-slovakian.

LADY

How interesting.

MAN

(Uncrosses legs)
He's drunk.

JOE

Tom, Pribor's a city in Czecho-slovakia.

TOM

Oh.

(Pause)
You sure were nice to her, Joe.

JOE

Kitty Duval? She's one of the finest people in the world.

TOM

It sure was nice of you to hire an automobile and take us for a drive along the ocean-front and down to Half Moon Bay.

JOE

Those three hours were the most delightful, the most somber, and the most beautiful I have ever known.

TOM

Why, Joe?

JOE

Why? I'm a student.

(Lifting his voice)

Tom.

> (*Quietly*)

I'm a student. I study all things. All. All. And when my study reveals something of beauty in a place or in a person where by all rights only ugliness or death should be revealed, then I know how full of goodness this life is. And that's a good thing to know. That's a truth I shall always seek to verify.

LADY

Are you sure he's drunk?

MAN

> (*Crossing his legs*)

He's either drunk, or just naturally crazy.

TOM

Joe?

JOE

Yeah.

TOM

You won't get sore or anything?

JOE

> (*Impatiently*)

What is it, Tom?

TOM

Joe, where do you get all that money? You paid for the automobile. You paid for supper and the two bottles of champagne at the Half Moon Bay Restaurant. You moved Kitty out of the New York Hotel around the corner to the St. Francis Hotel on Powell Street. I saw you pay her rent. I saw you give her money for new clothes. Where

148

do you get all that money, Joe? Three years now and I've never asked.

JOE

> (*Looking at* TOM *sorrowfully, a little irritated, not so much with* TOM *as with the world and himself, his own superiority. He speaks clearly, slowly and solemnly*)

Now don't be a fool, Tom. Listen carefully. If anybody's got any money—to hoard or to throw away—you can be sure he stole it from other people. Not from rich people who can spare it, but from poor people who can't. From their lives and from their dreams. I'm no exception. I *earned* the money I throw away. I stole it like everybody else does. I hurt people to get it. Loafing around this way, I *still* earn money. The money itself earns more. I *still* hurt people. I don't know who they are, or where they are. If I did, I'd feel worse than I do. I've got a Christian conscience in a world that's got no conscience at all. The world's trying to get some sort of a *social* conscience, but it's having a devil of a time trying to do *that*. I've got money. I'll always have money, as long as this world stays the way it is. I don't work. I don't make anything.

> (*He sips*)

I drink. I worked when I was a kid. I worked *hard*. I mean hard, Tom. People are supposed to enjoy living. I got tired.

> (*He lifts the gun and looks at it while he talks*)

I decided to get even on the world. Well, you can't enjoy living unless you work. Unless you do something. I don't do anything. I don't *want* to do anything any more. There isn't anything I can do that won't make me feel embar-

149

rassed. Because I can't do simple, good things. I haven't the patience. And I'm too smart. Money is the guiltiest thing in the world. It stinks. Now, don't ever bother me about it again.

TOM

I didn't mean to make you feel bad, Joe.

JOE

(*Slowly*)
Here. Take this gun out in the street and give it to some worthy hold-up man.

LADY

What's he saying?

MAN

(*Uncrosses legs*)
You wanted to visit a honky-tonk. Well, *this* is a honky-tonk.
(*To the world*)
Married twenty-eight years and she's still looking for adventure.

TOM

How should I know who's a hold-up man?

JOE

Take it away. Give it to somebody.

TOM

(*Bewildered*)
Do I *have* to give it to somebody?

JOE

Of course.

150

TOM

Can't I take it back and get some of our money?

JOE

Don't talk like a business man. Look around and find
somebody who appears to be in need of a gun and give
it to him. It's a good gun, isn't it?

TOM

The man said it was, but how can I tell who needs a gun?

JOE

Tom, you've seen good people who needed guns, haven't
you?

TOM

I don't remember. Joe, I might give it to the wrong kind
of guy. He might do something crazy.

JOE

All right. I'll find somebody myself.
(TOM *rises*)
Here's some money. Go get me this week's *Life, Liberty,
Time*, and six or seven packages of chewing gum.

TOM

(*Swiftly, in order to remember each item*)
Life, Liberty, Time, and six or seven packages of chewing gum?

JOE

That's right.

TOM

All that chewing gum? What kind?

151

JOE

Any kind. Mix 'em up. All kinds.

TOM

Licorice, too?

JOE

Licorice, by all means.

TOM

Juicy Fruit?

JOE

Juicy Fruit.

TOM

Tutti-frutti?

JOE

Is there such a gum?

TOM

I think so.

JOE

All right. Tutti-Frutti, too. Get *all* the kinds. Get as many kinds as they're selling.

TOM

Life, Liberty, Time, and all the different kinds of gum.

(*He begins to go*)

JOE

(*Calling after him loudly*)
Get some jelly beans too. All the different colors.

152

TOM

All right, Joe.

JOE

And the longest panatela cigar you can find. Six of them.

TOM

Panatela. I got it.

JOE

Give a news-kid a dollar.

TOM

O.K., Joe.

JOE

Give some old man a dollar.

TOM

O.K., Joe.

JOE

Give them Salvation Army people in the street a couple of dollars and ask them to sing that song that goes—
    (*He sings loudly*)
Let the lower lights be burning, send a gleam across the wave.

TOM

    (*Swiftly*)
Let the lower lights be burning, send a gleam across the wave.

JOE

That's it.
    (*He goes on with the song, very loudly and religiously*)

153

Some poor, dying, struggling seaman, you may rescue, you may save.

(*Halts*)

TOM

O.K., Joe. I got it. *Life, Liberty, Time,* all the kinds of gum they're selling, jelly beans, six panatela cigars, a dollar for a news-kid, a dollar for an old man, two dollars for the Salvation Army.

(*Going*)

Let the lower lights be burning, send a gleam across the wave.

JOE

That's it.

LADY

He's absolutely insane.

MAN

(*Wearily crossing legs*)

You asked me to take you to a honky-tonk, instead of to the Mark Hopkins. You're *here* in a honky-tonk. I can't help it if he's crazy. Do you want to go back to where people aren't crazy?

LADY

No, not just yet.

MAN

Well, all right then. Don't be telling me every minute that he's crazy.

LADY

You needn't be huffy about it.

154

MAN *refuses to answer, uncrosses legs.*

When JOE *began to sing,* KIT CARSON *turned away from the marble game and listened. While the man and woman are arguing he comes over to Joe's table.*

KIT CARSON
Presbyterian?

JOE
I attended a Presbyterian Sunday School.

KIT CARSON
Fond of singing?

JOE
On occasion. Have a drink?

KIT CARSON
Thanks.

JOE
Get a glass and sit down.

> KIT CARSON *gets a glass from* NICK, *returns to the table, sits down,* JOE *pours him a drink, they touch glasses just as the Salvation Army people begin to fulfill the request. They sip some champagne, and at the proper moment begin to sing the song together, sipping champagne, raising hell with the tune, swinging it, and so on. The* SOCIETY LADY *joins them, and is stopped by her* HUSBAND.

Always was fond of that song. Used to sing it at the top of my voice. Never saved a seaman in my life.

(*Flirting with the* SOCIETY LADY *who loves it*)
I saved a seaman once. Well, he wasn't exactly a seaman. He was a darky named Wellington. Heavy-set sort of a fellow. Nice personality, but no friends to speak of. Not until I came along, at any rate. In New Orleans. In the summer of the year 1899. No. Ninety-eight. I was a lot younger of course, and had no mustache, but was regarded by many people as a man of means.

JOE
Know anything about guns?

KIT CARSON

(*Flirting*)
All there is to know. Didn't fight the Ojibways for nothing. Up there in the Lake Takalooca Country, in Michigan.

(*Remembering*)
Along about in 1881 or two. Fought 'em right up to the shore of the Lake. Made 'em swim for Canada. One fellow in particular, an Indian named Harry Daisy.

JOE

(*Opening the box containing the revolver*)
What sort of a gun would you say this is? Any good?

KIT CARSON

(*At sight of gun, leaping*)
Yep. That looks like a pretty nice hunk of shooting iron. That's a six-shooter. Shot a man with a six-shooter once. Got him through the palm of his right hand. Lifted his arm to wave to a friend. Thought it was a bird. Fellow named, I believe, Carroway. Larrimore Carroway.

156

JOE

Know how to work one of these things?

He offers KIT CARSON *the revolver, which is old and enormous.*

KIT CARSON

(*Laughing at the absurd question*)

Know how to work it? Hand me that little gun, son, and I'll show you all about it.

JOE *hands* KIT *the revolver.*

(*Importantly*)

Let's see now. This is probably a new kind of six-shooter. After my time. Haven't nicked an Indian in years. I believe this here place is supposed to move out.

(*He fools around and gets the barrel out for loading*)

That's it. There it is.

JOE

Look all right?

KIT CARSON

It's a good gun. You've got a good gun there, son. I'll explain it to you. You see these holes? Well, that's where you put the cartridges.

JOE

(*Taking some cartridges out of the box*)

Here. Show me how it's done.

KIT CARSON

(*A little impatiently*)

Well, son, you take 'em one by one and put 'em in the holes, like this. There's one. Two. Three. Four. Five. Six.

157

Then you get the barrel back in place. Then cock it. Then all you got to do is aim and fire.

> *He points the gun at the* LADY *and* GENTLEMAN *who scream and stand up, scaring* KIT CARSON *into paralysis.*
>
> *The gun is loaded, but uncocked.*

JOE
It's all set?

KIT CARSON
Ready to kill.

JOE
Let me hold it.

> KIT *hands* JOE *the gun. The* LADY *and* GENTLEMAN *watch, in terror.*

KIT CARSON
Careful, now, son. Don't cock it. Many a man's lost an eye fooling with a loaded gun. Fellow I used to know named Danny Donovan lost a nose. Ruined his whole life. Hold it firm. Squeeze the trigger. Don't snap it. Spoils your aim.

JOE
Thanks. Let's see if I can unload it.
(*He begins to unload it*)

KIT CARSON
Of course you can.

> JOE *unloads the revolver, looks at it very closely, puts the cartridges back into the box.*

158

JOE

    (Looking at gun)

I'm mighty grateful to you. Always wanted to see one of those things close up. Is it really a good one?

KIT CARSON

    It's a beaut, son.

JOE

    (Aims the empty gun at a bottle on the bar)

Bang!

WILLIE

    (At the marble game, as the machine groans)

Oh, Boy!

    (Loudly, triumphantly)

There you are, Nick. Thought I couldn't do it, hey? Now, watch.

> The machine begins to make a special kind of noise. Lights go on and off. Some red, some green. A bell rings loudly six times.

One. Two. Three. Four. Five. Six.

> An American flag jumps up. WILLIE comes to attention. Salutes.

Oh, boy, what a beautiful country.

> A loud music-box version of the song "America." JOE, KIT, and the LADY get to their feet.

    (Singing)

My country, 'tis of thee, sweet land of liberty, of thee I sing.

Everything quiets down. The flag goes back into the machine. WILLIE *is thrilled, amazed, delighted.* EVERYBODY *has watched the performance of the defeated machine from wherever he happened to be when the performance began.*

WILLIE, *looking around at everybody, as if they had all been on the side of the machine.*

O.K. How's that? I knew I could do it.
(*To* NICK)
Six nickels.

NICK *hands him six nickels.* WILLIE *goes over to* JOE *and* KIT.

Took me a little while, but I finally did it. It's scientific, really. With a little skill a man can make a modest living beating the marble games. Not that that's what I want to do. I just don't like the idea of anything getting the best of me. A machine or anything else. Myself, I'm the kind of a guy who makes up his mind to do something, and then goes to work and does it. There's no other way a man can be a success at anything.
(*Indicating the letter "F" on his sweater*)
See that letter? That don't stand for some little-bitty high school somewhere. That stands for me. Faroughli. Willie Faroughli. I'm an Assyrian. We've got a civilization six or seven centuries old, I think. Somewhere along in there. Ever hear of Osman? Harold Osman? He's an Assyrian, too. He's got an orchestra down in Fresno.
(*He goes to the* LADY *and* GENTLEMAN)
I've never seen you before in my life, but I can tell from the clothes you wear and the company you keep

>   (*Graciously indicating the* LADY)
that you're a man who looks every problem straight in
the eye, and then goes to work and *solves* it. I'm that way
myself. Well.
>   (*He smiles beautifully, takes the* GENTLEMAN'S *hand*
>   *furiously*)
It's been wonderful talking to a nicer type of people for
a change. Well. I'll be seeing you. So long.
>   (*He turns, takes two steps, returns to the table.*
>   *Very politely and seriously*)
Good-by, lady. You've got a good man there. Take good
care of him.

>   WILLIE *goes, saluting* JOE *and the world.*

KIT CARSON
>   (*To* JOE)
By God, for a while there I didn't think that young
Assyrian was going to do it. That fellow's got something.

>   TOM *comes back with the magazines and other*
>   *stuff.*

JOE
>   Get it all?

TOM
>   Yeah. I had a little trouble finding the jelly beans.

JOE
>   Let's take a look at them.

TOM
>   These are the jelly beans.

JOE puts his hand into the cellophane bag and takes
out a handful of the jelly beans, looks at them,
smiles, and tosses a couple into his mouth.

JOE

Same as ever. Have some.
(He offers the bag to KIT)

KIT CARSON

(Flirting)
Thanks! I remember the first time I ever ate jelly beans.
I was six, or at the most seven. Must have been in
(Slowly)
eighteen—seventy-seven. Seven or eight. Baltimore.

JOE

Have some, Tom.

(TOM takes some)

TOM

Thanks, Joe.

JOE

Let's have some of that chewing gum.
He dumps all the packages of gum out of the bag
onto the table.

KIT CARSON

(Flirting)
Me and a boy named Clark. Quinton Clark. Became a
Senator.

JOE

Yeah. Tutti-frutti, all right.

162

He opens a package and folds all five pieces into his mouth.

Always wanted to see how many I could chew at one time. Tell you what, Tom. I'll bet I can chew more at one time than you can.

TOM

> (*Delighted*)

All right.

> *They both begin to fold gum into their mouths.*

KIT CARSON

I'll referee. Now, one at a time. How many you got?

JOE

Six.

KIT CARSON

All right. Let Tom catch up with you.

JOE

> (While TOM's *catching up*)

Did you give a dollar to a news-kid?

TOM

Yeah, sure.

JOE

What'd he say?

TOM

Thanks.

JOE

What sort of a kid was he?

TOM

Little, dark kid. I guess he's Italian.

163

JOE

Did he seem pleased?

TOM

Yeah.

JOE

That's good. Did you give a dollar to an old man?

TOM

Yeah.

JOE

Was he pleased?

TOM

Yeah.

JOE

Good. How many you got in your mouth?

TOM

Six.

JOE

All right. I got six, too.

(*Folds one more in his mouth.* TOM *folds one too*)

KIT CARSON

Seven. Seven each.

They each fold one more into their mouths, very solemnly, chewing them into the main hunk of gum.

Eight. Nine. Ten.

164

JOE

    (Delighted)

Always wanted to do this.

    He picks up one of the magazines.

Let's see what's going on in the world.

    He turns the pages and keeps folding gum into his mouth and chewing.

KIT CARSON

Eleven. Twelve.

    KIT *continues to count while* JOE *and* TOM *continue the contest. In spite of what they are doing, each is very serious.*

TOM

Joe, what'd you want to move Kitty into the St. Francis Hotel for?

JOE

She's a better woman than any of them tramp society dames that hang around that lobby.

TOM

Yeah, but do you think she'll feel at home up there?

JOE

Maybe not at first, but after a couple of days she'll be all right. A nice big room. A bed for sleeping in. Good clothes. Good food. She'll be all right, Tom.

TOM

I hope so. Don't you think she'll get lonely up there with nobody to talk to?

JOE

    (*Looking at* TOM *sharply, almost with admiration, pleased but severe*)

There's nobody anywhere for her to talk to—except you.

TOM

    (*Amazed and delighted*)

Me, Joe?

JOE

    (*While* TOM *and* KIT CARSON *listen carefully*, KIT *with great appreciation*)

Yes, you. By the grace of God, you're the other half of that girl. Not the angry woman that swaggers into this water-front dive and shouts because the world has kicked her around. *Anybody* can have *her.* You belong to the little kid in Ohio who once dreamed of living. Not with her carcass, for money, so she can have food and clothes, and pay rent. With *all* of her. I put her in that hotel, so she can have a chance to gather herself together again. She can't do that in the New York Hotel. You saw what happens there. There's nobody anywhere for her to talk to, except you. They all make her talk like a whore. After a while, she'll *believe* them. Then she won't be able to remember. She'll get lonely. Sure. People can get lonely for misery, even. I want her to go on being lonely for you, so she can come together again the way she was meant to be from the beginning. Loneliness is good for people. Right now it's the only thing for Kitty. Any more licorice?

TOM

    (*Dazed*)

What? Licorice?

166

(*Looking around busily*)
I guess we've chewed all the licorice in. We still got Clove, Peppermint, Doublemint, Beechnut, Teaberry, and Juicy Fruit.

JOE

Licorice used to be my favorite. Don't worry about her, Tom, she'll be all right. You really want to marry her, don't you?

TOM

(*Nodding*)
Honest to God, Joe.
(*Pathetically*)
Only, I haven't got any money.

JOE

Couldn't you be a prize-fighter or something like that?

TOM

Naaaah. I couldn't hit a man if I wasn't sore at him. He'd have to do something that made me hate him.

JOE

You've got to figure out something to do that you won't mind doing very much.

TOM

I wish I could, Joe.

JOE

(*Thinking deeply, suddenly*)
Tom, would you be embarrassed driving a truck?

TOM

(*Hit by a thunderbolt*)

167

Joe, I never thought of that. I'd like that. Travel. Highways. Little towns. Coffee and hot cakes. Beautiful valleys
and mountains and streams and trees and daybreak and
sunset.

JOE

There *is* poetry in it, at that.

TOM

Joe, that's just the kind of work I *should* do. Just sit there
and travel, and look, and smile, and bust out laughing.
Could Kitty go with me, sometimes?

JOE

I don't know. Get me the phone book. Can you drive a
truck?

TOM

Joe, you know I can drive a truck, or any kind of thing
with a motor and wheels.

TOM *takes* JOE *the phone book.* JOE *turns the pages.*

JOE

(Looking)
Here! Here it is. Tuxedo 7900. Here's a nickel. Get me
that number.

TOM *goes to telephone, dials the number.*

TOM

Hello.

JOE

Ask for Mr. Keith.

168

TOM

     (Mouth and language full of gum)
I'd like to talk to Mr. Keith.

     (Pause)
Mr. Keith.

JOE

  Take that gum out of your mouth for a minute.

       (TOM *removes the gum*)

TOM

  Mr. Keith. Yeah. That's right. Hello, Mr. Keith?

JOE

  Tell him to hold the line.

TOM

  Hold the line, please.

JOE

  Give me a hand, Tom.

      TOM *helps* JOE *to the telephone.*

     (At phone, wad of gum in fingers delicately)
Keith? Joe. Yeah. Fine. Forget it.

     (Pause)

Have you got a place for a good driver?

     (Pause)

I don't think so.
     (To TOM*)*
You haven't got a driver's license, have you?

TOM

    (*Worried*)
No. But I can get one, Joe.

JOE

    (*At phone*)
No, but he can get one easy enough. To hell with the union. He'll join later. All right, call him a Vice-President and say he drives for relaxation. Sure. What do you mean? Tonight? I don't know why not. San Diego? All right, let him start driving without a license. What the hell's the difference? Yeah. Sure. Look him over. Yeah. I'll send him right over. Right.
    (*He hangs up*)
Thanks.
    (*To telephone*)

TOM

Am I going to get the job?

JOE

He wants to take a look at you.

TOM

Do I look all right, Joe?

JOE

    (*Looking at him carefully*)
Hold up your head. Stick out your chest. How do you feel?

    TOM *does these things.*

TOM

Fine.

170

JOE

You look fine, too.

> JOE takes his wad of gum out of his mouth and
> wraps Liberty magazine around it.

JOE

You win, Tom. Now, look.

> (He bites off the tip of a very long panatela cigar,
> lights it, and hands one to TOM, and another to
> KIT)

Have yourselves a pleasant smoke. Here.

> (He hands two more to TOM)

Give those slummers one each.

> (He indicates the SOCIETY LADY and GENTLEMAN)

> TOM goes over and without a word gives a cigar
> each to the MAN and the LADY.

> The MAN is offended; he smells and tosses aside
> his cigar. The WOMAN looks at her cigar a moment,
> then puts the cigar in her mouth.

MAN

What do you think you're doing?

LADY

Really, dear. I'd like to.

MAN

Oh, this is too much.

LADY

I'd really, really like to, dear.

> She laughs, puts the cigar in her mouth. Turns to
> KIT. He spits out tip. She does the same.

171

MAN

    (*Loudly*)

The mother of five grown men, and she's still looking for romance.

    (*Shouts as* KIT *lights her cigar*)

No. I forbid it.

JOE

    (*Shouting*)

What's the matter with you? Why don't you leave her alone? What are you always pushing your women around for?

    (*Almost without a pause*)

Now, look, Tom.

       The LADY *puts the lighted cigar in her mouth, and begins to smoke, feeling wonderful.*

Here's ten bucks.

TOM

Ten bucks?

JOE

He may want you to get into a truck and begin driving to San Diego tonight.

TOM

Joe, I got to tell Kitty.

JOE

I'll tell her.

TOM

Joe, take care of her.

JOE

She'll be all right. Stop worrying about her. She's at the St. Francis Hotel. Now, look. Take a cab to Townsend and Fourth. You'll see the big sign. Keith Motor Transport Company. He'll be waiting for you.

TOM

O.K., Joe.
    (Trying hard)
Thanks, Joe.

JOE

Don't be silly.
Get going.

    TOM goes.

    LADY starts puffing on cigar.

    As TOM goes, WESLEY and HARRY come in together.

NICK

Where the hell have you been? We've got to have some entertainment around here. Can't you see them fine people from uptown?
    (He points at the SOCIETY LADY and GENTLEMAN)

WESLEY

You said to come back at ten for the second show.

NICK

Did I say that?

WESLEY

Yes, sir, Mr. Nick, that's exactly what you said.

HARRY

Was the first show all right?

NICK

That wasn't a show. There was no one here to see it. How can it be a show when no one sees it? People are afraid to come down to the waterfront.

HARRY

Yeah. We were just down to Pier 27. One of the longshoremen and a cop had a fight and the cop hit him over the head with a blackjack. We saw it happen, didn't we?

WESLEY

Yes, sir, we was standing there looking when it happened.

NICK

(*A little worried*)
Anything else happen?

WESLEY

They was all talking.

HARRY

A man in a big car came up and said there was going to be a meeting right away and they hoped to satisfy everybody and stop the strike.

WESLEY

Right away. *Tonight.*

NICK

Well, it's about time. Them poor cops are liable to get nervous and—shoot somebody.
(*To* HARRY, *suddenly*)
Come back here. I want you to tend bar for a while. I'm going to take a walk over to the pier.

174

HARRY

    Yes, sir.

NICK

        (*To the* SOCIETY LADY *and* GENTLEMAN)
    You society people made up your minds yet?

LADY

    Have you champagne?

NICK

        (*Indicating* JOE)
    What do you think he's pouring out of that bottle, water
or something?

LADY

    Have you a chill bottle?

NICK

    I've got a dozen of them chilled. He's been drinking
champagne here all day and all night for a month now.

LADY

    May we have a bottle?

NICK

    It's six dollars.

LADY

    I think we can manage.

MAN

    I don't know. I *know* I don't know.

        NICK *takes off his coat and helps* HARRY *into it.*
        HARRY *takes a bottle of champagne and two glasses*
        to the LADY *and the* GENTLEMAN, *dancing, collects*

six dollars, and goes back behind the bar, dancing.
NICK gets his coat and hat.

NICK

(To WESLEY)
Rattle the keys a little, son. Rattle the keys.

WESLEY

Yes, sir, Mr. Nick.

NICK is on his way out. The ARAB enters.

NICK

Hi-ya, Mahmed.

ARAB

No foundation.

NICK

All the way down the line.
(He goes)

WESLEY is at the piano, playing quietly. The ARAB
swallows a glass of beer, takes out his harmonica,
and begins to play. WESLEY fits his playing to the
Arab's.

KITTY DUVAL, strangely beautiful, in new clothes,
comes in. She walks shyly, as if she were embarrassed by the fine clothes, as if she had no right to
wear them. The LADY and GENTLEMAN are very impressed. HARRY looks at her with amazement. JOE
is reading Time magazine. KITTY goes to his
table. JOE looks up from the magazine, without the
least amazement.

176

JOE

Hello, Kitty.

KITTY

Hello, Joe.

JOE

It's nice seeing you again.

KITTY

I came in a cab.

JOE

You been crying again?
  (KITTY *can't answer. To* HARRY)
Bring a glass.
      HARRY *comes over with a glass.* JOE *pours* KITTY *a*
      drink.

KITTY

I've got to talk to you.

JOE

Have a drink.

KITTY

I've never been in burlesque. We were just poor.

JOE

Sit down, Kitty.

KITTY

    (Sits down)
I tried other things.

177

JOE

Here's to you, Katerina Koranovsky. Here's to you. And Tom.

KITTY

(Sorrowfully)
Where is Tom?

JOE

He's getting a job tonight driving a truck. He'll be back in a couple of days.

KITTY

(Sadly)
I told him I'd marry him.

JOE

He wanted to see you and say good-by.

KITTY

He's too good for me. He's like a little boy.
(Wearily)
I'm— Too many things have happened to me.

JOE

Kitty Duval, you're one of the few truly innocent people I have ever known. He'll be back in a couple of days. Go back to the hotel and wait for him.

KITTY

That's what I mean. I can't stand being alone. I'm no good. I tried very hard. I don't know what it is. I miss—
(She gestures)

JOE

(Gently)
Do you really want to come back here, Kitty?

178

KITTY

I don't know. I'm not sure. Everything *smells* different.
I don't know how to feel, or what to think.

(*Gesturing pathetically*)

I know I don't belong there. It's what I've wanted all my
life, but it's too *late*. I try to be happy about it, but all
I can do is remember everything and cry.

JOE

I don't know what to tell you, Kitty. I didn't mean to
hurt you.

KITTY

You haven't hurt me. You're the only person who's ever
been good to me. I've never known anybody like you. I'm
not sure about love any more, but I know I love you, and
I know I love Tom.

JOE

I love you too, Kitty Duval.

KITTY

He'll want babies. I know he will. I know *I* will, too. Of
course I will. I can't—

(*She shakes her head*)

JOE

Tom's a baby himself. You'll be very happy together. He
wants you to ride with him in the truck. Tom's good for
you. You're good for Tom.

KITTY

(*Like a child*)

Do you want me to go back and wait for him?

JOE

I can't *tell* you what to do. I think it would be a good idea, though.

KITTY

I wish I could tell you how it makes me feel to be alone. It's almost worse.

JOE

It might take a whole week, Kitty.

(*He looks at her sharply, at the arrival of an idea*)
Didn't you speak of reading a book? A book of poems?

KITTY

I didn't know what I was saying.

JOE

(*Trying to get up*)
Of course you knew. I think you'll like poetry. Wait here a minute, Kitty. I'll go see if I can find some books.

KITTY

All right, Joe.

He walks out of the place, trying very hard not to wobble.

Fog-horn. Music. The NEWSBOY comes in. Looks for JOE. Is broken-hearted because JOE is gone.

NEWSBOY

(*To* SOCIETY GENTLEMAN)
Paper?

MAN

(Angry)
No.

The NEWSBOY *goes to the* ARAB.

NEWSBOY

Paper, Mister?

ARAB

(*Irritated*)
No foundation.

NEWSBOY

What?

ARAB

(*Very angry*)
No foundation.

The NEWSBOY *starts out, turns, looks at the* ARAB,
shakes head.

NEWSBOY

No foundation? How do you figure?

BLICK *and* TWO COPS *enter.*

NEWSBOY

(*To* BLICK)
Paper, Mister?
(BLICK *pushes him aside. The* NEWSBOY *goes*)

BLICK

(*Walking authoritatively about the place, to* HARRY)
Where's Nick?

HARRY

He went for a walk.

BLICK

Who are you?

181

HARRY

    Harry.

BLICK

        (*To the* ARAB *and* WESLEY)
Hey, you. Shut up.

        (*The* ARAB *stops playing the harmonica,* WESLEY
the piano)

BLICK

        (*Studies* KITTY)
What's your name, sister?

KITTY

        (*Looking at him*)
Kitty Duval. What's it to you?

        *Kitty's voice is now like it was at the beginning
of the play: tough, independent, bitter and hard.*

BLICK

        (*Angry*)
Don't give me any of your gutter lip. Just answer my
questions.

KITTY

    You go to hell, you.

BLICK

        (*Coming over, enraged*)
Where do you live?

KITTY

    The New York Hotel. Room 21.

BLICK

    Where do you work?

    182

KITTY

I'm not working just now. I'm looking for work.

BLICK

What kind of work?

　　　　(KITTY *can't answer*)

What kind of work?

　　　　(KITTY *can't answer*)

　　　　(*Furiously*)

WHAT KIND OF WORK?

　　　　(KIT CARSON *comes over*)

KIT CARSON

You can't talk to a lady that way in my presence.

　　　　BLICK *turns and stares at* KIT. *The* COPS *begin to*
　　　　move from the bar.

BLICK

　　　　(*To the* COPS)

It's all right, boys. I'll take care of this.

　　　　(*To* KIT)

What'd you say?

KIT CARSON

You got no right to hurt people. Who are you?

　　　　BLICK, *without a word, takes* KIT *to the street.*
　　　　Sounds of a blow and a groan. BLICK *returns,*
　　　　breathing hard.

BLICK

　　　　(*To the* COPS)

O.K., boys. You can go now. Take care of him. Put him

183

on his feet and tell him to behave himself from now on.

(*To* KITTY *again*)

Now answer my question. What kind of work?

KITTY

(*Quietly*)

I'm a whore, you son of a bitch. You know what kind of work I do. And I know what kind you do.

MAN

(*Shocked and really hurt*)

Excuse me, officer, but it seems to me that your attitude—

BLICK

Shut up.

MAN

(*Quietly*)

—is making the poor child say things that are not true.

BLICK

Shut up, I said.

LADY

Well.

(*To the* MAN)

Are you going to stand for such insolence?

BLICK

(*To* MAN, *who is standing*)

Are you?

MAN

(*Taking the* WOMAN's *arm*)

I'll get a divorce. I'll start life all over again.

184

(*Pushing the* WOMAN)
Come on. Get the hell out of here!

The MAN *hurries his* WOMAN *out of the place,*
BLICK *watching them go.*

BLICK

(*To* KITTY)
Now. Let's begin again, and see that you tell the truth.
What's your name?

KITTY

Kitty Duval.

BLICK

Where do you live?

KITTY

Until this evening I lived at the New York Hotel. Room
21. This evening I moved to the St. Francis Hotel.

BLICK

Oh. To the St. Francis Hotel. Nice place. Where do you
work?

KITTY

I'm looking for work.

BLICK

What kind of work do you do?

KITTY

I'm an actress.

BLICK

I see. What movies have I seen you in?

KITTY

I've worked in burlesque.

185

BLICK

You're a liar.

> WESLEY *stands, worried and full of dumb resentment.*

KITTY

> (*Pathetically, as at the beginning of the play*)

It's the truth.

BLICK

What are you doing here?

KITTY

I came to see if I could get a job here.

BLICK

Doing what?

KITTY

Singing—and—dancing.

BLICK

You can't sing or dance. What are you lying for?

KITTY

I can. I sang and danced in burlesque all over the country.

BLICK

You're a liar.

KITTY

I said lines, too.

BLICK

So you danced in burlesque?

KITTY

Yes.

186

BLICK

All right. Let's see what you did.

KITTY

I can't. There's no music, and I haven't got the right clothes.

BLICK

There's music.
    (*To Wesley*)
Put a nickel in that phonograph.
        (WESLEY *can't move*)
Come on. Put a nickel in that phonograph.
        (WESLEY *does so. To* KITTY)
All right. Get up on that stage and do a hot little burlesque number.
        KITTY *stands. Walks slowly to the stage, but is unable to move.* JOE *comes in, holding three books.*
Get going, now. Let's see you dance the way you did in burlesque, all over the country.

        KITTY *tries to do a burlesque dance. It is beautiful in a tragic way.*

BLICK

All right, start taking them off!

        KITTY *removes her hat and starts to remove her jacket.* JOE *moves closer to the stage, amazed.*

JOE

        (*Hurrying to* KITTY)
Get down from there.
        (*He takes* KITTY *into his arms. She is crying*)
        (*To* BLICK)
What the hell do you think you're doing!

187

WESLEY

>   (*Like a little boy, very angry*)
> It's that man, Blick. He made her take off her clothes.
> He beat up the old man, too.

>>   BLICK *pushes* WESLEY *off, as* TOM *enters.*
>>   BLICK *begins beating up* WESLEY.

TOM

>   What's the matter, Joe? What's happened?

JOE

>   Is the truck out there?

TOM

>   Yeah, but what's happened? Kitty's crying again!

JOE

>   You driving to San Diego?

TOM

>   Yeah, Joe. But what's he doing to that poor colored boy?

JOE

>   Get going. Here's some money. Everything's O.K.
>   (*To* KITTY)
>   Dress in the truck. Take these books.

WESLEY'S VOICE

>   You can't hurt me. You'll get yours. You wait and see.

TOM

>   Joe, he's hurting that boy. I'll kill him!

JOE

>   (*Pushing* TOM)

188

Get out of here! Get married in San Diego. I'll see you when you get back.

> TOM and KITTY go. NICK enters and stands at the lower end of bar. JOE takes the revolver out of his pocket. Looks at it.

I've always wanted to kill somebody, but I never knew who it should be.

> He cocks the revolver, stands real straight, holds it in front of him firmly and walks to the door. He stands a moment watching BLICK, aims very carefully, and pulls trigger. There is no shot.

> NICK runs over and grabs the gun, and takes JOE aside.

NICK

What the hell do you think you're doing?

JOE

(Casually, but angry)
That dumb Tom. Buys a six-shooter that won't even shoot once.

> JOE sits down, dead to the world.

> BLICK comes out, panting for breath.

> NICK looks at him. He speaks slowly.

NICK

Blick! I told you to stay out of here! Now get out of here.

(He takes BLICK by the collar, tightening his grip as he speaks, and pushing him out)
If you come back again, I'm going to take you in that

189

room where you've been beating up that colored boy, and **I'm going to murder** you—slowly—with my hands. Beat it!

(*He pushes* BLICK *out*)

(*To* HARRY)
Go take care of the colored boy.

> HARRY *runs out.*

> WILLIE *returns and doesn't sense that anything is changed.* WILLIE *puts another nickel into the machine, but he does so very violently. The consequence of this violence is that the flag comes up again.* WILLIE, *amazed, stands at attention and salutes. The flag goes down. He shakes his head.*

WILLIE
(*Thoughtfully*)
As far as I'm concerned, this is the only country in the world. If you ask me, nuts to Europe!
(*He is about to push the slide in again when the flag comes up again. Furiously, to* NICK, *while he salutes and stands at attention, pleadingly*)
Hey, Nick. This machine is out of order.

NICK
(*Somberly*)
Give it a whack on the side.

> WILLIE *does so. A hell of a whack. The result is the flag comes up and down, and* WILLIE *keeps saluting.*

WILLIE

    (Saluting)

Hey, Nick. Something's wrong.

> *The machine quiets down abruptly.* WILLIE *very stealthily slides a new nickel in, and starts a new game.*

> *From a distance two pistol shots are heard, each carefully timed.*

> NICK *runs out.*

> *The* NEWSBOY *enters, crosses to Joe's table, senses something is wrong.*

NEWSBOY

    (Softly)

Paper, Mister?

> JOE *can't hear him.*

> *The* NEWSBOY *backs away, studies* JOE, *wishes he could cheer* JOE *up. Notices the phonograph, goes to it, and puts a coin in it, hoping music will make* JOE *happier.*

> *The* NEWSBOY *sits down. Watches* JOE. *The music begins. "The Missouri Waltz."*

> *The* DRUNKARD *comes in and walks around. Then sits down.* NICK *comes back.*

NICK

    (Delighted)

Joe, Blick's dead! Somebody just shot him, and none of the cops are trying to find out who.

JOE doesn't hear. NICK steps back, studying JOE.

NICK

(*Shouting*)
Joe.

JOE

(*Looking up*)
What?

NICK

Blick's dead.

JOE

Blick? Dead? Good! That God damn gun wouldn't go off. I *told* Tom to get a good one.

NICK

(*Picking up gun and looking at it*)
Joe, you wanted to kill that guy!

(HARRY *returns.* JOE *puts the gun in his coat pocket*)

I'm going to buy you a bottle of champagne.

NICK goes to bar. JOE rises, takes hat from rack, puts coat on. The NEWSBOY jumps up, helps JOE with coat.

NICK

What's the matter, Joe?

JOE

Nothing. Nothing.

192

NICK

How about the champagne?

JOE

Thanks.

(Going)

NICK

It's not eleven yet. Where you going, Joe?

JOE

I don't know. Nowhere.

NICK

Will I see you tomorrow?

JOE

I don't know. I don't think so.

KIT CARSON *enters, walks to* JOE. JOE *and* KIT *look at one another knowingly.*

JOE

Somebody just shot a man. How are you feeling?

KIT

Never felt better in my life.

(Loudly, bragging, but sombre)

I shot a man once. In San Francisco. Shot him two times. In 1939, I think it was. In October. Fellow named Blick or Glick or something like that. Couldn't stand the way he talked to ladies. Went up to my room and got my old pearl-handled revolver and waited for him on Pacific Street. Saw him walking, and let him have it, two times. Had to throw the beautiful revolver into the Bay.

193

HARRY, NICK, the ARAB and the DRUNKARD close in around him.

JOE searches his pockets, brings out the revolver, puts it in Kit's hand, looks at him with great admiration and affection. JOE walks slowly to the stairs leading to the street, turns and waves. KIT, and then one by one everybody else, waves, and the marble game goes into its beautiful American routine again: flag, lights, and music. The play ends.

CURTAIN

194

HOW AND WHY TO BE A PLAYWRIGHT

The first show I ever saw was called *Punch and Judy*. I'd heard about *Punch and Judy* for weeks. All the kids were talking about *Punch and Judy* all the time and then finally the day before Xmas they took us all there and the lights went down and I looked where the light was strong and in no time at all the curtains parted and there they were: Punch and Judy. Made of wood. Crazy. But as real as anything could be. Very funny and tragic and sad, too.

Naturally, I thought it was swell.

The second show I saw was a movie in which covered-wagon people fought Indians.

That was fine, too.

A fellow named Charlie used to come around and tell us stories. He was very famous to all of us. He wasn't exactly a show all by himself, but his voice had a good range and when he got going I could see the play, the stage, the theater, and so on, beyond the words. I could see the players, too.

Long before all this, however, a few of us were already established as actors. Myself, I enjoyed a reputation as something of a clown, although I never deliberately sought to establish myself in that field. It happened inevitably. Everybody got a kick out of the loping manner in which I walked, the incredible length of my arms, and the swiftness with which I met (and usually solved) all problems. It seemed as if there was nothing I could do that did not make the others laugh. There was nothing I could say, either, that did not make them laugh. In fact, I was doomed. When we all went to Sunday School, they used to put me in the last row so nobody could see me because they knew there would be laughter all of a sudden—maybe in the middle of a prayer.

This was a confusing state of affairs for a boy of seven who was by nature melancholy, serious, and very eager to learn something about what was going on everywhere.

I mean to say that in the larger sense I have always been connected with the theater, the art of inventing roles to play, the art of playing them, and so on. It is true that I began without knowing about all this, but I remember very clearly that by the time I was eight I was beginning to understand that there was something to the art, and that I had the privilege of controlling it. This I did.

When I was eight the field of my life was greatly enlarged. I had traveled two hundred miles by train from one place to another. I had left one kind of life for another. I had been at school several years, and now was actively a member of the population of the world, and a worker: one who belonged in the world. Selling papers was at first a kind of role I did not understand very much or like very much, but after two days I had everything under control, especially my voice, which was one of the purest headline-hollering voices in the San Joaquin Valley. The art of carrying twenty afternoon papers under the left arm I had also learned. And I was swiftly learning nonchalance, ease, poise, repartee, and the art of entrance and exit, particularly into and out of saloons and gambling joints. I had learned by the end of the first seven days that to enter a saloon and belong you had to be completely aloof. I got the idea from alley cats, whom I had watched carefully. I had learned also that it was infinitely smarter not to have anything to say, or sell, until someone invited speech or sale.

By the time I was nine and in the third grade I was well along in the art of satire, parody, subtle contempt for ignorance or pomposity, and kindly recognition of virtue and charm, or lack of virtue and charm, either of which I continuously championed and protected in my contemporaries.

All this was theater, as all living is, as I say, in the larger sense. It was all drama. It was all for my own amusement in a region where amusement was rare and difficult, and for the amusement of any others who could see it that way. This included few teachers who, I still maintain, are the dullest and most ignorant and least imaginative people in the world.

In addition to my own acting, there was the regular theater. When I was ten the year of the new calendar was 1918 and movies were silent but great in number. I saw them all because I could get into any of them free, or by sneaking in. I take pride in my having sneaked into every theater in my home town, Fresno, California; into every circus that came to town; into the County Fairs; into the Summer stock company shows. It was completely out of the question for me to think of paying admission into anything. It simply never occurred to me, although I wanted very much to see everything that happened to come to town.

I am not one to hide any influences. I was very much impressed by all the movies I saw, good and bad. The vaudeville at the Hippodrome Theatre was a source of infinite delight to me. The musical comedies there in the Summers: the same. The circuses were magnificent. The automobile races at the County Fairs were full of drama: plot, personalities, atmosphere, style, suspense, climax, profound meaning.

I saw drama in everything because there was drama in everything—because there was drama in myself. School itself, which I always despised, and still despise, was full of drama: a strange, pathetic, miserable drama of its own, which became furious and amazing because of my presence in it, a matter of great alarm to the teachers. If there was a rule, I would break it. This style of behavior continues to this day because I believe rules are made only for those who need them, must have them, or are willing to be buffaloed by them.

Good vaudeville came to town along about when I was twelve or so. Orpheum Circuit vaudeville. I remember Trixie Friganza and Sophie Tucker and a lot of acts that were wonderful whose players I do not remember by name.

I saw *Othello*, billed *Otello*, played in Armenian. It was a great experience, and although I was taken by my uncle and although he had paid for our tickets and although we sat away up in the gallery, it was a fine experience. I understood less than ten per cent of the words, but I remember one word very clearly: *sarsapelli*, which was hissed by Othello, and which means *amazing* or *astounding* or *unbelievable*.

I read *Lady Windemere's Fan* when I was fourteen, and the same day wrote a very good play in imitation of that worldly and brilliant style. It didn't seem right for me,

198

however. I had that much sense. But it was very easy to do. I had all the wit for it, but the environment was wrong. My world was a world of plain and poor people, broken-down houses, casualness, good health, poverty, and uproarious laughter, rather than a world of complex and wealthy people, magnificent houses, cultivated ease, pretended health, and sophisticated and discreet laughter. I knew it wouldn't do for me to write plays after the manner of Oscar Wilde.

My uncle had acted in Fresno High School's (Class of 1916) presentation of Ibsen's *Ghosts*, so the play was always around, along with others by that great and magnificently dull dramatist: *A Doll's House*, I remember, and *The Lady of the Sea*. I read these plays, and from not understanding them too well, enhanced or enlarged their greatness. But I didn't care to try to imitate the style. It was too cagey, crafty, and calculating. Vaudeville pleased me more, and seemed more real. It was easygoing and didn't try for too much and as a result very often achieved things Ibsen himself couldn't achieve. Vaudeville was American, too, which made a great difference.

These are a few of the most easily remembered realities which I know contributed to my becoming, at thirty, a writer of plays. I have put these things down by way of clarifying the matter of how to be a playwright, and as you see it must begin very early and the education must include many things, the least of which is, as you will have observed, a course in a school or university on the art.

That, I'd say, would be the very worst way to be a playwright—that taking of a course. That would be the way, I believe, for any dullard in the world, and it would no doubt lead to the writing of plays of some kind, but I should imagine they would be plays better left unwritten. I know some good men have come out of the classroom, but the classroom was at best an afterthought. They just thought they'd take a look at what the scholars had to offer. O'Neill was O'Neill anyhow; and the others were themselves anyhow; the classroom didn't do anything for them, unless it tangled them up a little. I'd say it did that: tangled them up. I'd say they would have done better or would now be doing better had they maintained their pride and ignored the classroom.

You begin being what you become—in *time*—at the beginning. Not in a classroom.

As for the "Why" part. Well, I know why for myself, and if you're a writer or a playwright you know why for yourself, which is all you need to know. The reasons all come together and become one: one reason. It is a matter of staying alive in an interesting way—by which you provide staying alive in an interesting way for others. Or at least, with the others, *help* provide. There are other angles to it, too, of course. But on the whole it's something like this.

Love's Old Sweet Song

To Richard Watts, Jr.

OF ALL THE THINGS I LOVE

I love to see the sun come smiling to the world;
I love to hear the wind go singing through a field;
I love to hear a love-bird singing in a tree,
And I love to see a lovely face light up with love for me.

CHORUS

Of all the things I love,
I love the most
Sleeping in the shade of love.
Sleeping in the shade of love,
I love the most, my love.

Of all the things I love to taste,
Sweetest is the kiss of love.
Dreaming in the shade of love,
The kiss of love
I love the most, my love.

My love, of all the lovely things,
Loveliest of all is you,
Dreaming in the shade of love.
Sleeping in the shade of love, my love,
I love the most, my love.

I love to breathe the scent of earth and new-mown hay;
I love to taste the peach and berry ripe in May;
I love to feel the spray as I walk beside the sea,
And I love to see a lovely face light up with love for me.

THE YEARS

The years, the years, they come and go,
And go and go, and oh, my heart!
The years have gone with my heart.

The days, the days still come and go,
And I still breathe,
But oh, my heart!
The years have gone with my heart.

The years, the days, the nights
Still come and go,
And I still dream,
But oh, my heart is gone,
My heart is gone with the years.

The hours, the hours, the long, dreaming hours
Still come and go,
And I still dream.
But the light is gone from my dream,
And the love is gone from my heart!

The two foregoing songs have been published by Chappell.
Music by Paul Bowles, words by William Saroyan.

PREFACE

"Love's Old Sweet Song," in addition to being a theatrical entertainment, intended primarily to delight the eye and ear and the heart and mind of the beholder, is *literally* a song. The singers of the song are the few people in the play selected from the many in the world, but any who see the play are likely to be the singers of the song also, inasmuch as the song is living itself. It is an old song, but the time is our time, the people are our people, and the environment is our environment. All the sources of the song are contemporary, but still the song is the oldest song in the world, as love is the most basic emotion of life. There could be no mortality without love, and no dimension to living without song. Love is an inevitable part of the bargain of the living in the inexplicable exchange of nothingness for mortality, and poetry is man's defense against being swindled in that bargain. Any man who is an alien to poetry, no matter who he is, *is* swindled in that bargain. Instinct demands love of all who live, and good living demands imagination and faith.

The line of the play is melodic, the same as the line of a song. It is a simple play, as the song is the simplest of music's various forms. While its theme is love, in a number of variations, the play is without love-sickness, no doubt simply because I do not feel things sickly. I find the tenderest or strongest emotions of a man inextricable from every-

5

thing else that is a man's: understanding, a sense of proportion, love of comedy, and intelligence. The arrival of a fresh emotion, or a fresh dimension of an old emotion, or a magnification of a constant emotion, does not, as I remember things, nullify all other emotions or qualities a man possesses. Characters in drama have been generally unrounded-out, most likely for the convenience of the dramatist, and for the security of the meaning of the play. It is difficult to have rounded-out characters in a play and to have a satisfying play at the same time, but at this stage of the game that appears to be something very essential to try for. The character of man is neither steady nor predictable. Even one whose life is limited by willfully accepted rules, such as a saint, is not free of variation in impulse, thought, or act. Man's greatness and man's insignificance are both the consequence of his being inevitably free. Nothing can limit man. And yet, with all his freedom, religion in men (and I mean primarily the inherent sense of rightness, grace, beauty, and so on) compels, usually, a noble exercise of freedom, so that murder, for instance, is always rarer than delight. The people in "Love's Old Sweet Song" are free people. The freedom they enjoy, and the freedom which carries them sometimes to disaster, is a freedom which art, with all its limits, has never been able to shift from the living to the dead. We can be grateful for this failure. Freedom is not essential: it is *inevitable*. It cannot be taken from the living without literally taking life from them. For this reason any idea, however noble or base, which depends for its strength or validity on the regimenting of life is an unsound idea, temporary, and scheduled for ultimate failure. As the limits in living are good taste, the limits in art cannot be anything more severe.

The play is simultaneously naive and sophisticated. I be-

6

lieve the living are simultaneously naive and sophisticated, because no matter how naive a man may be there is somewhere in him great sophistication, and no matter how sophisticated he may be there is great naïveté in him. In the nature of things I cannot understand anyone in the world as well or as fully as I understand myself, and I know this simultaneous reality of sophistication and naïveté exists in myself. It is true and inevitable. It is impossible for me not to be sophisticated. It is also impossible for me not to be naive. I cannot abandon one for the other merely to simplify things. I must therefore recognize the validity of both, and, in my own work at least, I must assume that naïveté and sophistication are simultaneous in everybody. Neither are *cultivated* in myself. Neither are unnatural. I must assume, therefore, that this condition is general.

The variations of love are great, but they are not really variations. Love is the one thing that is constant, even when the variation of it appears to be hate. In reality there is no such thing as hate. Hate is love kicked in the pants. It is love with a half-nelson on itself. The deepest and most general love is love of God, the defining of which I leave to you, as you please. Love of God includes regard of self. All the kinds of love, in fact, are regard of self. As long as a man is alive, he is alive for himself. It is foolish to be buffaloed by embarrassment into not accepting this truth. In the nature of things a man cannot cease to be himself, and therefore whatever he does, good or bad, he does for himself. Doing good things is the ultimate selfishness, and as love is the best of the better things, *it* is the ultimate selfishness. I can see no reason why it shouldn't be. No morality is worth anything that doesn't understand that all behavior is selfish. Selfishness is correct by all standards.

7

The necessity to defend my work again and again is embarrassing to me, and yet I have no alternative. To ignore criticism, as many writers do, I regard as an evasion of my responsibility to my work. In fairness to my critics, I acknowledge the *partial* truth and validity of every charge brought against my work, against myself personally, and against my methods of making my work public. What is lacking in their criticism is the fullness and humanity of understanding which operates in myself, in my work, and in my regard for others. The essence of my work is honor, honesty, intelligence, grace, good humor, naturalness, and spontaneity, and these things do not appear to be nicely balanced in my critics. Consequently, it is difficult for them to make sense in themselves of that which is complicated and unusual for them. What should delight them because of its honesty, shocks them. What should enlarge them because of its understanding, drives them more completely behind the fort of their own limitations.

I will take up each of the commonest charges the critics have made against myself and my work. In a sense the charge of exhibitionism is a valid one. No creative activity could possibly deny the validity of exhibitionism, and it is a mistake to regard exhibitionism as something improper. The implication that it *is* something improper, and something characteristic only of my work, is that which I object to. The creative impulse itself is exhibitionistic. The fulfilling of the impulse is even more so. And the placing of that which has been created before others is still more so. If you want no exhibitionism (if that is what you choose to call it), you want no creation. After the creation of my work, it is true that I have been more energetic than many others in my attack upon the problem of making my work as public as possible. This has been necessary because my work has been unfamiliar, and because making it public *has* been a problem. If I did not believe in my work I would not bring it about in the first place. Since I do believe in it, I must do whatever I am able to do to make it known to as many people as possible. It is probably my enjoyment of living and working, however, which is offensive to so many, and which they put down as exhibitionism. As I understand things, acceptance of our life is the first law of living, and enjoyment of it (and I know all about its unenjoyables) is the first necessity of artful and gracious living.

To the charge of mindlessness, it would be unkind of me to ask where is the mindfulness in the work of other men, not only of our time but of other times? Where is the mindfulness of Shakespeare, if need be? By mindlessness I believe the critics mean absence of *specific* instruction to society or the state on how to behave, and *presence* of immediate living. In the play form, among other things, there must be play. It is impossible to exclude thought or belief or faith from a play, but these things are in a play after living is in it, and they are in a play as tone, not as things by themselves. Since the theater is not an adult continuation school, those who come to the theater must be entertained before they are instructed. The difference between my thinking, it would appear, and the thinking of others is that mine operates from beginnings long ago and not from headlines and news in today's paper. What appears to the glib and superficial mind or sensibility as mindlessness is, in reality, a depth and fullness so far removed from cheap thinking that it bewilders. The critic with political bias, for instance, cannot accept my thought simply because it puts him out of work.

No ambition for the living, for the individual, for the

9

weak and stupid and the strong and wise, is loftier than mine. No affection for the ugly and base and the beautiful and noble in man is more generous than mine. No scorn for the cruel, the miserable, the wretched, the cowardly, the insane—wherever they may occur, in the good or in the bad— is greater than my scorn. No faith in grace is steadier or more encouraging than mine. Therefore, I must take it, my work is mindless. The truth is, I am not unbalanced.

It is charged, further, that my work is formless. The form of my work is simply unfamiliar. It has very definite form. The compulsion within myself for wholeness, for balance, and for grace is so great that form is the first demand I make of my work and the first demand my work makes of me. It is probable that the critics cannot see the form for the full-ness. If there were nothing in the form they would see the form, but since the form is full, they cannot see it.

It is charged further that I am crazy, an ego-maniac, a charlatan, that I will write anything to celebrate my name, that I am an enemy of the people, especially the working-class, that my intention is merely to make money and rise in the world, that I have bad taste or no taste at all, and a good many other things. These charges come from men too dull, too vulgar and too inferior for me to bother with.

LOVE'S OLD SWEET SONG

"Love's Old Sweet Song," like "The Time of Your Life," was produced by Eddie Dowling in conjunction with The Theatre Guild, and directed by Mr. Dowling and myself. It was first performed in Princeton, New Jersey at the Mc-Carter Theatre, Saturday evening, April 6, 1940. This was followed by two weeks at the Forrest Theatre in Philadelphia, beginning Monday, April 8. The play next went to Ford's Theatre in Baltimore for one week. It opened in New York at The Plymouth Theatre on West 45th Street, Thursday evening, May 2, and closed Saturday evening June 8th, after a run of 44 New York performances.

This is the cast which opened the play in New York:

Ann Hamilton	JESSIE ROYCE LANDIS
Georgie Americanos	PETER FERNANDEZ
Barnaby Gaul	WALTER HUSTON
Tom Flora	JAMES S. ELLIOTT
Demetrios	ANGE DE POLOK
Cabot Yearling	ARTHUR HUNNICUTT
Leona Yearling	DORO MERANDE
Newton Yearling	REINEIR BITTS
Velma Yearling	BARBARA HASTINGS
Selma Yearling	ARDELL E. HASTINGS
Al Yearling	THOMAS JORDAN
Henry Yearling	ERIC ROBERTS
Jesse Yearling	JACKIE AYERS
Lucy Yearling	KATER O'SHEA
Ella Yearling	MAE GARNER
Susan Yearling	PATRICIA ROY

343

NOTE

"Love's Old Sweet Song," like "The Time of Your Life," was produced by Eddie Dowling in conjunction with The Theatre Guild, and directed by Mr. Dowling and myself. It was first performed in Princeton, New Jersey, at the Mc-Carter Theatre, Saturday evening, April 6, 1940. This was followed by two weeks at the Forrest Theatre in Philadelphia, beginning Monday, April 8. The play next went to Ford's Theatre in Baltimore for one week. It opened in New York at The Plymouth Theatre on West 45th Street, Thursday evening, May 2, and closed Saturday evening, June 8th, after a run of 44 New York performances.

This is the cast which opened the play in New York:

Ann Hamilton	JESSIE ROYCE LANDIS
Georgie Americanos	PETER FERNANDEZ
Barnaby Gaul	WALTER HUSTON
Tom Fiora	JAMES S. ELLIOTT
Demetrios	ANGI O. POULOS
Cabot Yearling	ARTHUR HUNNICUTT
Leona Yearling	DORO MERANDE
Newton Yearling	EUGENE FITTS
Velma Yearling	BARBARA HASTINGS
Selma Yearling	ARDELE HASTINGS
Al Yearling	THOMAS JORDAN
Henry Yearling	ERIC ROBERTS
Jesse Yearling	JACKIE AYERS
Lucy Yearling	PATSY O'SHEA
Ella Yearling	MAE GRIMES
Susan Yearling	PATRICIA ROE

Maud Yearling	CAROL ESA
Lemmie Yearling	BOB WHITE
Mae Yearling	ELEANOR DREXLER
Harry Yearling	MICHAEL ARTIST
Wilbur Yearling	GERALD MATTHEWS
Richard Oliver	LLOYD GOUGH
Elsa Wax	BEATRICE NEWPORT
David F. Windmore	ALAN HEWITT
Daniel Hough	JOHN A. REGAN
Mr. Smith	NICK DENNIS
Mr. Harris	GEORGE TRAVELL
Pass Le Noir, Sheriff	HOWARD FREEMAN
Stylianos Americanos	ALAN REED
Pericles Americanos	JOHN ECONOMIDES

The out-of-town Sheriff was Pass Le Noir, whose performance I admired so much I have given his name to the part.

I wish to thank every member of the cast, including those who, for one reason or another, did not appear in the play when it reached New York, especially Jules Leni who was not old enough, according to law, to stay in the play as Wilbur Yearling. Mr. Leni I regard as one of the finest actors of our time. It would be a serious oversight for me not to acknowledge the great contribution of Eric Roberts to the play, as Henry Yearling. He himself created the delightful mockery of Fascism during the *Time Magazine* episode, which was to me one of the pleasantest moments of the play.

Every player, in fact, brought something personal and special to his role, and many, not excluding children, helped direct the play. An usher in Baltimore also helped direct the play. Mr. Dowling brought to the play from his family the idea of the Happy Birthday song during Barnaby Gaul's pitch for the Yearling family. Mr. Langner of The Theatre Guild is responsible for several of the most important scenes

14

in the play, which I wrote upon his suggestion. Mr. Arthur Hunnicutt's presence impelled me to expand the part of Cabot Yearling, which Mr. Hunnicutt performed magnificently. His discovery was, I believe, one of the most fortunate events, both for this play and for the theater in general. Mr. Huston, it goes without saying, brought to his part a fine quality which could not have come from any other American player. Jessie Royce Landis, with perhaps the most difficult role in the play and wholly without direction, made Ann Hamilton both real and delightful. Peter Fernandez, as the Messenger, was perfect. Angi O. Poulos, as an American citizen, was beyond direction, and consequently impossible to improve. Alan Hewitt, as the man from *Time*, was exactly what I had in mind. John Economides, the famous Greek actor, as Pericles Americanos, not only translated my lines into Greek, but brought to his part the comic solemnity and gentle anger which the role called for. And finally, Alan Reed, as the simple wrestler, accomplished the difficult task of being, every night, both a skillful acrobat and a sensitive actor.

The settings by Watson Barratt could not have been closer to what I wanted.

The music and two songs by Paul Bowles contributed so much to the play, but were so integrated in the material, that I am afraid critics and theatergoers alike were not sufficiently aware of their importance. I must say, however, that I am aware.

Armina Marshall, as Production Assistant, did most of the hard work.

To these, and to all others, including the Musicians and Stage Hands, my sincere thanks.

THE PEOPLE

ANN HAMILTON, *44, a beautiful unmarried small-town woman*

GEORGIE AMERICANOS, *a Postal Telegraph messenger*

BARNABY GAUL, *51, a pitchman*

TOM FIORA, *another messenger*

DEMETRIOS AMERICANOS, *an American citizen*

CABOT YEARLING, *a family man*

LEONA YEARLING, *44, his wife*

NEWTON YEARLING, *19, their half-wit son*

VELMA YEARLING
SELMA YEARLING } *twins*

AL YEARLING
ELLA YEARLING
HENRY YEARLING
JESSE YEARLING
SUSAN YEARLING
MAUD YEARLING
LEMMIE YEARLING
MAE YEARLING
HARRY YEARLING
WILBUR YEARLING
LUCY YEARLING } *their children*

RICHARD OLIVER, *an unpublished writer*

ELSA WAX, *a photographer for Life Magazine*

DAVID F. WINDMORE, *a college man*

DANIEL HOUGH, *a farmer*

17

MR. SMITH, a representative of the West Coast Novelty
   Amusement Company
MR. HARRIS, his associate
PASS LE NOIR, a sheriff
STYLIANOS AMERICANOS, 41, Georgie's father, a wrestler
PERICLES AMERICANOS, 71, Stylianos' father

THE PLACE

Outside Ann Hamilton's House at 333 Orchard Avenue,
Bakersfield, California.
The parlor of the Americanos home.

THE TIME

Late morning and afternoon of Friday, September 15,
1939.

18

ACT ONE

AN old-fashioned house with a front porch, at 333 Orchard Avenue in Bakersfield, California. A large front yard, with rose bushes in bloom near the house. An orange and a lemon tree. A palm. Two eucalyptus. A cement statue of a lion on the lawn.

A homeless family goes by in the street: MAN, WOMAN, THREE CHILDREN.

ANN HAMILTON, a beautiful and rather elegant woman in her early forties, comes out of the house, looks around, walks about in the yard, to the gate, smells and cuts several roses, singing "the years, the years, they come and go," and so on; goes up onto the porch, sits down in the rocking-chair with a love-story magazine, waiting for nothing, least of all a telegram.

GEORGIE AMERICANOS, Greek-American Postal Telegraph messenger, arrives, skidding, on a bicycle.

GEORGIE
You Miss Ann Hamilton?

19

ANN

I am.

GEORGIE

Well, a fellow by the name of Barnaby Gaul is coming out from Boston to visit you. He sent you this telegram. Know him?

ANN

Barnaby Gaul? May I read the telegram?

GEORGIE

It's collect. A dollar and eighty cents. It's a long night-letter. Lots of people can't pay for collect telegrams nowadays, but they always want to know what's in them just the same, so I *memorize* everything and let them know. *Free.* That's my little gift to society. People are poor. A dollar and eighty cents is a lot of money. Know him?

ANN

I'm afraid there must be some mistake.

GEORGIE

Oh, no, there isn't.

ANN

I don't know anybody in Boston. Are you sure the telegram's for me?

GEORGIE

If you're Ann Hamilton, it's for you. Otherwise it ain't. Mistakes sometimes happen.

ANN

What's that name again?

GEORGIE

Barnaby Gaul. B-a-r-n-a-b-y, Barnaby. G-a-u-l, Gaul. We get a lot of different kinds of telegrams, but this is the best *I've* ever seen. This telegram is about love.

ANN

Love?

GEORGIE

That's right. L-O-V-E, love. I'll recite the message to you. It's against the rules of the company, but to hell with the company. My sympathies are with the poor, not the rich. To tell you the truth, I'm a radical.

ANN

Are you?

GEORGIE

Of course I'm an American, too. My father's Greek. He used to be a wrestler. My father's *father* used to be a tobacco-grower in Smyrna, in the old country. We read philosophy. My name's Georgie Americanos.

ANN

How do you do?

GEORGIE

How do you do?

ANN

Won't you sit down, Georgie?

GEORGIE

That's all right. You lived in this house twenty-seven years?

21

ANN

I've lived in this house all my life. My goodness, I'm forty-four years old.

GEORGIE

You're the lady, all right. My father's been reading Greek philosophy to me for three years. Consequently, I'm intelligent. If he comes out here from Boston, like he says he's going to, will you let me come out and look at him?

ANN

If somebody's coming here.

GEORGIE

He'll be here.

ANN

All right, Georgie, you can come out. What does the telegram say?

GEORGIE

Can I bring my father? He likes to meet people who've traveled.

ANN

All right, Georgie, your father, too.

GEORGIE

The telegram goes like this.
        (Reciting the telegram)
Boston, Massachusetts. September 7, 1939.

ANN

September 7? Today's September 15.

GEORGIE

Well, to tell you the truth, I lost the telegram. It was in

22

my pocket. I don't know *how* it got there. I always put telegrams in my hat.

ANN

Good gracious, Georgie, tell me what's in the telegram, even if it *is* eight days old.

GEORGIE

Has anybody walked by in front of this house whistling *Love's Old Sweet Song* lately?

ANN

No, Georgie. Please recite the telegram.

GEORGIE

Well, let me think a minute. Get everything straight. He sure is a nut. O.K. Here it is. "If you remember me, I am the young man with the red hair who walked in front of your house twenty-seven years ago whistling *Love's Old Sweet Song*." Do you remember him?

ANN

No, I don't. Please recite the *whole* telegram.

GEORGIE

How could you forget a guy like that? He goes on to say: "You were sixteen years old at the time. You had half a dozen roses in your hand. Four red and two white. I hardly noticed you when I went by, and then I came back and said hello, and you said hello. I said what is your name and you said Ann Hamilton. You didn't ask my name. We talked a minute or so and that was all. I made a note of the number of your house and the name of the street and went away. I am now fifty-one years old and want you to know I love you." Now, do you remember him?

23

ANN

No, Georgie. Is there anything more?

GEORGIE

Plenty! There's plenty more. He says: "I am coming back to you, even if you're married and have five children." How about it? Are you? Have you?

ANN

I'm not married.

GEORGIE

Aren't you married?

ANN

No. Please finish the telegram, Georgie.

GEORGIE

Well, he says: "Get rid of everybody. Love is everything. I know, now. Nothing else matters. I will walk in front of your house again very soon and I will be whistling the same old sweet song of love." They don't usually send telegrams this way, even when they're collect. They usually try to say everything in ten words. He says: "If you remember me, speak to me. If you do not speak, I shall know you have forgotten. Please remember and please speak to me. I love you. BARNABY GAUL." That's the whole message, word for word. A dollar and eighty cents. Know him?

ANN

No, I don't.

GEORGIE

Are you Ann Hamilton?

24

ANN

My name is Ann Hamilton.

GEORGIE

Well, *he* knows you. He sent you this message all the way from Boston. You're going to speak to him, aren't you?

ANN

No, I'm not.

GEORGIE

Doesn't love mean *anything* to you?

ANN

No, it doesn't. Besides, the man's crazy.

GEORGIE

Why? Just because he hasn't forgotten?

ANN

A girl of sixteen is liable to be polite and say a few words to any man who speaks to her.

GEORGIE

This is different. You must have been very pretty at the time. You're not bad now. Don't you remember holding half a dozen roses in your hand? Four red and two white?

ANN

I've cut roses from these bushes hundreds of times. I don't remember any *particular* time.

GEORGIE

Don't you remember a guy with red hair, whistling?

ANN

No, I don't. I'm not sixteen, Georgie. I'm forty-four.

25

GEORGIE

Well, all I know is you mean everything in the world to this nut. This Barnaby Gaul. And by all rights he ought to mean everything in the world to you, too.

ANN

Well, he doesn't mean *anything* to me.

GEORGIE

I wouldn't be so sure about that. He may come by here and sweep you right off your feet.

ANN

No, he won't.

GEORGIE

Why not?

ANN

I'm perfectly happy.

GEORGIE

Oh, no, you're not. You can't fool me. You may be satisfied but you're not happy. You've got to be a little unhappy to be perfectly happy. Satisfied's one thing, and happy's another.

(*Pause*)

Socrates.

(PEOPLE go *by*)

Poor people. Homeless. No place to go.

ANN

What's he say in that telegram?

GEORGIE

That's more like it. Listen carefully.

26

(Reciting)

"If you remember me, I am the young man with the red hair who walked in front of your house—"

(Whistling)

Listen.

(At the gate)

It's *him*. Barnaby Gaul. He's come back to you, just like he said he would. This is the greatest love story that's ever taken place in the streets of Bakersfield, California. Speak to him.

ANN

I don't remember anybody like that.

GEORGIE

Speak to him. The man's come all the way from Boston to see you again. He's moved everything back twenty-seven years where it belongs. Say a kind word.

ANN

I don't know what to say.

GEORGIE

Say *anything*. He'll understand.

ANN

(At the gate)

Here he comes. Don't go away, Georgie.

GEORGIE

Go away? I wouldn't miss this for anything in the world.

(The PERSON *who appears is a handsome man of fifty whose years are instantly irrelevant. He is, in fact, youth constant and unending. His hair is reddish, if not exactly red. His face is still the face of*

27

a young man. His figure is still that. His clothes
are the casual clothes of a young man who has better things to think about. He is wearing an old
straw hat, and he is carrying a straw suitcase. He is
walking jauntily, and he is whistling. He notices
ANN, stops whistling and stands)

ANN

Good morning.

GAUL

How do you do?
        (ANN and GAUL stare at one another a moment)

GEORGIE

Wow!

GAUL

Your son?

ANN

Yes. No.

GAUL

A handsome boy.

ANN

He's Greek.

GAUL

A classic and noble people. You have others?

ANN

No. He's a messenger. He brought your telegram.

GAUL

Telegram?

28

GEORGIE

Sure. From Boston.

GAUL

Boston?

(ANN *turns and rushes into the house*)

GEORGIE

Weren't you just whistling *Love's Old Sweet Song?*

GAUL

I was *whistling*. I don't know what it was. It's a beautiful morning. The least a man can do is whistle.

GEORGIE

Didn't you walk down this street twenty-seven years ago?

GAUL

My boy, I've never been in this town before.

GEORGIE

Ah, for the love of Mike.

(ANN *comes out of the house, holding half a dozen roses. Four red and two white*)

GAUL

Roses! I have never seen roses more beautiful to behold. Nor have I seen anyone hold roses more beautifully. Nor have I seen them held any way at all by anyone more beautiful.

GEORGIE

It's him, all right.

GAUL

Him? Who?

GEORGIE

Who? You. Don't you recognize her?

ANN

Four red and two white.

GEORGIE

She remembers you. Don't you remember her?

(GAUL stares at ANN)

All right.
(He tears open the telegram)
Let me read the telegram for you, too.

GAUL

Telegram? What telegram?

GEORGIE

What telegram! The collect telegram from Boston.
(Reading)
Boston, Massachusetts. September 7, 1939.

(GAUL takes the telegram and reads it silently,
glancing at ANN every once in a while)

GAUL

"I love you. BARNABY GAUL."

GEORGIE

Now don't try to tell me you're not Barnaby Gaul.

GAUL

Is this Bakersfield, California?

ANN

Yes, it is.

30

GAUL

Is *this* Orchard Avenue?

ANN

Yes. 333.

GAUL

How can I ever ask you to forgive me?

GEORGIE

You are Barnaby Gaul, aren't you?

GAUL

Words fail me.

ANN

Oh, that's all right.

GEORGIE

Were you ever in Bakersfield before?

GAUL

Please try to understand.

GEORGIE

Were you in Boston eight days ago?

GAUL

Forgive me. Both of you. I thought I was in Fresno. Let's
start all over again. From the beginning.
      (*He takes his suitcase and hurries away*)

GEORGIE

Do you remember anybody like that?

ANN

I don't know how I ever could have forgotten.

31

GEORGIE

Are you sure this is the nut?

ANN

As sure as I'm breathing.

GEORGIE

Well, get ready, then. Whoever he is, here he comes again, and this time he means it. This time he knows where he is and who he is, and who you are. Don't forget to speak to him or else he'll just walk away and maybe not send a telegram again for another twenty-seven years.

> (GAUL *appears again, whistling* "Love's Old Sweet Song")

ANN

Good morning.

> (GAUL *stops, turns, looks at* ANN, *sets down his suitcase, hurries to* ANN *and kisses her. She drops the roses one by one*)

GAUL

Ann. I knew you'd remember. I knew you'd never forget.

ANN

I thought I *had* forgotten, Barnaby. I even believed there was no one in the world like you.

GAUL

There is, however. There is.

ANN

And then when I saw you, I knew how foolish I had been to think you would never come back. I couldn't help it, Barnaby. The years moved away, slowly and then swiftly,

32

and always I stayed here alone, living in this house, rocking back and forth in this chair on this porch. The roses bloomed and faded.

GAUL

The poor roses.

ANN

The song died.

GAUL

The poor song.

ANN

The children I wanted were never born.

GAUL

The poor children.

ANN

Barnaby, why have you stayed away so long?

GAUL

Ann, you may remember there were wars.

ANN

Oh!

GAUL

And you may remember, Ann, there were great troubles. There were panics in which a man rushed with the crowd to no place. No place at all. And I, with the million others, ran, and ran, forgetting love, forgetting everything but the need for escape. Protection from police and disease. Hide-aways in fifty-cent rooms in large cities, in small villages. There were famines, Ann.

33

ANN

Oh, Barnaby, you were hungry?

GAUL

Hungry? Days, weeks, months, years of hunger. Hunger for bread, not love. Hunger for ease and comfort, not glory.

(*He embraces her*)

There were disasters at sea. Shipwreck and storm. Floods and hurricanes, and a man off-balance falling in the street. Fear and shouting. No songs, Ann. There were distances, and barking dogs. Mountains to cross, and rivers and prairies and deserts. And wherever a man stood, his heart was far away, and wherever he went, his heart was not there. There was cold and few coats. There was ice and no fire. There was fury and stupor in the heart. As you dreamed here through the years, there was pain and forsakenness. There were accidents, Ann, with a man's body embarrassed by helpless and ugly posture, the arm twisted, the leg out of joint, and the heart in fever of disgust, raging against the mice.

GEORGIE

What mice?

GAUL

Mice? Go away, boy. And the foolish people asking, Are you hurt? Hurt? My God, I have been attacked by an army of termites as big as Japanese, and marching in the same military formation. There was snow and quiet, with the eyes of men staring out from secrecy and crime. There was *hate*, with the rain drenching the streets and the wind roaring around the buildings.

34

ANN

Oh, Barnaby.

GAUL

There were many things, Ann, to keep me away from you, as you dreamed here through the years. I remember the thirst I knew in Kansas City, and the bar-flies driving me mad. There were small things, Ann, insects and little words. Frowns and sneers. And big things. The stairway of the hotel on fire, and a man in his bare feet. There were moments, repeated a million times, that were useless to the years. And years that were meaningless to any moment. But I knew—always I knew, Ann—that you would not forget. I've come a long way, through many things, and still your face is bright. Your eyes still young. Your hand warm. Your lips soft and full. The errors that have been, I dismiss. Here, in your presence, I deny all I have known but good, since you are still by sweetness molded sweet. I here cease movement and begin dream, because here dream is real. Ann, I've traveled across half the world.

(*Solemnly*)

I'm tired, Ann. Now I must lie down in the sweet shade of love, and dream into the years of youth. The years of our youth, Ann. The years we have lost and shall now regain in the embrace of love.

(BARNABY *embraces* ANN. *They go into the house.* BARNABY *turns and throws* GEORGIE *a coin*)

GAUL

My luggage, boy.

35

(GEORGIE *picks up the suitcase and puts it just inside the house*)

(TOM FIORA, *another Postal Messenger, arrives and settles his bike next to* GEORGIE'S)

TOM

Telegram for you, Georgie.

GEORGIE

Telegram for me?

TOM

Yes, you. Here. Read it.

GEORGIE

(Reading telegram)

"I told you I'd get even with you some day, so how do you like that? The telegram to Miss Ann Hamilton is not real. Ha, ha, ha. Your pal, Tom Fiora." Ha ha ha? What's the big idea?

TOM

I told you I'd get even on you.

GEORGIE

You put that telegram in my coat pocket?

TOM

That's right. That'll teach you to play tricks on me.

GEORGIE

You wrote that telegram?

TOM

I didn't write it. My brother Mike did.

36

GEORGIE

That's what I call a low-down dirty trick, and a guy in the house there getting ready to sleep in the sweet shade of love.

TOM

Serves you right. I told you I'd get even.

GEORGIE

Well, what about that lady? What about that wonderful lady who told him I was her son?

TOM

Tell her the truth.

GEORGIE

The truth? Ah, Tom, I never did like Italians. Greeks never did like Italians. How did your brother Mike ever happen to write a telegram like that?

TOM

Mike gets all kinds of funny ideas. He cut this lady's lawn one day. She told him the story of her life. He knew she was lonely.

GEORGIE

Well, who the hell is this guy, then? He's not just anybody. Giving me a Canadian dime. Tom, I'm going to tell the Manager.

TOM

Go ahead. He'll fire you, too. Then he'll come out here and make a personal call and explain everything.

GEORGIE

No, he can't do that. It's too late to do *that*.

37

TOM

  Come on. Let's go back to work.

GEORGIE

  O.K., you rat.

      (TOM goes)

  If that guy breaks her heart I'm going to tell my father
  to get a half-nelson on him and teach him some manners.
  Good-by, Miss Hamilton.

ANN'S VOICE

  Good-by, Georgie.

GEORGIE

  Is he sleeping?

ANN'S VOICE

  No, he wants to shave first.

GEORGIE

  Aaah. I'll be back to see how you're getting along first
  chance I get.

ANN'S VOICE

  All right, Georgie. And thanks ever so much.

GEORGIE

  Any time at all.
      (He rides away)

      (GAUL, with lather on his face, comes out on the
      porch, followed by ANN. GAUL sings to ANN)

GAUL

      (Singing)
  I love to see the sun come smiling to the world;

I love to hear the wind go singing through a field;
I love to hear a love-bird singing in a tree,
And I love to see a lovely face light up with love for me.

CHORUS

> Of all the things I love,
> I love the most
> Sleeping in the shade of love.
> Sleeping in the shade of love,
> I love the most, my love.
>
> Of all the things I love to taste,
> Sweetest is the kiss of love.
> Dreaming in the shade of love,
> The kiss of love
> I love the most, my love.
>
> My love, of all the lovely things,
> Loveliest of all is you,
> Dreaming in the shade of love.
> Sleeping in the shade of love, my love,
> I love the most, my love.

I love to breathe the scent of earth and new-mown hay;
I love to taste the peach and berry ripe in May;
I love to feel the spray as I walk beside the sea,
And I love to see a lovely face light up with love for me.

CHORUS

> (GAUL guides ANN into the house. DEMETRIOS, a
> small middle-aged Greek with a big black mus-
> tache, pushes a lawn-mower into the yard, begins
> to cut the lawn, suddenly notices the roaring lion,
> roars back at it. GAUL opens an upstairs window)

39

GAUL

Hey. You. That grass does not need cutting.

DEMETRIOS

I am American citizen.

GAUL

Even so, the grass does not need cutting. Have you got your first or second papers?

DEMETRIOS

Second papers next month.

GAUL

All right, come back and cut the grass next month.

DEMETRIOS

Is this official?

GAUL

Official. Now get your lawn-mower and get the hell out of here.

> (DEMETRIOS *hurries away with his lawn-mower.*
> *There is a moment of peaceful silence. Then* CABOT
> YEARLING *and his family arrive, one by one.* CABOT
> *thoughtfully smells a rose and surveys the terrain.*
> CABOT'S *family consists of* LEONA, *his wife;* NEWTON,
> *nineteen;* AL, *seventeen; the* TWINS, SELMA *and*
> VELMA, *sixteen;* ELLA, *thirteen;* HENRY, *twelve;*
> JESSE, *eleven;* SUSAN, *ten;* MAUDE, *nine;* LEMMIE,
> *eight;* MAE, *seven;* HARRY, *six;* WILBUR, *five; and*
> LUCY, *four.* LEONA *is pregnant. The family is ac-*
> *companied by* RICHARD OLIVER, *a newspaper man*
> *who is collecting material for a book. He is an old-*
> *ish, partially bald young man who is very troubled.*

Also ELSA WAX, *a large, plain young women wearing spectacles, who is a photographer for* Life Maga-zine)

CABOT

Leonie, here we rest.

OLIVER

But, Mr. Yearling, this is somebody's front yard.

CABOT

Don't aim to do no harm. Just aim to rest a spell. Leonie's going to have a baby soon, you know.

> (*Spreads his old blanket on the lawn and lies down*)

OLIVER

Another baby? When?

CABOT

Leonie, when?

LEONA

Two or three months, most likely. He'll be my fifteenth.

ELSA

You're aiming to stay here till the little fellow comes, of course?

CABOT

Don't know why not.
> (*To* AL)

Here, you. What are you always reading books for? Shake-speare and things like that?

> (ELSA *takes a picture*)

41

LEONA

When do you folks aim to leave us?

ELSA

I can't answer for Mr. Richard Oliver here. He's aiming to write a novel about you folks, I believe. He'll be with you for the next two or three years, most likely. I won't be half that long.

LEONA

I don't reckon we could undertake to feed another mouth, what with the children growing up and needing things all the time, and another coming.

ELSA

Mr. Oliver won't be no trouble, hardly.

CABOT

Well, it ain't so much the extra mouth to feed. It's always having somebody around asking questions.

(*Knocks notebook out of* OLIVER's *hand*)

It's more like never being able to lie down and sleep in the afternoon, without somebody waking up a body to ask if we know how to read or not, or if we want better working conditions.

(ELSA *takes a picture of* CABOT)

Or somebody else taking pictures of us all the time. We ain't publicity mad. We know we ain't society folk. If it's pictures you want, there's a world full of people who're always fussing with soap and water, keeping themselves clean and nice-looking all the time.

OLIVER

I have no intention of getting in the way. Miss Wax! If

42

you please. The pitiable plight of these unfortunate people is not the concern of one man alone, but of the whole nation.

CABOT

Unfortunate? I've got my driver's license.

OLIVER

Something's got to be done for them.

ELSA

All right, *do* something. What can you do?

CABOT

We ain't asking much.

LEONA

That's so. We don't want nothing from nobody—hardly. Food. A place to sleep. A roof over our heads. Clothes. A little land to walk around in. Cows. Chickens. A radio. A car. Something like that. We aim to shift for ourselves, the same as ever.

CABOT

A handful of vines to pick grapes off of to eat. A small melon patch. Good climate. Working conditions? We aim to *hire* our help fair and square.

ELSA

I don't hardly guess this family's typical.

LEONA

Oklahomans. That's what we are. Don't belong to no religious sex. Mind our own business.

CABOT

Live and let live. When do you folks aim to let us rest?

43

LEONA

We like to be neighborly and all, but this following us around and spying on us don't seem just right.

ELSA

I won't be much longer. We're going to call these pictures "Life Goes to a Garden Party."

OLIVER

You're making fun of these people.

ELSA

Don't be silly. I'm not making fun of anybody, except you. Because you think these people are pathetic. Well, they're not. You are. Look at these people. Nothing can stop them. They've got the stubbornness and fertility of weeds. And they're not common, either. I'm a photographer and I've learned to see *into* things. Your vision is so bad, the only thing you ever see is the surface, and I don't think you see that very clearly. For all we know one of these kids is a genius.

(Looking at AL)

This fellow *looks* like a genius: he reads Shakespeare.

(Looking at NEWTON)

On the other hand they may all be idiots. But how do we know the world isn't supposed to be inhabited by idiots, instead of silly people who want to get everything organized—like you?

OLIVER

You're a Fascist.

CABOT

Talk! Talk! Talk! That's all I hear, ever since you intellectuals started following us around.

44

OLIVER

I'm trying to *help* you people. With my novel, I hope to improve migratory agricultural labor conditions.

CABOT

Conditions are all right. I'm a little tired, that's all. I brought this family all the way from Muskogee, Oklahoma, in seven weeks, in a broken-down old Ford that cost sixty-seven dollars and fifty cents.

OLIVER

It's not a question of a broken-down old Ford—

> (HENRY *hits* OLIVER *with a stick.* OLIVER *falls, and three boys leap on him*)

CABOT

No kicking, now! Fair and square! No gouging! No biting!

> (BARNABY GAUL *opens an upstairs window*)

GAUL

What's going on around here? Ann. Are these people relatives of yours?

ANN

I've never seen them before.

GAUL

Don't worry. I'll get them out of here in two minutes.

HENRY

Oh, yeah!

> (*Three boys run into the house.* GAUL *appears with the boys hanging on him*)

45

GAUL

Ann, come out here. For the love of God, save me.
(*He falls to his knees*)

ANN

(*Appearing*)
Barnaby! What's the matter?

CABOT

Here, you kids. Henry. Jesse. Get off that boy. Get off
him before I come over there and break your arms.

(HENRY *and* JESSE *release their holds on* GAUL. *He
rises to his feet*)

GAUL

What're all you people doing in this front yard?

CABOT

We aim to rest a while and catch our breath.

(HENRY *leaps on* GAUL's *leg*)

GAUL

You aim to rest a while and catch your breath?
(*To* HENRY)
Get away from me, you bashi-bazouk!
(*To* CABOT)
Call off your children.

CABOT

Henry. Leave the boy alone.

GAUL

My God! You're not all one family, are you?

46

CABOT

All excepting him and her. He's a writer, and she's a photographer.

GAUL

All the others yours?

CABOT

More than half of them are. Every one of them's my wife's, though.

GAUL

Well, it's been pleasant chatting with you. Now clear out of here. Go on up the street somewhere a couple of blocks.

(He starts to enter house, singing "Of All the Things I Love")

CABOT

We ain't aiming to go no further just now.

GAUL

When are you aiming to?

CABOT

After Leonie has the baby.

GAUL

After Leona has the baby. When will that be?

CABOT

That won't be for a couple of months.

GAUL

A couple of months? My God!

(He moves to go)

47

ANN

Barnaby!

GAUL

I can't stand noise and confusion and crowds of people in my private life.

ANN

Barnaby! You're not *going*?

GAUL

I'm not staying.

ANN

I've already waited for you twenty-seven years. You just arrived.

GAUL

Ann, you've got the most beautiful spirit in the world, but I can't hang around a house that's surrounded by Indians.

LEONA

Oklahomans.

GAUL

Same thing.

(*To* ANN)

I can tell you now, and truthfully, that I shall never forget you.

ANN

You're angry and excited, Barnaby. You don't know what you're saying.

(GAUL *goes*)

48

Barnaby! Don't go! Wait for me! Let me get my hat and coat. I'm coming with you. Barnaby!

(*She runs after him*)

HENRY

(*At the upstairs window*)
The whole house is ours.

(*Everybody rushes into the house*)

OLIVER

But, Mr. Yearling, you'll get in trouble. This is still private property. Of course after the revolution—

CABOT

Ah, to hell with the revolution.

AL

(*Alone, on the steps*)
What am I doing here? I don't belong to this man and this woman. I'll go away. I'll be truly alone, as every man must be. Good-by, my father. Good-by, my mother. Good-by, my sisters and my brothers.

(JESSE, *in one of* ANN's *hats, comes out and sees his brother going away*)

JESSE

Al!

(AL *stops, turns*)
Where you going?

AL

Nowhere. Jesse, go on back!

JESSE

No. I know you're going away. I'm going with you. I don't want to be alone.

49

AL

Jesse, go on back! You can't go with me.

JESSE

(Grabs his brother around the waist)
No. I won't go back. I am going with you.

AL

Jesse! Listen! I can't take care of you. I don't even know
if I'll be able to take care of myself. Now go on back.

JESSE

Al, please take me with you. Please.

AL

I can't, Jesse. Now go on back!
(He pushes JESSE, turns and runs)

JESSE

You're a hell of a brother!

(JESSE sits down in front of the cement lion. Suddenly he stretches out on the lawn, face downward.
ELSA comes out of the house. OLIVER's hat and
portable typewriter follow. Then OLIVER, who stumbles out and falls on the ground, pushed by CABOT
and NEWTON)

CABOT

You stay away from us with your God-damn propaganda.
We voted for Roosevelt.

(CABOT and NEWTON go back into the house)

OLIVER

I don't know how I'm going to be able to write this and
give it social significance.
(Gets to his feet)

ELSA

Don't be foolish. You just write what you wanted to write in the first place, and forget all these little complications.

OLIVER

I'm disappointed.

ELSA

You've been betrayed. How dare they have personalities of their own? It would be a little cruel if one of the brighter children wrote a novel about you. One of them might, you know.

OLIVER

Sometimes it seems impossible to be of help.

ELSA

Be of help to who? No one wants to help anybody but himself.

OLIVER

I can't figure you out.

ELSA

You can't even figure out those simple people in the house. How do you expect to figure me out?—A Vassar girl!

OLIVER

The trouble with you Vassar girls is, you've got no faith.

ELSA

And the trouble with you unpublished writers is, you *have*. Faith belongs to the great only. Foolish people aren't entitled to faith. They make trouble with it, for themselves and for everybody else. They gather their

51

feebleness into crazy mobs that don't understand anything except to *insist*. If you want the world to be better, be better yourself.

OLIVER

Shut up!

ELSA

What?

OLIVER

Shut up! That's what! I don't want to hear any more of this chit-chat.

ELSA

You know it's the truth.

OLIVER

Shut up, I said! I love you!

JESSE

Ha-ha-ha!

> (OLIVER *studies* JESSE. JESSE *studies* OLIVER. OLIVER *takes some money out of his pocket*)

OLIVER

Here! Here's half-a-dollar.

> (JESSE *takes the coin*)

JESSE

What for?

OLIVER

Get yourself an education and be like me.

JESSE

You two going along?

OLIVER

Yes. And to help you with your novel, I'm going to marry
her.

(*To* ELSA)

That's right.

JESSE

Are you coming back?

OLIVER

No, I'm not.

JESSE

Why?

OLIVER

Because I don't like you.

JESSE

Couldn't you make it seventy-five cents?

OLIVER

(*Starts to bring out more money. Changes his
mind*)

No! Why should I?

JESSE

Ah, come on. Just two bits more.

OLIVER

No!

JESSE

(*Picks up a rock and gets set to throw it*)

Two bits.

OLIVER

You throw that rock, and I'll break your neck.

53

ELSA

Richard, be careful!

OLIVER

Shut up, I said. I can take care of myself.

JESSE

(*Making a line with his foot*)
Cross this line and see what happens.

OLIVER

It so happens, I'm going the other way.

JESSE

Well, you better if you know what's good for you.

OLIVER

(*Turns to* ELSA)
What's more, we'll have kids, too. The God-damnedest punks in the world. Don't talk. You've said everything. To hell with the people in the house! Let God take care of them, the same as ever. To hell with art! To hell with propaganda! To hell with you! I love you, so shut up and let's try to live.

> (JESSE *watches them go, then rushes into the house. Inside the house there is a great commotion. The children are singing "My Country 'Tis of Thee."* GEORGIE *arrives on his bike, listens, and runs to the lower window*)

GEORGIE

Hey. Cut out that racket.

> (HENRY *comes out on the porch in one of* ANN's *dresses*)

54

Who are you? What are you doing in that dress?

HENRY

I'm a society lady!
(*He does a bump*)

GEORGIE

Society lady? Where's Miss Ann Hamilton?

HENRY

Who?

GEORGIE

Miss Ann Hamilton.

HENRY

Annie doesn't live here any more.

GEORGIE

(*To* CABOT *in upper window*)
What are you people doing in this house?

CABOT

We aim to rest a while and catch our breath.

GEORGIE

Where's Barnaby Gaul?

HENRY

You mean that fellow with the straw hat? He went away.

(SELMA, *one of the twins, comes out and studies* GEORGIE)

SELMA

Hello!

GEORGIE

Where's Miss Hamilton?

55

SELMA

She went with the man. We're living here now.

GEORGIE

(To HENRY)

Get away from that wheel!

SELMA

You aiming to come back and pay us another visit some time?

GEORGIE

This house don't belong to you people.

SELMA

I hope you're aiming to come back.

VELMA

(The other twin, comes out and studies GEORGIE)

Hello!

GEORGIE

Hello, nothing!

VELMA

What's your name?

GEORGIE

Never mind what my name is. You people get out of this house!

VELMA

My name's Velma.

GEORGIE

What do I care what your name is? You people are house-wreckers.

56

WILBUR

No, we're not.

VELMA

I'm sixteen. How old are you?

GEORGIE

What do I care how old you are? You people are mice.

WILBUR

No, we're not.

GEORGIE

You folks get out of this house. It belongs to Miss Ann Hamilton and Mr. Barnaby Gaul. It belongs to true love.

> (VELMA and SELMA come toward GEORGIE. He pushes down on the pedal of his bike and rides off. The big boy, NEWTON, breaks out of the house, holding half a loaf of French bread, a piece of cheese and other miscellaneous items of food)

NEWTON

The whole house is full of things to eat. I got mine.

> (The TWINS hurry back into the house. HENRY follows them. There is great noise in the house, then silence)

> (GAUL returns to the house, gets his suitcase, and tries to escape. ANN catches up with him at the gate)

ANN

Barnaby! You've come back.

GAUL

Dear lady, you shame me. Your poetic words pierce me

57

like arrows. I am sweetly wounded by your devotion! I would be the lowest of the low to leave you here in this garden of disorder, except—except, I repeat—that there are things stronger even than love, if one can only discover them. I am *not* your man, except when I am. That is the truth, and the truth is hard. Forgive me, dear lady. The lies I tell are never for the purpose of hurting others. There is murder in such lies. In mine there is birth. I say only what others wish me to say. I have said what you have wished to hear. Gentle deceit is best for the moment, but for the year, truth is best. Stay, I beg of you. Do not leave yourself. To be vagrant, dear lady, you must be swift. Stay. I shall remember you. I promise. Good-by, dear lady.

(GAUL *goes.* LEONA *comes out on the porch. There is noise and confusion in the house.* ANN *walks slowly after* GAUL)

CURTAIN

ACT TWO

Several hours later, about two in the afternoon.
Everything has quieted down. CABOT YEARLING *is*
on the lawn in front of the house, sleeping in the
shade.

LEONA *is rocking in* ANN's *rocking-chair on the*
porch. Miscellaneous CHILDREN *are at miscellaneous*
games.

The scene is bright and somnolent. Cries of "Ice
Cream" from far away.

The TWINS *come out of the house, each in one of*
ANN's *dresses, each wearing high-heeled shoes, each*
powdered and rouged.

MR. SMITH *and* MR. HARRIS, *walking by in the street,*
pause a moment to notice the girls.

VELMA

Look, Ma. We bathed, too.

LEONA

Hear that, Cabot? They bathed, too.

SELMA

Look, Pa. Look at me!

59

CABOT

Selma, you look like a picture actress. Leonie, why don't you dress up, too?

LEONA

Now, Cabot!

VELMA

There must be ten or eleven more dresses in the closet, Ma.

CABOT

Why, sure, Leonie. Does a woman good to dress up fancy once in a while. Any men's clothes in there?

SELMA

No men's clothes, but lots of dresses.

CABOT

Go on inside, Leonie, and get into some pretty things.

LEONA

Well, all right, Cabot.

(She goes into the house)

VELMA

We're going to walk around town, Pa.

CABOT

Well, all right. Be careful.

VELMA

(To SELMA, lifting her dress)
Are my stockings straight?

SELMA

(Lifting her dress)
Uh-huh. Mine?

60

VELMA

Uh-huh. Well, come on.

(*The* GIRLS *walk away.* CABOT *gets up on an elbow to watch.* MR. SMITH *and* MR. HARRIS *walk by in the street, following the girls*)

CABOT

I'll be losing them girls soon. Get married, or go on the stage, or meet somebody, or something. They grow up and leave you. They grow up and go away. First they're little children you can hardly recognize, and then all of a sudden they're women. It's moving pictures that does it. Moving pictures. They was always the nicest children I ever knew. Sweet and thoughtful and courteous. Now, they're women. It's moving pictures! Clark Gable and all them different men coming into their lives. All those heroes jumping on horses all the time, saving people from drowning, winning wars. All them good-looking men putting their heads close to women, talking confidentially. Reciting poetry. Whispering in their ears. I remember a picture where the fellow *bit* her ear. *Bit it!* All them well-dressed men with millions of dollars, doing all kinds of brave things. You can't hardly blame the children. They don't know there ain't any people like that. They get impatient to grow up, so they can meet moving picture millionaires. I've been through ten states, and I've never seen anybody like Clark Gable, fixing everything up everywhere. I've seen 'em in one state the same as in another, working, or tired, or worried, or sick. It's moving pictures, making promises they can't keep. I'll be losing them girls soon. I can see it in their eyes. No matter what a man does, it just seems like

61

he's always going to lose something. It scares a man. Gives him a lonely feeling.

(He lies back. GEORGIE AMERICANOS arrives on his bicycle)

Telegram for me?

GEORGIE

Telegram for you! I want to talk to Miss Hamilton.

CABOT

Ain't nobody here but us.

GEORGIE

What right have you got to move into somebody else's house?

CABOT

We aim to rest a while and catch our breath.

GEORGIE

What kind of people are you, anyway?

CABOT

Migratory workers.

GEORGIE

Well, why don't you work? Or migrate?

CABOT

Leonie can't work. She's going to have a baby. The big boy gets tired easy. The twins—they just went to town— they don't like farm work. The others are all too little.

GEORGIE

Well, why don't you work?

CABOT

Can't get a job.

GEORGIE

Ah. You're just no good. What made you come to California from Oklahoma?

CABOT

Dust.

GEORGIE

Dust! Where'd you get that from?

CABOT

The writer told me.

GEORGIE

You could have gone the other way. You could have gone to Kansas or somewhere down around in there.

CABOT

Nope. California.

GEORGIE

Aaaah. You people are no good, that's all. Well, you better get out of this house in a hurry, and don't forget it.

CABOT

Ain't your house.

GEORGIE

Ain't yours either.

CABOT

Ain't yours.

GEORGIE

Ain't yours either. You're taking advantage of Miss Hamilton—driving her out of her own house. You ought to be ashamed.

CABOT

We didn't drive nobody from nowhere. He just went, and then *she* just went. No use leaving the house empty.

GEORGIE

How do you expect anybody to live in a house with a million people like you hanging around?

CABOT

Sixteen people. We was in the front yard, minding our own business—

(ANN *arrives*)

GEORGIE

What's the matter, Miss Hamilton?

ANN

He's gone.

GEORGIE

Gone? Where'd he go?

ANN

I don't know. He said he was going back to Boston.

GEORGIE

Boston?

ANN

He said for me to forget him.

GEORGIE

Aaah.

ANN

I begged him to take me with him, but he wouldn't do it. I told him I'd sell the house. I told him to give me two or

64

three days and I'd sell the house and we'd go away together, but he said he had to start going right away.

GEORGIE

How'd he go? By train?

ANN

He went running.

GEORGIE

How can a man run to Boston?

ANN

I ran after him a while, and then I couldn't run any more.
Now, I don't know what to do.

GEORGIE

Listen, Miss Hamilton. He's just a good-for-nothing tramp,
like everybody else around here.

CABOT

Migratory worker.

ANN

He's an itinerant merchant.

GEORGIE

Yeah? What does he sell?

ANN

Medicine. He gave me a bottle of it.
        (ANN *hands the bottle to* GEORGIE)

GEORGIE

        (*Reading the label*)
Dr. Greatheart's Five-Star Multi-Purpose Indian Remedy.
Good for all kinds of aches, pains and sores. Works ex-

65

ternally as well as internally. Quiets nerves. Stimulates super-human powers in tired men. Excellent for female nervous wrecks. Cures backaches. Contains numerous secret vitamins. Good for epilepsy, toothache, social diseases, earache, stomach disorders, insanity. Aaaah, this is a lot of hooey.

CABOT

Son, let me have a look at that bottle.

GEORGIE

One dollar a bottle. Is that what he sells?

ANN

Yes. He's got a suitcase full of them. He's gone.

GEORGIE

Well, you better forget him.

ANN

Forget him? I'm going to sell this house and go to Boston.

GEORGIE

He isn't going to Boston. He'll go to some town near here somewhere: Visalia, or Hanford, or Coalingo, or some other little town where there are lots of poor, *ignorant* people in the streets who will buy his medicine.

CABOT

Uninformed.

ANN

Well, wherever he goes, I'm going, too.

GEORGIE

Listen, Miss Hamilton, that telegram wasn't a real telegram.

66

ANN

Of course it was real.

GEORGIE

No, it wasn't. That man's name isn't Barnaby Gaul.

ANN

Now, Georgie, don't tell lies just to comfort me.

GEORGIE

I'm not comforting you.

ANN

Georgie, I know the truth.

GEORGIE

O.K., then. I'll get Barnaby Gaul.

ANN

Will you, Georgie?

GEORGIE

Sure, I will. I'll bring him back here, if that's what you
want.

ANN

Oh, I do, Georgie. Will you get him?

GEORGIE

If you'll get these people out of your house, I will.

ANN

(To CABOT)
You get out of here. Go away.
(To GEORGIE)
They won't go.

67

GEORGIE

Listen, you. You heard her. This is her house. Pack up your junk and get out of here.

> (LEONA YEARLING *comes out of the house in one of* ANN'S *dresses*)

ANN

You take off my dress and get out of my house.

LEONA

My dress.

ANN

It's not your dress. I bought that dress at Gottschalk's in Fresno three years ago.

LEONA

My dress.

GEORGIE

Aaaaaaah.

> (HARRY *comes out of the house with a book and lies down on the lawn*)

ANN

Georgie, help me.

GEORGIE

Listen, you riff-raff!

> (THREE BOYS *appear at upper windows*)

Get out of this lady's house! Do you hear?

LEONA

You hush, child. You're just a boy. You don't understand things.

CABOT

That's right, son. You go along and deliver your telegrams. This is a matter that don't concern you.

GEORGIE

Aaaah.

ANN

I'm going into my house.

HENRY

(In upper window)

It's our house now. Loosers weepers; finders keepers.

(ANN goes into the house)

GEORGIE

You people leave that lady alone. You people are gangsters.

HARRY

No, we're not.

(ANN comes out of the house)

ANN

Georgie, they're all over the house. They've eaten everything. Broken everything. Stolen everything. And they won't go.

GEORGIE

I'll go get the police.

ANN

What'll I do? Where'll I go?

GEORGIE

You go over to my house. My father's there. His name's

69

Stylianos. The address is 137 Vine Street. You know where that is?

ANN

137 Vine Street. I'll find it.

GEORGIE

Tell my father everything, and wait there for me.

ANN

All right, Georgie. Thanks ever so much.

GEORGIE

Any time.

ANN

137 Vine Street.

(*She goes*)

GEORGIE

That's right. I'll get the police to come here and make them go away. I'll get a writ of some kind.

CABOT

Writ? The whole nation's behind us.

(GEORGIE *rides off*)

(LEONA *sits down in the rocking-chair.* CABOT *stretches out in the shade. Everything is quiet and peaceful. Then* DAVID F. WINDMORE *arrives. He speaks swiftly, but enunciates his words very carefully, so that they have the effect of sounding unreal and foreign*)

WINDMORE

Good afternoon, sir.

CABOT

Good afternoon.

WINDMORE

How do you do, ma'am.

LEONA

How do.

WINDMORE

A lovely day. A beautiful countryside. A rich and fertile valley. A benevolent warmth. A delightful pressure of air. My name is David F. Windmore. Think of wind for wind. Think of more-or-less for more: Windmore. Think of David and Goliath for David, and think of Frank for F, although the F is actually for Fenimore.

CABOT

Hear that, Leonie?

WINDMORE

(Opening brief-case)
No home life is a full home life unless included among its general activities is the special and important activity of r-r-r-reading.

CABOT

Hear that?

WINDMORE

A well-read man is a well-bred man. He is a man who can carry on a lively and intelligent conversation on any topic with anybody, and therefore his company is desirable on all sides.

CABOT

What must I do?

71

WINDMORE

(*Bringing out a copy of* Time Magazine)
Time Magazine—curt, clear, complete—brings to your home every Friday all the news of the world:
(*Children running*)
Art, books, business, cinema, education, medicine, music, people, press, radio, religion, science, sport, and theater. National affairs: The President, the Congress, Labor, the States, crime, politics, and so on. World War, Poland, Germany, France, England, Russia, Finland, and the others. Military events at sea. Sinking of ships. Submarines and mines. China and Japan.
(HENRY *goose-steps, followed by* WILBUR, *arms raised in Fascist salute*)
Time marches on.

CABOT

How do they get that news? Telegraph?

WINDMORE

Time Magazine is assembled every week by intelligent men all over the world. Editor of the magazine is Henry R. Luce.

CABOT

Henry R. Luce. College man, I suppose. Educated.

WINDMORE

The managing editors are: Manfred Gottfried—

CABOT

Manfred Gottfried.

WINDMORE

Frank Norris.

72

CABOT

Norris.

WINDMORE

T. S. Matthews.

CABOT

Matthews.

WINDMORE

The *Associate* Editors are Carlton J. Balliett Jr.—

CABOT

Junior.

LEONA

Cabot, let the man talk.

WINDMORE

Carlton J. Balliett Jr., Robert Cantwell, Laird S. Goldsborough, David W. Hulburd Jr., John Stuart Martin, Fanny Saul, Walter Stockly, Dana Tasker, Charles Weretenbaker. The *Contributing* Editors of *Time Magazine* are: Roy Alexander, John F. Allen, Robert W. Boyd Jr., Roger Butterfield, Whittaker Chambers, James G. Crowley, Robert Fitzgerald, Calvin Fixx, Walter Graebner, John Hersey, Sidney L. James, Eliot Janeway, Pearl Kroll, Louis Kronenberger, Thomas K. Krug, John T. McManus, Sherry Mangan, Peter Matthews, Robert Neville, Emeline Nollen, Duncan Norton-Taylor, Sidney Olsen, John Osborne, Content Peckham, Green Peyton, Williston C. Rich Jr., Winthrop Sargeant, Robert Sherrod, Lois Stover, Leon Svirsky, Felice Swados, Samuel G. Welles Jr., Warren Wilhelm, and Alfred Wright Jr.

73

(GAUL *arrives and stands at the gate, a little drunk*)

The Editorial *Assistants* of *Time Magazine* are:

LEONA

Yes. Tell us who *they* are.

WINDMORE

Ellen May Ach, Sheila Baker, Sonia Bigman, Elizabeth Budelman, Maria de Blasio, Hannah Durand, Jean Ford, Dorothy Gorrell, Helen Gwynn, Edith Hind, Lois Holsworth, Diana Jackson, Mary V. Johnson, Alice Lent, Kathrine Lowe, Carolyn Marx, Helen McCreery, Gertrude McCullough, Mary Louise Mickey, Anna North, Mary Palmer, Tabitha Petran, Elizabeth Sacartoff, Frances Stevenson, Helen Vind, Eleanor Welch, and Mary Welles.

LEONA

No more names?

WINDMORE

No, that just about winds up the editorial department.

LEONA

What were some of those nice names again?

WINDMORE

Duncan Norton-Taylor. Williston C. Rich Jr.

LEONA

Yes, yes. My name's Leona. I don't know what you could think of for Leona. Could you tell me?

WINDMORE

Oh, I'll remember it all right. Leona. It's an easy name to remember.

74

LEONA

Leona Yearling. What could you think of for Yearling?

WINDMORE

Yearling. That's easy, too. I'll remember it all right. Now, Mrs. Yearling, *Time Magazine*, I think you'll agree, is something you and Mr. Yearling should read.

CABOT

Is that so?

WINDMORE

The subscription rate is five dollars for one year. All you have to do is sign this form and next Friday the mailman will bring you your first copy of *Time*.

CABOT

Is that all I've got to do?

WINDMORE

That's all. We'll bill you later.

CABOT

Give me a pencil.

WINDMORE

Oh. Life will be so much more interesting for you after *Time Magazine* begins to arrive every Friday. So much more dramatic and exciting.

(Filling in the form)

Mr. Cabot Yearling. 333 Orchard Avenue. Bakersfield, California.

CABOT

That's right. Where do I sign?

75

WINDMORE

On this line, Mr. Yearling. Wouldn't you rather sit up?

CABOT

No. I just want to sleep a little. I enjoy sleeping in the afternoon. Here?

WINDMORE

Yes, Mr. Yearling.

CABOT

(Signing)

X——X.

(Hands the form back)

There you are, son. You haven't got a cigar, have you?

WINDMORE

No, I'm sorry, I haven't. I don't smoke.

CABOT

It don't matter, really. I just thought you might have one.

WINDMORE

Until next Friday, then.

CABOT

Next Friday.

WINDMORE

It's been a pleasure, Mr. Yearling.

CABOT

Not at all.

WINDMORE

Mrs. Yearling.

76

LEONA

Couldn't you just say a few more of those names?

WINDMORE

Henry R. Luce, Manfred Gottfried, Carlton J. Balliett Jr.

LEONA

My gracious.

WINDMORE

Whittaker Chambers. Calvin Fixx. Louis Kronenberger. Oh, yes, Mrs. Yearling. Laird S. Goldsborough.

LEONA

Laird S. Goldsborough.

WINDMORE

Oh, yes, Mrs. Yearling, Laird S. Goldsborough.
(*He bends over* CABOT *briskly, extending his hand*)

CABOT

What do you want?

WINDMORE

Just to shake your hand, Mr. Yearling.

CABOT

Oh.
(*He holds up his hand, which* WINDMORE *grasps and shakes violently*)
Mrs. Yearling?
(*He shakes her hand, too*)
Until next Friday, then.

LEONA

Just one more name.

77

WINDMORE

Well, let me see. Felice Swados?

LEONA

Felice Swados.

WINDMORE

And last but not least, my own personal gift to my clients.
>   (*He brings out a toy horn; blows it; tosses one to*
>   LEONA)

Mrs. Yearling.
>   (*Blows another, tosses it to* CABOT)

Mr. Yearling. And now, good-by.
>   (WINDMORE *turns to go*)

GAUL

Just a moment.
>   (HENRY *is running around the house. He stops and*
>   *turns.* CABOT *gets to his elbow and turns.* LEONA
>   *stops rocking.* WINDMORE *halts.* GAUL *sets up his*
>   *suitcase*)

My friend, my fellow worker in the field, and, I believe but regret, my contemporary. With no intention in the world of being rude to you, or to these good and humble people of the earth, I could not help overhearing part— and perhaps the greater part—of that which I shall generously call your pitch.

>   (JESSE *puts his head out of an upstairs window*)

Step up just a little closer, please.

>   (WINDMORE *moves forward.* CABOT *stands up.*
>   HENRY *and* LUCY *and other children move forward*

78

a little. JESSE *climbs out of the window onto the roof. To* CABOT)

For the purpose of the amazing demonstration I am about to make, I must trouble you for a silver dollar. One silver American dollar.

(CABOT *has no money.* GAUL *takes a dollar from* WINDMORE'S *fingers*)

Thank you.

WINDMORE

For the demonstration?

GAUL

For the demonstration.

WINDMORE

What kind of a demonstration is it?

GAUL

A most amazing demonstration. Now, will you be good enough to take a card. Any card at all.

(WINDMORE *takes a card*)

Thank you. What card have you?

WINDMORE

The Nine of Clubs.

GAUL

The Nine of Clubs. Will you place the Nine of Clubs on the table face down. Madam, will you be good enough to take a card?

(LEONA *takes a card*)

Thank you. What card have you?

LEONA

The Nine of Clubs.

(WINDMORE *reaches for his dollar*)

GAUL

One moment, please.

(*To* LEONA)

Will you kindly hold the Nine of Clubs aloft? Step up a little closer, please. On this card I will place this silver dollar. Around the card and the silver dollar, I will place these three candles, and I will light them. One. Two. Three.

LUCY

(*Sings*)

Happy birthday to you. Happy birthday to you.

GAUL

Thank you, dear child. Now. The card is on the table. The dollar is on the card. The three candles are burning. Step up just a little closer, please.

WINDMORE

I'm sorry. I must go. Give me back my dollar.

GAUL

Please do not interrupt. Never interrupt a pitch. At least not a high pitch. You are no doubt a Harvard man. A man only recently turned loose into the world from one of the larger and more exclusive Universities of the East: Harvard, Yale, Princeton, or Dartmouth. My association with Universities has been comparatively meager. I have only seen a University. A Baptist University, I believe, somewhere

80

or other in the State of Ohio. Furthermore, you are a reader of *Esquire Magazine*.

WINDMORE

This suit was given to me by my mother.

GAUL

Your mother is a reader of *Esquire Magazine*. I read religious pamphlets, brochures on the lesser known arts, catalogues, and for relaxation the labels on bottles of various kinds, usually empty.

WINDMORE

This is nonsense.

GAUL

Nonsense? No, my friend. You are nonsense. I only dwell in a world of nonsense. I have neither degree nor diploma, and yet it is I, not you, who goes about with tidings of hope. I heal the wounds of people. I instruct them in courage and fortitude, not you.

CABOT

Hear that, Leonie? He's a preacher.

GAUL

No, my good friend, you are mistaken. My father was a preacher. I am a doctor. There is no other word for it. At the same time, I am more than a doctor.

CABOT

Well, Doc. What about them pains in my head?

GAUL

Stop thinking, my friend, stop thinking. I heal those mysterious ailments in the living which science itself has

81

not been able to isolate or identify. I destroy death in the living. That is my work. Step up just a little closer, please.

> (*Everybody moves forward a little. A husband and wife in the street stop to listen*)

WINDMORE

Will you please give me back my dollar?

GAUL

Not another word. Not another word. You are not one who is exempt from the illnesses it is my purpose here to cure. You are not exempt. I have returned to say a gentle word to the woman whose good heart I have hurt.

> (LEONA *stands*)

You may put the card down, Madam. Ann! Ann!

CABOT

She ain't here, Doc.

GAUL

Where is she?

CABOT

She came back, Doc, but she went away again.

GAUL

I quarreled with her in the streets. I ran from her as though she were death itself. I came to plead with this woman. I came hoping she would be established in her home again. I came to see these good and honest people.

> (*To* CABOT *and* LEONA)

Yes, you. And you.

82

(To LUCY*)*

And you. You are honest and you are good.

(To LEONA*)*

As the world has made you, so must I understand you, for as the world has made me, so must I be understood. Understanding you, I know that this house is yours, no less than hers. You were commanded to be fruitful, and by God you have been fruitful. No man may say the fruit you have brought forth is not the finest in the world, since it is yours, and you could bring forth no other. But it is mine, too, and mine is yours. Love is selfish. I returned hoping you would be gone.

CABOT

We aim to rest a while and catch our breath.

GAUL

I know. I know. I returned knowing that you would *not* be gone. There is nowhere for you to go. *I* can go where I please, but when there is homelessness, *I* am homeless. I am not separated from any part of life. Here in this front yard, I must wage with others the war in Europe, even. I am encumbered by you in the depths of my sleep. When there is hunger, I am hungry, and when the children weep, they are my children.

(To WINDMORE*)*

You have studied, no doubt, the reasons for things: for disgrace, for wretchedness, for disease and for stupor.

WINDMORE

I studied business administration.

GAUL

You would have done better to study sleep, as—

83

(*Indicating* CABOT)

—this man has.

(*To* WINDMORE)

I have studied the reasons for things: for disgrace, for wretchedness, for disease, for stupor. No man in the world knows better than I why these tragic things occur in that most miraculous and magnificent creation of the hand of God: the noble body which is man. You bring news of world-wide madness and horror to the living every Friday. You make of universal crime a topic for idle reading. You tell the people of foolishness everywhere, every week. That's fine. *I* bring *hope* to the people. I have here in these bottles a medicine. The juices of certain roots and barks are extracted and boiled together—

(HUSBAND *whispers in* GAUL's *ear*)

Is this the lady?

(HUSBAND *nods*, GAUL *slaps a bottle into his hand*)

It has never failed, my friend. It has never failed.

(HUSBAND *hands* GAUL *a dollar*)

Thank you, my friend.

(HUSBAND *and his* WIFE *leave*)

May the Good Lord bless you. This mixture, which has an appropriately bitter flavor, cannot, I am sure, cure anything. It can do no harm, but it can cure nothing. What this fluid actually is only God knows. But the taking of this fluid is the taking of faith. And with these bottles I carry to the people that which they need most. *Faith.* Do you understand?

WINDMORE

No, I do not understand.

GAUL

This humble medicine can restore a kind of faith as long as the bottle is not empty. I know of no other way in which to do anything about the wretchedness I see everywhere I go. The regular cost is two dollars. For this area of California only, and for this day only, the cost has been reduced one half. One dollar for one bottle. The bottle is yours.

(*He slaps a bottle into* WINDMORE's *hand*)

WINDMORE

I do not want it.

GAUL

You would reject Jesus, I believe.

(*He blows out the candles*)

WINDMORE

I don't need any medicine, whatsoever.

GAUL

You are the sickest man in the world.

(*He begins to pack up his suitcase*)

WINDMORE

You are a charlatan.

GAUL

There were many who said the same of the Son of Man.

WINDMORE

What about the Nine of Clubs?

85

GAUL

It is still here, as you see.

WINDMORE

What about the dollar on the Nine of Clubs?

GAUL

It is gone, as you see. Drink and go away.

WINDMORE

Where is my dollar?

GAUL

Your dollar? Whose image is engraved upon the dollar?

WINDMORE

I don't know. I haven't looked carefully lately. But I will not drink and I want my dollar.

GAUL

Ah—ha. Just as I thought. You are not a student. I gave to Caesar long ago that which belongs to Caesar. Go.

WINDMORE

Give me back my dollar.

GAUL

(*Closing his suitcase*)
Go. I lose my patience.
(*To* CABOT)
Here is the dollar.
(*He slides the dollar off the Nine of Clubs, and tosses the card away*)
Purchase commodities for the children. Buy ridiculous things. This is a ridiculous world. Drink this.
(GAUL *hands* CABOT *a bottle, turns to go*)

86

WINDMORE

Give me back my money, you thief.

GAUL

Thief? I am a missionary.
       (*To* CABOT)
If I find other college men in the streets, I will come back
later with more money.
       (*To* WINDMORE)
Until next Friday then.
       (GAUL *goes*)

WINDMORE

Henry R. Luce. Curt, clear, complete. Laird S. Goldsborough. National affairs. Crime. Politics. Religion. Louis
Kronenberger. Business administration. World War. $5.00
a year. You don't need to wait till next Friday.
       (*Throws Time Magazine to* CABOT, *and goes.* CABOT
       *picks up the magazine, looks at it a moment, blows
       the whistle* WINDMORE *gave him. Then throws maga-
       zine away*)

CABOT

It don't make sense.
       (CABOT *takes a drink of* GAUL's *medicine, and gets
       to his feet*)

LEONA

       (*Blowing the horn* WINDMORE *gave her*)
Do you remember any of the names, Cabot?

CABOT

What names?

LEONA

The wonderful names the magazine man said.

87

CABOT

I forgot 'em all, Leonie. But did you ever hear a man talk the way that man with the bottles talked?

LEONA

I never heard anything like it before. What's going on in the world, Cabot?

CABOT

Leonie, I'm glad you asked me that. You see, the way things are. You know, about industry and all. One thing and another, they don't hardly ever match up equivalent or comparative.

LEONA

Why, Cabot, I never heard you talk like that before.

CABOT

Oh, sure, Leonie. I just don't meet the right people. The law of averages, don't you see, like when you take two and two, and subtract one, somehow or other it don't make no difference. Oh, I can think along with the best of them, Leonie. I *do* get the ideas sometimes. You remember the way I talked to that writer. I said all those things, where he came in about social security. Social security. Oh, sure. I said all those things. Economic stability and things like that. You remember how I said propaganda right to his face. Exploitation. You remember that. Land erosion and all those different things. Oh, I can talk to 'em, Leonie. I can talk right up to 'em. Educational systems and all those.

LEONA

My, Cabot. You do sound good to hear.

88

CABOT

(Takes another drink from bottle)

Oh, hell fire, yeah, Leonie. I'm not so old. Leonie, you look good. Young and beautiful—

LEONA

Oh, hush, Cabot!

CABOT

You do, Leonie. Yes, you do. Come sit by my side.

(LEONA sits down beside CABOT. The big boy, NEWTON, comes around the house)

NEWTON

Pa! What are you doing with that pretty woman? I'm going to tell Ma.

CABOT

Newt, this is your Ma.

NEWTON

Is that you, Ma?

LEONA

Yep.

NEWTON

I thought Pa was carrying on with some pretty woman again.

LEONA

Shucks, no, Newt. It's just me, bathed and dressed.

NEWTON

Did you bathe again, Ma?

89

LEONA

Yep.

CABOT

Smells like soap. Clean and sweet.

LEONA

Now, Cabot.

CABOT

Newt, go away somewhere. I want to talk to your Ma.

NEWTON

No. I want to listen.

CABOT

Now do as I say. Go away.

NEWTON

Why?

CABOT

I've got things to talk over with your Ma.

NEWTON

I'm tired, Ma. Can I put my head on your lap and go to sleep, like I used to?

LEONA

Newt, you're too big a boy for that.

NEWTON

I ain't.

CABOT

Now, get the hell out of here, Newt.

NEWTON

I won't.

90

CABOT

You get the hell out of here, or I'll up and spank you.

NEWTON

No, you won't.

CABOT

(*Threatening to get to his feet*)

I won't, won't I?

LEONA

Now, Cabot.

NEWTON

No, you won't. She's my mother, and I guess I got a right to rest my head on her lap.

CABOT

And I'm your father, and I guess I got a right to get up and kick your pants.

NEWTON

Ma, tell him to stop.

LEONA

Cabot, let the boy rest his head.

NEWTON

Sure, Pa.

(GEORGIE *arrives, unseen. Gets off his bike, watching and listening. He keeps out of sight*)

CABOT

You go away, Newton Yearling.

NEWTON

Ah, Pa, I'm tired. I want to go to sleep.

91

CABOT

Go in the house and sleep. There's a time and place for everything.

LEONA

Let the poor boy rest his head, Cabot.

CABOT

Leonie, you're my wife.

NEWTON

She's my mother.

LEONA

Now, now.

CABOT

I won't have you spoiling a full-grown boy. Go away, Newt. Hurry, now.

NEWTON

I won't! I won't! I won't!

CABOT

(Getting up)
You won't, won't you?
(CABOT breaks into a trot, chasing NEWTON. LEONA sits alone. WILBUR comes out of the house, and puts his head on LEONA's lap)

LEONA

My, it's good to be alive and bathed.

CABOT'S VOICE

(From behind the house)
Newt, you son of a bitch, drop that club or I'll break your arm.

92

NEWTON'S VOICE

Don't come any closer, Pa, or I'll knock your head off.

CABOT'S VOICE

Drop that club, Newt, and run for your life, now.

NEWTON'S VOICE

Don't you fool with me, Pa. I'll hit you down. Look out
now, Pa. I'm warning you. Don't come any closer.

CABOT'S VOICE

Drop that club, I tell you, and run.

> (*The sound of human substance struck by a club
> is heard*)

Newt!

NEWTON'S VOICE

I warned you, Pa.

LEONA

My, it's peaceful and wonderful here.

> (NEWTON *returns, drops club alongside lion, picks
> up* WILBUR, *lies down and puts his head on* LEONA's
> *lap.* WILBUR *goes into the house*)

NEWTON

Ma.

LEONA

Newt. Where's your Pa?

NEWTON

In the back yard. I hit him over the head with a club.

LEONA

Is he hurt?

NEWTON

I think he's dead.

LEONA

Now, Newt, you shouldn't ought to have done that.

NEWTON

Maybe he ain't.

LEONA

A good son shouldn't ought to hit his Pa with a club.

NEWTON

Well, why wouldn't he let me rest my head on your lap?

LEONA

All right. Sleep now.

(A FARMER comes into the yard)

FARMER

Excuse me, ma'am? Anybody around here looking for work?

LEONA

What kind of work?

FARMER

Picking grapes. That man there. I can pay him thirty cents an hour. If he doesn't want to work by the hour I can give him three cents a box. A fast worker can pick fourteen or fifteen boxes an hour. That's about forty-five cents. I've got a heavy crop this year.

LEONA

No, I guess not.

94

FARMER

I need help bad this year, ma'am. He looks like a big man.

LEONA

No, he gets tired easy. Go talk to my husband. He's in the back yard somewhere.

FARMER

All right, ma'am.
(Going to back of house)
I sure could use a few good hands.

NEWTON

Who was it, Ma?

LEONA

Just a farmer, looking for workers.

(The TWINS return, accompanied by MR. SMITH and MR. HARRIS)

VELMA

Ma, this is Mr. Harris. He's going to put me on the stage.

SELMA

Ma, this is Mr. Smith. He's going to put me on the stage, too.

LEONA

Well, that's nice. I knew you two would get somewhere in the world some day. I'm proud of you.

MR. HARRIS

You're entitled to be proud of these girls, Mrs. Yearling. Two or three months of instruction is all they need. After that, fame and fortune.

95

MR. SMITH

We'll take all responsibility for the girls, Mrs. Yearling. Don't you worry about anything.

MR. HARRIS

(Handing LEONA a card)
Our card. We're with the West Coast Novelty Amusement people. Branches in all major cities of the Pacific Coast. Our school's in San Francisco. We'll see that the girls are properly cared for, instructed, and protected from unsuitable companions.

MR. SMITH

You have nothing to worry about, Mrs. Yearling. Mrs. Cavanaugh will escort the girls to San Francisco, and look over them like a mother. In the meantime, we want to advance a little something to you on their future earnings.
(He counts out crisp new bills)
One, two, three, four, five. Six, seven, eight, nine, ten.

LEONA

Did you say novelty people?

MR. SMITH

(He makes an acrobatic flip-over)
Yes, novelty.

VELMA

Gee!

LEONA

My! It's certainly good to see something unusual once in a while.

VELMA

Isn't it wonderful, Ma?

96

LEONA

I'm proud of you.

MR. SMITH

We've only got a few minutes to catch the train.

LEONA

Now you take good care of them.

MR. SMITH

Oh, we will, Mrs. Yearling. Don't you worry about that.

GEORGIE

I've been waiting for you, Sheriff. Gosh! I thought you'd never get here. These are the people.

(A SHERIFF in plain, untidy clothing, wearing a badge, appears)

SHERIFF

Don't you worry, Georgie. I'll straighten out everything in a minute or two. Law and order in the Sovereign State of California.

(The YOUNG MEN and the TWINS go)

FARMER

(Returning)
Ma'am, I think that man's dead.

SHERIFF

Somebody been killed?

FARMER

Yes. Her husband.

SHERIFF

Who killed him?

97

NEWTON

I did. I hit him over the head with a club.

GEORGIE

No, he didn't!

SHERIFF

Well, how did he die, then?

GEORGIE

He tripped and fell—off the back porch—on his head.

SHERIFF

Let me make an official investigation.
>   (*To* LEONA)
Get your family together.
>   (*Goes behind the house*)

NEWTON

Ma, he didn't fall. I hit him.

GEORGIE

He fell.

NEWTON

>   (*Getting up, showing club*)
I hit him with this.

GEORGIE

Give me that club.
>   (*Takes club from* NEWTON, *hides it behind rose bushes*)
If you don't want a lot of trouble, ma'am, get your family together and go away.

FARMER

He killed his father!

GEORGIE

He didn't kill anybody.

FARMER

He said he did.

GEORGIE

What do you expect a great big idiot like that to say?

NEWTON

I did too kill him.

GEORGIE

Ah, shut up!

LEONA

You be quiet, Newton Yearling. Children! Children! We're moving along.

HENRY

(*Appearing*)
Come on, everybody. We're on our way again.

(*One by one, the* CHILDREN *join their mother*)

SHERIFF

(*Returning*)
He's dead all right. Fell on his head all right.

FARMER

No, he didn't! That big fellow hit him over the head.

SHERIFF

Did you see it happen?

FARMER

I didn't see it happen, but he *said* he did it.

99

SHERIFF

Well, then shut up! Now, let's see. Get in touch with the Coroner and have him cart the body away.

GEORGIE

Thanks, Sheriff.

SHERIFF

Now, she can come back to her house.

FARMER

I tell you, there's been a murder!

SHERIFF

(*Taking out notebook and pencil*)
What's your name?

FARMER

Daniel Hough.

SHERIFF

How do you spell it?

FARMER

H-o-u-g-h.

SHERIFF

Age?

FARMER

Sixty-two.

SHERIFF

Married?

FARMER

Yes.

100

SHERIFF
Number of children?

FARMER
Five.

SHERIFF
Occupation?

FARMER
Farmer.

SHERIFF
What kind of a farm?

FARMER
Malaga and Muscat grapes.

SHERIFF
How many acres?

FARMER
Forty.

SHERIFF
That's all. Get out of here.
(*He throws paper away*)

FARMER
I don't know what a man ever wants to be a farmer for.
If I don't get workers, I'll lose my whole crop. It's murder.

SHERIFF
Get out of here.
(*The* FARMER *goes. To* LEONA)
Ready to go? All you people arriving from all over the

101

country, making trouble, breaking laws, no respect for private property.

GEORGIE

Sheriff, you don't need to bawl them out, just because they're poor. They're just as good as any other people.

SHERIFF

Georgie, what is this anyhow? I get up out of a good pinochle game and come out here to try to help you. You want me to get these people out of her house, don't you?

GEORGIE

Yeah, but I thought you could do something for them. You're a big important man.

SHERIFF

No, Georgie, I'm not big. And I'm not important. I'm a Republican.
    (*To* LEONA *and the children*)
Now clear out of here.

GEORGIE

    (*To* LEONA)
You've got some place to go, haven't you?

LEONA

We'll just walk along to a front yard in the next block somewhere.

GEORGIE

Why do you always want to go to places where people don't want you? Go over to my father's house. 137 Vine Street.

102

LEONA

We wouldn't want to bother anybody.

GEORGIE

You won't be bothering anybody. Go over there, will you?

LEONA

All right, children!

(*They start to go. The* SHERIFF *follows them*)

SHERIFF

Now get out, all of you. Law and order in the Sovereign State of California.

(GEORGIE *stands watching them go.* CABOT *comes from behind the house, holding his head*)

CABOT

Leona!
(Sees GEORGIE)
What happened?

GEORGIE

Your boy hit you over the head with a club.

CABOT

Is that what that crazy Newt did?

GEORGIE

Yeah, and everybody thought you were dead, too.

CABOT

I ain't, though. Where's Leonie?

103

GEORGIE

I sent them over to my father's house. You go there, too.
137 Vine Street.

(CABOT *goes.* GEORGIE *sits on the steps of the house.*
GAUL *arrives*)

GEORGIE

(*Running up to* GAUL)
Well, it's about time you came back to her.

GAUL

My God! The messenger of love again. My boy, forgive
me. I have not come back to remain. I have come back to
depart.

GEORGIE

Doesn't love mean anything to you?

GAUL

Anything? Everything.

GEORGIE

Then why have you come back to depart? Why haven't
you come back to remain?

GAUL

To depart is to remain, and to remain is very often to depart. My heart will stay here.

GEORGIE

What good is your heart, if you're not here with it?

GAUL

I am a traveler.

104

GEORGIE

What about Miss Hamilton?

GAUL

My heart is broken. Need I tell you my heart is broken?—
You, who are Cupid itself. This is her world, not mine.
I am a traveler.

GEORGIE

Well, why don't you stop traveling? What do you always
want to be running around for?

GAUL

I am one who seeks, and seeking all these years, I have
never found until this day, and having found, I am *still*
one who seeks.

GEORGIE

What do you seek?

GAUL

What all men seek and never find. One's self and one's
companion. My boy, you, with your morning telegram
from Boston, a city I have never so much as seen, today
revealed to my companion and to myself. I am not Barnaby Gaul, but no man in the world is Barnaby Gaul
more than I. Barnaby Gaul is he for whom shy and lonely
love waits in shy and lonely house—this house—guarded
these many years by this magnificent Abyssinian lion. You
have revealed me. I am a fraud.

GEORGIE

No, you're not.

GAUL

I am. Be good enough to tell this woman that I came to say good-by.

GEORGIE

Go over to my father's house, will you, and talk to her? She's waiting there. 137 Vine Street.

GAUL

Forgive me. I am on my way again. Messenger, bring the good woman back to her trees and roses and songs and dreams. Bring the good woman home. *Home?*

(*Smoke and flames in the lower window*)

My God! *This* house is on fire. Run down to the corner and turn in the alarm.

(GEORGIE *goes*)

Now the poor woman has no home to come back to.
(*He goes into the house*)
Anybody in here?

LUCY

(*Inside the house*)
I want my Mama.

GAUL

(*Reappearing with the* CHILD *in his arms*)
All right. Don't cry. I'll find your Mama for you. This is a hell of a mess for a traveling man to be in.
(*He goes*)

CURTAIN

106

ACT THREE

The parlor of the STYLIANOS AMERICANOS home.
About three the same afternoon. The room is typical of the parlors of almost all peoples of the Near
East in America. Oriental rug. An old Army rifle,
crossing a sword in its sheath, over an enormous
photograph of eleven men, ranging in age from
15 to 70, all with mustaches of one sort or another; each in a military uniform or part of one;
each holding a gun. American and Greek flags,
crossed. A big photograph of a naked baby on a
table covered with velvet. The baby is GEORGIE,
aged three months. Another photograph of a bride
and groom, GEORGIE's father and mother, standing stiffly in unnatural clothes. A piano. A phonograph. A few large books. A map of the world as
it was about twenty-five years ago, bordered with
the flags of the various nations, as well as pictures
of the kings, emperors and presidents of the time.
Also two large photographs of STYLIANOS in wrestler's tights.

STYLIANOS is at the center of the room, seated on
crossed legs, smoking a nargilah. He is an enormous man of forty-one or so, thick-necked, with
heavy arms, big hands, and a naive, spiritual face.

PERICLES, his father, a man in his early seventies, comes in noisily, walks about mumbling discontentedly to himself, sits down and lights a cigarette.

The two men smoke in silence a moment, and then begin to speak, the father in Greek, the son in broken English.

PERICLES
Aaaahkh, aaaahkh.

STYLIANOS
Don't worry, Papa. Everything's going to be satisfactory.

PERICLES
Home. Home.

STYLIANOS
The whole world is a man's home.

PERICLES
My home is Smyrna. I was born in Smyrna. I want to die in Smyrna.

STYLIANOS
Papa, you are a strong man. Maybe some day we will go back to Smyrna together.

PERICLES
No. No.
    (He finishes his cigarette, gets up)
The years are all gone. I have given them to you and Georgie.
    (He points to himself in the photograph. STYLI-
ANOS gets up, puts his arm around his father)
That was me, Stylianos. Aaahkh, aaahkh. The infidel Turks.

STYLIANOS

My papa. He is still fighting the Turks.

PERICLES

My son, if I had my youth. If I only had my youth. Give my love to Georgie. I will come back later, and we will sit together and remember the old country. Good-by.

> (*He goes to door.* STYLIANOS *puts needle to an old Greek phonograph record.* PERICLES *listens, returns to his chair*)

No. I will stay.

> (*He sits down*)

STYLIANOS

That's right, Papa. You stay here. We got Smyrna here, too.

> (*The doorbell rings.* STYLIANOS *shuts off the phonograph,* PERICLES *goes to the door*)

ANN'S VOICE

Mr. Americanos?

PERICLES

> (*In English*)

Yes, come in, please.

ANN

> (*Coming in*)

Excuse me, Mr. Americanos?

STYLIANOS

Yes, lady.

ANN

I'm Miss Ann Hamilton. I live at 333 Orchard Avenue. Your son Georgie told me to come here until the police

drive the people away from my house. They won't go.
They just won't budge. It's my house. Georgie went to
get the police.

STYLIANOS

Don't worry. Everything's going to be satisfactory.

ANN

I'm so confused. It seems like I've been walking years.
It's because *he's* gone. I guess I got lost, too. Everything's
changed. A few hours ago I was happy. Then the people
came. Then they wouldn't go. Then *he* went. Then I
went after him. So many things have happened to me
today.

STYLIANOS

Lady. Please cool down. It's not good to be so exciting.

PERICLES

What's the matter?

STYLIANOS

(*Pours wine*)
Papa, the lady's got trouble.
(*To* ANN)
It's nothing. Please sit down.

ANN

Oh, thank you, Mr. Americanos. It's wonderful people
like you— I begged him to stay.

STYLIANOS

Here, lady. Please take this. It will do you good.
(*He hands drink to* ANN)

110

ANN

I told him to wait, and we'd go away together. I told
him I'd sell the house.

(ANN *drinks*)

STYLIANOS

Lady, don't sell the house now. Keep the house. Ask my
Papa.—He don't know nothing. Prices are bad. Please
cool down.

ANN

Oh, I'm so ashamed. He ran.—Right in the street. And I
ran after him.

(*Starts to rise.* STYLIANOS *holds her down*)

I couldn't help it. I couldn't do anything else. I tried not
to run, but I just couldn't stand still. I love him.

STYLIANOS

She's in love, Papa.

ANN

I walked here. Never in all my life have I walked that
way. That's why I am so confused. I got lost, looking for
him. Then Georgie—Mr. Americanos, your son is a wonderful, wonderful boy.

(DEMETRIOS *breaks into the room*)

DEMETRIOS

Hello, my cousin.

STYLIANOS

Demetrios! Out!

DEMETRIOS

How is you, Miss Hamilton? Troublous?

111

STYLIANOS

Out! Good-by, please!

(DEMETRIOS *goes into kitchen*)

Lady. Don't sell the house. Five years ago I paid four thousand dollars for this house. Two stories. Today I can't get thirty-seven hundred.

ANN

When I went into my house everything was ruined. I was born in that house. I don't know why he had to run. My mother and my father built that house when they were married. I didn't want people like that in my house. All Mama's things ruined. And they wouldn't go.

(ANN *takes another drink*)

PERICLES

Is she an actress?

STYLIANOS

No, Papa. The lady is not an actress. Lady, please cool down, please.

ANN

They just wouldn't go. Georgie told me to come here and wait.

(*She brings Dr. Greatheart's bottle out of her bag, unscrews the top*)

He gave me a bottle of this. "Any time you feel miserable," he shouted—we were running down the street— "just take a swig of the stuff in that bottle. Won't do you any harm." I don't know what it is. I guess it's medicine, though.

(*She starts to take a swig*)

STYLIANOS

Don't drink that patent medicine.
> (*He takes bottle*)

That's not good. Drink this wine.
> (*Places bottle on piano*)

ANN

> (*Taking glass*)

Oh, thank you, Mr. Americanos. A toast. To love.
> (ANN *and* STYLIANOS *drink together.* PAPA *takes bottle and drinks*)

I feel so strange. I'm scared. I used to live so peacefully. Everything was quiet and nice. Last night I dreamed of lions.

STYLIANOS

Lions!
> (*He fills* ANN's *glass quickly*)

ANN

> (*Drinks*)

The lions ran after me, and then they became friendly. Then they begged me to be friendly. Lions begging me to be friendly. This morning, Georgie came with the telegram. And then he came. Barnaby Gaul.

STYLIANOS

Lions? Georgie? Telegram? Papa, don't drink that patent medicine.

PERICLES

What's the difference? She's crazy. I'll be crazy, too.
> (*He drinks*)

113

ANN

He's nice. It's so nice talking to you, Mr. Americanos. You're just like your beautiful son. At first I didn't understand anything. Boston. Barnaby Gaul. Six roses. But he didn't remember. I was so scared, because I thought I'd lose everything, all those years. But little by little he remembered, and then my heart— It sang and sang. Then I remembered the beautiful friendly lions.

STYLIANOS

Lady, drink more.

ANN

Thank you, Mr. Americanos.

(*To* PERICLES)

To love.

PERICLES

(*Takes bottle*)

Homeland.

(ANN *tries to repeat Greek word. They drink*)

ANN

I know something's happening. I don't know what it is. He came up onto the porch and kissed me. It was like he had kissed me every day for twenty-seven years. And when he walked through the house, I thought he'd been there all those years. One beautiful thing after another, as if I were still dreaming, but I wasn't scared any more. He sang to me.

(*She sings. Stops*)

I don't know what's happened.

STYLIANOS

Lady, please go into this room and lie down. Try to sleep.

ANN

 (*Going*)

Thank you very much, Mr. Americanos.

PAPA

 Stylianos!

STYLIANOS

 Papa, the lady's got trouble.

  (*He closes the door, sits on the floor and begins to puff at the nargilah.* GEORGIE *runs into the room*)

GEORGIE

 Is she here, Pa?

STYLIANOS

 Sleeping.

GEORGIE

 Her house is on fire, Pa.

STYLIANOS

 House on fire?

GEORGIE

 They set fire to it. And that guy. He didn't leave town.

STYLIANOS

 Wait, Georgie! Please cool down, Georgie.

GEORGIE

 He's in the White Fawn saloon, Pa. You've got to go get him.

STYLIANOS

 Georgie! *Please* cool down.

GEORGIE

Pa, he may run away.

STYLIANOS

Georgie, sit down a minute. Then we talk. Don't talk now. Just sit. Quiet!

(GEORGIE *tries to quiet down*)

Now, what's the matter?

GEORGIE

(*Jumping out of chair*)
Tom Fiora—

STYLIANOS

(*Pushing him back into chair*)
Quiet, Georgie.
(STYLIANOS *folds his arms and waits for* GEORGIE *to calm down*)
All right, Georgie, go ahead.

GEORGIE

Tom Fiora—he's another messenger—put a telegram in my pocket. It wasn't a real telegram. He was sore at me. His brother Mike wrote it. The telegram was for her.

PERICLES

Georgie, is war in Europe?

GEORGIE

Yes, Grandpa. But this isn't about the war.

STYLIANOS

Cool down, Georgie. Speak slow.

116

GEORGIE

I recited the telegram to her. I talked to her. I made her believe it was all real.

STYLIANOS

Georgie! What this telegram say?

GEORGIE

Here's the telegram, Pa. You read it. I don't like to think about it any more.

(STYLIANOS *takes the telegram from* GEORGIE.

DEMETRIOS *enters and stands looking at telegram which* GEORGIE *has handed to* STYLIANOS.

STYLIANOS *sees him and orders him out of the room.* DEMETRIOS *goes*)

PERICLES

(*Rises*)
Georgie. Is the Greeks in the war?

GEORGIE

No, Grandpa. Germany and Poland.

STYLIANOS

(*Quoting telegram*)
Love's Old Sweet Song. Twenty-seven years. Six roses. Four red. Two white. Five children. Get rid of everybody. Remember me. Speak to me. I love you. It's very romantical, Georgie. Why you exciting?

GEORGIE

Romantical, my eye. Don't you see, Pa, the guy went into the house, and I thought everything was going to be all right. But he ran away from her.

117

STYLIANOS

Don't worry. Everything's going to be satisfactory.

GEORGIE

How's everything going to be satisfactory?

STYLIANOS

You leave everything to me.

(DEMETRIOS *comes into the room again. He doesn't speak, but looks expectantly towards* STYLIANOS)

Demetrios, out! Can't you see I've got trouble?

DEMETRIOS

Stylianos, for why you tell me "Out! Out!" I am your cousin?

STYLIANOS

Yes, you are my cousin.

DEMETRIOS

(Going)

I am your cousin no more. I quit!

STYLIANOS

All right, Georgie. Tell the romance.

GEORGIE

I told her to wait here until I could come and take her home. But now there's no home to take her to, and the man's gone.

STYLIANOS

That man. What kind of man is he?

118

GEORGIE

I *thought* he was a great man, Pa, on account of the telegram. It's all my fault.

STYLIANOS

Georgie, when that man went into the house—

(GEORGIE nods)

I don't want you to feel bad, Georgie. It's not your fault.

GEORGIE

I started it all.

STYLIANOS

Georgie, be philosopher, please.

GEORGIE

What good is philosophy? Her house is burned down. The
man's gone. How are we going to get out of this with
philosophy?

STYLIANOS

Easy as peachy-pie, Georgie. I go get that man.

GEORGIE

He won't come. He's drinking. He won't come.

STYLIANOS

No? I carry him here. I make him talk to her. If she still
wants him, I make him marry her.

GEORGIE

I told him everything at the fire. I told him to come here.
Then I followed him to the White Fawn. He won't
come.

119

STYLIANOS

You go for ride. You forget everything.

GEORGIE

All right, Pa.

(*Starts to go*)

STYLIANOS

I go get that man.

GEORGIE

He's a big guy, and he carries a straw suitcase.

STYLIANOS

I find him, all right.

GEORGIE

Thanks, Pa. Gosh! I sure make a lot of trouble.

(*He goes*)

(STYLIANOS *does limbering-up exercises and half a
minute of fancy wrestling*)

PERICLES

Bravo.

(GEORGIE *breaks into the room with a brand-new
bicycle*)

GEORGIE

Look, Pa!

STYLIANOS

Georgie! Where you get that bike?

GEORGIE

(*Honks horn*)

He gave it to me.

120

STYLIANOS

Who?

GEORGIE

That guy, Pa.

STYLIANOS

You mean the man?

GEORGIE

(*Setting the bike beside the piano*)
Yeah. Barnaby Gaul. He rode the bike out here. He was riding like everything, zigzagging all over the place, blowing the horn, ringing the bell.
(*He honks the horn and rings the bell*)
He tried to ride one-handed through the hedge. You can't do that with both hands. He hurt himself, I guess, but he didn't hurt the bike. He's drunk. He's sitting on the lawn, holding his leg. I'm supposed to get him a drink of water.
(*Begins to go, stops, sits down*)
Gosh, Pa! I sure am a dope.

STYLIANOS

Dope? Why dope?

GEORGIE

I forgot everything, just because he gave me a lousy brand-new bike.

STYLIANOS

Don't worry. Everything's going to be satisfactory. Georgie, I gonna rassle that man.

GEORGIE

Ah, Pa. What do you want to rassle him for?

121

STYLIANOS

He's drunk. I gonna teach him manners.

GEORGIE

He's got manners, Pa.

STYLIANOS

Georgie, I gonna get head-lock, half-nelson, toe-hold and scissor-hold on that man.

GEORGIE

Ah, Pa, you'll ruin him.

STYLIANOS

That's all right. I be careful.

GEORGIE

Careful? He can't even stand up, I don't think. He's sitting on the lawn holding his leg, and you want to get a half-nelson on him. I'm supposed to get him a glass of water.

(*He goes.* BARNABY GAUL, *limping, comes in*)

GAUL

For the love of God! Bring me a glass of water. I'm dying.

STYLIANOS

Who are you?

GAUL

(*Sits*)

Nobody. A wretch. A man without a home. Neither son, nor brother, nor husband, nor father. A man without an address. A man who gets no mail. A traveler. A tourist.

(GEORGIE *brings him a glass of water*)

A failure.

122

(GAUL *drinks the water*)

STYLIANOS

Georgie, why is he bragging?

GEORGIE

He's not bragging. That's the way he talks.

STYLIANOS

What is your name?

GAUL

My name's Jim. I am a swindler who is himself swindled every day. Every minute.

STYLIANOS

Georgie, is this the man?

GEORGIE

Yeah, Pa.
(To GAUL)
I don't want the bike.

GAUL

I'm the man. Dr. Greatheart. A fraud. Barnaby Gaul. Never heard of Barnaby Gaul in my life. Who invented that incredible name?

GEORGIE

Mike Fiora.

GAUL

Mike Fiora! What'd he do it for?

GEORGIE

So his brother could get even on me.

123

GAUL

My name's Jim. Just plain ordinary Jim. Where is she?

STYLIANOS

Georgie, I gonna rassle that man.

GAUL

Rassle? Who's going to rassle who?

STYLIANOS

I gonna rassle you.

GAUL

Why? I'm hurt.

STYLIANOS

I gonna teach you manners. You ain't hurt.

GAUL

Manners? What's the matter with my manners?

STYLIANOS

(Limbering up)
You get ready, now. I give you chance.

PERICLES

Bravo!

GEORGIE

You can't rassle *him*.

STYLIANOS

Why not, Georgie?

GEORGIE

Suppose she still loves him?

GAUL

Yes. Suppose she still loves me?

124

GEORGIE

A lot of good he'll be after you get through with him. Come on, Pa. Leave him alone.

STYLIANOS

Why you come here? Tell the truth.

GAUL

I came to tell her her house is burned down. The poor woman's alone in the world.

GEORGIE

What did you do with the little girl?

GAUL

She's with the Sheriff. I tried to find her mother, but I couldn't, so I took her to the police. I told them the truth, but they wouldn't believe me. They said she was my daughter. They said she looks like me. They're keeping her until I know what to do with her. She needs Ann. And I need Ann.

(To GEORGIE)
Why don't you want the bike?

GEORGIE

I've made a lot of trouble. Just because you gave me a bike, I forgot everything.

STYLIANOS

Georgie, you go away.

GAUL

Why? Why send the boy away?

(STYLIANOS *gestures to* GEORGIE. GEORGIE *goes into the kitchen.* STYLIANOS *gives* GAUL *a long meaning-*

125

ful look and gestures for him to come forward and
wrestle)

Now, Mr. Papakapoulos—

STYLIANOS

Mr. What?

GAUL

Mr. Arkapapoulos—

STYLIANOS

What?

GAUL

My dear sir.

STYLIANOS

You better try hard.

GAUL

I can't rassle.

STYLIANOS

You can't rassle!

(He lifts GAUL and spins him around)

GAUL

One moment.

STYLIANOS

This airplane spin.

GAUL

For the love of God, Greek.

PERICLES

Stylianos, who is this great man?

126

(STYLIANOS *swings* GAUL *around to* PERICLES. GAUL *and* PERICLES *shake hands*)

GAUL

Be good enough to set me down on my feet. I can't stand height.

STYLIANOS

(*Sets* GAUL *on his feet. Commanding*)
Rassle!

GAUL

I'm in love. How can I rassle when I'm in love?

(STYLIANOS *gets full-nelson on* GAUL)

STYLIANOS

You not in love. Why you run away from that lady?

GAUL

I don't know.

STYLIANOS

Why you start trouble?

GAUL

I didn't know I was starting trouble.

STYLIANOS

Why you go in the house?

GAUL

She wanted me to.

STYLIANOS

She wanted you to?

GAUL

One moment, please.

127

STYLIANOS

This full-nelson.

GAUL

All right. Full-nelson.

(STYLIANOS *lets him go*)

I didn't know who she was. Your son told me. I didn't send her a telegram from Boston. Your son said I did. I love her. I need her.

STYLIANOS

(*Getting head-lock on* GAUL)

Poor lady. Handsome man like you, telling lies all the time. This head-lock.

GAUL

All right. Head-lock. I'm not Dr. Greatheart. I'm not Barnaby Gaul. My name's Jim. Jim Doherty. Even so, I love her.

(STYLIANOS *grips him tighter*)

Would you mind loosening your arm a little? Your son's going to be a great man some day.

STYLIANOS

Georgie?

GAUL

Yes, sir.

STYLIANOS

Georgie Americanos?

GAUL

Yes, sir. Georgie Americanos.

128

(GEORGIE *comes in*)

GEORGIE

Ah, Pa! Let him go, will you?

GAUL

Yeah. The boy's got the right idea. Let him go.

(STYLIANOS *releases* GAUL)

GEORGIE

All I wanted to do was make things a little better. Now they're worse.

STYLIANOS

No. I rassle him. Everything's going to be satisfactory. He loves her. Don't you?

GAUL

Of course I love her.

GEORGIE

If you really loved her, you'd love everybody. You can't go around loving one person and hating everybody else.

GAUL

Who said anything about hating anybody? I've always loved everybody.

STYLIANOS

How about that, Georgie?

GEORGIE

You ran away when you knew she loved you.

STYLIANOS

You trouble-maker!

(STYLIANOS *gets another hold on* GAUL)

129

GAUL

All right. What's this?

STYLIANOS

This Australian jaw-breaker.

GEORGIE

Leave him alone, Pa. It's not his fault.

STYLIANOS

(Releasing GAUL)
No, Georgie? Whose fault is it?

GEORGIE

I don't know, Pa. It sure is a keen wheel, though.

STYLIANOS

You love this woman, you liar?

GAUL

Of course, I love her. I more than love her. We have a child.

STYLIANOS

You got money?

GAUL

Some. I spent most of my money today.

STYLIANOS

How much you got?

GAUL

Oh, ten, eleven, twelve dollars.

STYLIANOS

Ten, eleven, twelve dollars!

130

GAUL

It's not a lot, but when a man's in love—

(STYLIANOS *approaches threateningly*)

One moment! Will you kindly take a card. Any card at all.

(STYLIANOS *takes a card*)

You are a wrestler, I believe. You have wrestled in the arena.

STYLIANOS

World's Heavyweight Champion Kern County.

GAUL

I, too, am a wrestler.

STYLIANOS

All right. Let's rassle.

GAUL

I do not wrestle as you wrestle, my friend.

STYLIANOS

You rassle women?

GAUL

You shame me. The card you have taken is the Nine of Clubs, I believe. Three times three is nine. You are also a member of the Greek Orthodox Church, I believe. The number three, therefore, is not meaningless to you.

(STYLIANOS *and* GEORGIE *cross themselves*)

Georgie, will you take a card?

GEORGIE

(*Taking card*)

131

We don't want any of your medicine.

GAUL

You don't need any of it, I believe. Now what card have you?

GEORGIE

The Nine of Clubs. I guess that's all you've got in that deck.

GAUL

No. Here. Look at the cards. All different. All different.

(GEORGIE *looks*)

You are a messenger.

GEORGIE

Yeah.

GAUL

I, too, am a messenger.

STYLIANOS

Rassler. Messenger. What else?

GAUL

I am a missionary. This elderly gentleman here, I believe, is your father?

STYLIANOS

Papa, I want you to meet—

GAUL

Dr. Greatheart. Dr. Greatheart!

(*They shake hands*)

GEORGIE

Ah, that's not your real name. What are you bluffing for?

132

STYLIANOS

Yes, tell the boy why you bluff. This is not poker game.

GAUL

My good man, *life* is a poker game, among other things.

STYLIANOS

Georgie, this man is philosopher.

GEORGIE

Philosopher, my eye. Don't you see, Pa, that's the way he gathers a crowd around him, and then sells his medicine. He makes them think something very mysterious is going to happen.

GAUL

Something mysterious *does* happen. Every time. Your father is right. I am a philosopher.

STYLIANOS

What philosophy you have?

GAUL

You shall see in a moment.
 (*To* PERICLES)
Will you kindly take a card?

PERICLES

He is a Christian. I can tell from the way he speaks.

GAUL

I beg your pardon. I do not speak Greek. It is embarrassing to me that I am not able to speak such a magnificent language. You will forgive me, I am sure.
 (PERICLES *and* GAUL *bow*)
What did your father say?

133

STYLIANOS

He said you are a Christian.

GAUL

I am.

STYLIANOS

He said he can tell from the way you speak.

GAUL

Your father is a noble man.

STYLIANOS

He used to be a peasant in the old country.

GAUL

I, too, am a peasant.

　　　(To PERICLES)

I need not tell you the card you have taken is the Nine of Clubs.

GEORGIE

Yeah, it's the Nine of Clubs all right. How come everybody takes the Nine of Clubs?

　　　(ANN comes in)

GAUL

Now, for the amazing demonstration I am about to make—

ANN

Barnaby!

　　　(GAUL embraces her)

Barnaby!

134

GEORGIE

His name isn't Barnaby, Miss Hamilton.

ANN

Oh, Georgie. How can I ever thank you?

STYLIANOS

His name is Jim.

ANN

And you, Mr. Americanos? You *did* come back, Barnaby.

STYLIANOS

Jim!

ANN

I never want to see this town again. I'll sell the house, and we'll go to Boston.

GAUL

Ann, your house is burned down.

ANN

What?

GAUL

Yes, Ann.

ANN

I don't care. I don't care about the house. I don't care about anything. I'm happy, Barnaby. You've come back to me.

(*Doorbell rings and the* SHERIFF *enters with* LUCY)

SHERIFF

Your daughter's been asking for her father.

(LUCY *runs to* GAUL's *arms*)

135

ANN

Oh, what a beautiful child, Barnaby. Come here, darling.
(*Opens her arms to child, who rushes into them*)
Why didn't you tell me? Why, Barnaby, she looks just
like you.

GAUL

It's nothing. Nothing at all. Sheriff, this little girl is not my
daughter.

SHERIFF

She *looks* like you.

GAUL

She belongs to that family from Oklahoma. I looked all
over for her mother, but I couldn't find her.

SHERIFF

She *likes* you. Don't you like *her?*

GAUL

I love her more than anyone in the world, except this
woman, but I love the truth, too. I want you to know, because I want to be her father. I want to see her grow into
grace and loveliness. I have never before felt the affection
I feel for this woman and this child.

SHERIFF

Well, she *looks* like you.

GAUL

She's mine in spirit, at least.
(*To* LUCY)
You do love me, don't you, child?

136

LUCY

Yes. I love the way you smell.

GAUL

(Taking child in his arms)

I don't care why you love me, just so you do.

SHERIFF

Well, if I ever saw a father, there he is.

GAUL

And this woman, child? You love her, too, don't you?

ANN

(Holding out her arms to LUCY)

You love me, darling, don't you?

LUCY

(Running into ANN's arms)

Yes. I love you, too.

SHERIFF

There you are. A father, a mother, and a beautiful child.

(The doorbell rings. All the CHILDREN enter, followed by MRS. YEARLING)

GEORGIE

Pa, these are the people.

STYLIANOS

Come in. Come in.

(STYLIANOS takes all the CHILDREN to the sofa)

GAUL

(To LEONA)

137

Dear lady, here is your daughter. If the child is willing, and if you are willing—

LEONA

Well, you take good care of Lucy.

ANN

Oh, we will, we will!

LEONA

(To GEORGIE)

I just came to thank you. Children, we'll be going along now.

STYLIANOS

No, lady. You stay here. Everybody stay here. We all sit down and have supper together. Demetrios! My cousin, Demetrios!

(DEMETRIOS appears)

You go get bread. Get meat. Get wine. We all gonna sit down and have supper together. Hurry up! We wait for you.

DEMETRIOS

I am your cousin again?

STYLIANOS

Yes. Everybody is my cousin.

(DEMETRIOS goes)

(The doorbell rings and CABOT YEARLING comes in)

LEONA

Why, Cabot! I thought you was dead.

138

CABOT

Dead? Leona, you look good.

(*To* GAUL)

Doc, I want to tell you that medicine saved my life.

GAUL

Thank you, my good man.

(CABOT *goes to* LEONA)

Ann, I'm a pitchman. I sell this medicine to people. I sometimes drink it myself. I sometimes believe in it myself. Take a card, please.

(ANN *takes a card*)

Thank you. What card have you?

ANN

The Queen of Hearts.

GAUL

The Queen of Hearts. Ann, I love you. I'll do anything I can to make you happy. I'll do anything you want me to do. I'll throw away my suitcase. I'm alone in the world. I hardly ever see a face twice, and I hardly ever see a face I want to see twice. I like people, but I don't like the disgrace they've fallen into. The only way I know how to do anything about it is to set up my suitcase in the streets, get behind it, and talk to them. Ann, tell me what you want me to do, and I'll do it.

ANN

I want to do whatever you want me to do, Barnaby.

GAUL

My name's Jim, Ann. You could help me a lot. I wouldn't

spend so much time in saloons, Ann. I'd drink some, of course, but I wouldn't drink so much. After a while we could get a trailer, and you could stand up on the platform with me. You and the little girl. You'd just stand there, Ann. It does them good to look upon beauty. I know it does, because it does me good. We'd go from town to town. The highways are beautiful all the year around.

ANN

Jim, we're going to be so happy.

GAUL

Mr. Americanos, I shall always be grateful to you on account of this boy: this Postal Telegraph messenger who carries to the world the only message worth carrying.

(*To* CABOT)

My good man, I want you to be a living testimonial to the wonderful powers of Dr. Greatheart's Five-Star Multi-Purpose Indian Remedy. I want *all* of you to be that living testimonial. Now, Mr. Yearling, if you will line up the children, we will rehearse the amazing demonstration I am going to make from now on all over the country.

(CABOT *lines up the* CHILDREN)

Children, will each of you kindly take a card. Any card at all.

(*He gives each child a card*)
Hold the cards aloft.

(*Each card is the Nine of Clubs.* GAUL *starts to sing "Of All the Things I Love."* ANN *joins him. Finally the* CHILDREN *join in*)

(*To the audience, while the* CHILDREN *are singing*)

Ladies and gentlemen, I have here on this platform, Dr. Greatheart's World Famous A Capelle Choir, and while the children are singing this lovely little ballad, I'm going to ask you to step up a little closer. I have gathered these children from the four corners of the earth. Each child is a natural-born singer. Also each child is a genius. Beyond this platform and across the street is the world. What will happen to each child as it wanders into the world only God knows, but now each child is a genius.

> (*He takes a bottle out of his coat pocket and holds it aloft*)

I have here in this bottle a medicine. The juices of certain roots and barks are extracted—

CURTAIN

THE ONE EASY LESSON

It is always worth while to listen to an ignorant man on a theme of great-seeming complexity, because he will not be confused by the mysterious malarkey normally identified with the theme, but will speak of it as nothing, as I shall now proceed to do.

I know nothing about the mysterious theater, the theater which consists of several hundred superstitions, fancy laws, high-tone theories, and dozens of other spurious things. I know absolutely nothing about the dubious art of writing plays—as far as I am concerned there is as much art in peeling and eating an onion. What you must have for one is an onion, and for the other a play.

Everybody knows where onions come from, but there is a great deal of confusion in the world as to where plays come from. I keep telling the professors and infant prodigies of the theater that plays come from everywhere, are always everywhere; that the world is truly theater and play; that living is truly drama; that every minute of the twenty-four hours of every day is Shakespeare, Ibsen, Chekhov, O'Neill, O'Casey, and Saroyan. Naturally, they cannot understand this kind of plain talk. They insist on being confused. They aren't equal to simplicity. They aren't ready for wisdom. They must seem special, because they are not special. They must give an impression of being extraordinary, because in reality they are a dime a dozen. Above all things they should be doing something else instead of wanting to write plays, or instead of writing lousy ones. I can think of few American playwrights who oughtn't to be in some truly more mysterious field of activity, such as selling real estate.

This is only part of the trouble with the theater, but it is the most serious part, and it is the part which is least likely ever to be changed. There is something to be done, but it isn't something brilliant like social ostracism, banishment to Utah, or murder. The thing to do about the trouble with the theater is not to preach at other playwrights and demand that they wake up or anything cataclysmic like that; the simple thing to do is for me to go ahead and write good plays. The others can go ahead and write anything they like. Nine times out of ten they will be a cinch to write something that appears to be more truly a play than anything I write, but that will be nothing more than bluff, heroic and pathetic. Any man who must bluff must bluff, and in some cases should be admired for the virtuosity or something of his special method of triumph; but for my part bluff will always remain an important element or device in stud poker and occasionally in polite relations with charming people whose lovely ignorance has been spoiled by travel, education, money, and social position. Otherwise, no bluff.

There are sixty-four subdivisions beneath the main general theme of what is wrong with the theater. I could go down the whole line of subdivisions, but it wouldn't be anything like a scoop and it wouldn't change any of the child geniuses from heroes to workers, so I shall let the whole thing go until tomorrow or next Thursday.

But if any reader of this essay is a young man who is absolutely sure that he is a great playwright and all he needs is something to get him going, I may have something to tell him which will be just what he needs to hear.

1. Look at the world. Look at people. Listen to the world. Listen to people. Uncover the magnificent and unending drama in the most ordinary environments, events, and people.

2. Write a great deal. Never be careful. Never try to achieve style, because even if you do so it won't really be style because style is something which is there from the beginning and doesn't have to be achieved. Always know what you're doing, but at the same time never get so bright that you know what you're doing so fully that even Walter Winchell will be able to understand exactly what you have done after you've done it. That condition spells, I believe, The End.

3. Don't ever take Professor Baker's course on Drama. Don't take anybody's course on anything. Eat simple food and drink the kind of liquor you seem to like most, and if you see a pretty face, smile and let her know there's still love of poetry in the world. Don't study the books, unless you are still under twenty. If you are under twenty, study *all* the books, but don't forget yourself. Don't believe that any of the boys who have done their work are terribly great, even if they are. Don't be a fool about any man who was himself never a fool about any other man. Don't be a student of a writer at any time, but do be a student of everything all your life, even when it appears that you have a simple, modest understanding of everything, including American money, and what makes it so surrealistic. Never stop being amazed by human beings. By what passes for reality. By what is unquestionably religion in all things.

4. Don't be mistaken about yourself. If you're really great,

145

the realization that you are won't floor you. It won't even impress you. If you're not great, don't let that floor you either. Just stay fresh in heart, energetic in spirit, and eager about everything, good or bad. If you write something that is great, take it for granted, but tell everybody you know, and a few people you don't know. Tell them casually. Say, "I have just written the greatest play since the early O'Neill," as if you were saying, "From Times Square to 57th Street is about fifteen blocks." If you write something that is lousy, take this for granted also, but don't tell it to anybody, unless it's somebody you are in love with and can count on to be delighted with such a preposterous and unlikely thing.

5. Don't try to do much in a big way. Just do enough in a little way. If you have somebody say, "Ah, to hell with everything," because he is drunk or has lost two dollars on a bangtail named Fluke, let what he says also possibly mean the world stinks, here and there, and that, as far as he is concerned, big-shots ought to have their heads examined or hit with an inflated bladder.

6. Don't try to be a success. Only failures and inconsequential people can become successes and enjoy it. Success is never constant in their lives. It is always something acquired, usually willy-nilly, which ends mournfully in about two weeks. If your work thrills dopes and dizzy people with lots of class, don't let it bother you. Just be nice to them and go about your business.

7. Take it easy.

I think that's all for this year.